The One Year® Experiencing God's Presence
DEVOTIONAL

The One Year®
Experiencing God's Presence
DEVOTIONAL

365 Daily Encounters to Bring You Closer to Him

CHRIS TIEGREEN

Tyndale House Publishers, Inc.
Carol Stream, Illinois

Visit Tyndale online at www.tyndale.com.

TYNDALE, Tyndale's quill logo, and The One Year are registered trademarks of Tyndale House Publishers, Inc.

The One Year Experiencing God's Presence Devotional: 365 Daily Encounters to Bring You Closer to Him

Copyright © 2011 by Chris Tiegreen. All rights reserved.

Cover photo of pier copyright © alle12/iStockphoto. All rights reserved.

Designed by Jacqueline L. Nuñez

Edited by Jonathan Schindler

Published in asssociation with the literary agency of Mark Sweeney & Associates.

Unless otherwise indicated, all Scripture quotations are taken from the Holy Bible, New Living Translation, copyright © 1996, 2004, 2007 by Tyndale House Foundation. Used by permission of Tyndale House Publishers, Inc., Carol Stream, Illinois 60188. All rights reserved.

Scripture quotations marked The Message are taken from The Message by Eugene H. Peterson, copyright © 1993, 1994, 1995, 1996, 2000, 2001, 2002. Used by permission of NavPress Publishing Group. All rights reserved.

Scripture quotations marked NIV are taken from the Holy Bible, New International Version,® NIV.® Copyright © 1973, 1978, 1984, 2011 by Biblica, Inc.™ Used by permission of Zondervan. All rights reserved worldwide. www.zondervan.com.

Scripture quotations marked NKJV are taken from the New King James Version.® Copyright © 1982 by Thomas Nelson, Inc. Used by permission. All rights reserved. NKJV is a trademark of Thomas Nelson, Inc.

ISBN 978-1-4143-3955-9

Printed in the United States of America

17   16   15   14   13   12   11
7   6   5   4   3   2   1

INTRODUCTION

All of us long for God's Presence, and we sense it—occasionally. But for most of us, our faith tends to slip easily into a religion of theological beliefs about God and His Word, biblically derived precepts, step-by-step principles, and common "best practices." There are times when what we call a "relationship with God" feels like nothing more than a relationship with these beliefs and behaviors. We relate to printed words on a page, to people at church, to devotional practices, to ministry activities, and to our own sense of obligation to do what's right—and then we call *that* a relationship with God. What's missing? Real encounters with Him. Certainty that we have heard His voice. A sense of His palpable Presence.

This sense of God's Presence is what all of us truly crave. Most of us get glimpses of it from time to time, and we know it won't be full and complete this side of eternity. Still, we want more. We need to feel His touch. And we can. There are things we can do to become more aware of Him and to posture ourselves to experience Him more—if we understand where He is and how He shows Himself.

God is everywhere. We couldn't get away from Him if we wanted to—which, of course, we don't. So if He's always with us, why discuss His Presence as though it fluctuates? Because there's a difference between His Presence and our experience of it. We aren't as aware of Him as we'd like to be. We don't just want Him to be present; we want to actually encounter Him.

Our awareness is half of what we need in order to experience God's Presence; the other half is up to Him. He comes to us. Though He is in every place at all times, He isn't *manifestly* present in every place at all times. Scripture is clear in this distinction: sometimes He is "present," and sometimes He isn't (see, for example, Exodus 33:3, 14-15). Scripture must be referring not to His omnipresence but to some aspect of His Presence that is more intense, more evident, more tangible and real in some moments than in others. Sometimes He shows up in remarkable ways.

This devotional is about both sides of the issue: becoming more aware of God's Presence and experiencing Him when He comes closer. The first is what is often referred to as "practicing the Presence of God"—that is, tuning in to the knowledge of His nearness. The second is positioning ourselves to encounter His Presence when He shows up—having the attitudes and expectations that prepare us to encounter Him. We'll explore what it means when He says that His Presence will go with us, or that He is near to the humble and the brokenhearted but far from the proud, or that He draws near to us when we draw near to Him. Without compromising that He is always present, we'll consider the various levels and degrees of His Presence and how to experience "more" of Him. If Scripture can speak in these terms, so can we.

Toward those two ends—our awareness and His nearness—each day's reading concludes with a prayer to be drawn closer to God's Presence or for His Presence to become more real to us. These prayers are an invitation to enter into the truth of the devotional and to engage God about that truth. If you feel led to another response or another prayer, pray accordingly. Sometimes prayers like this seem contrived because, though they may be the heartfelt request of the writer, they aren't necessarily the heartfelt request of the reader. But some people need ideas or encouragement in taking the next step after they have read or received a spiritual truth. These prayers are offered as that next step. If you actually pray them—even if that feels awkward at first—and own them in some profound way, they can radically change your life. Over time, you will become constantly aware of His nearness, hear Him more clearly, and experience His touch more easily.

Some might consider this idea of experiencing God's Presence to be somewhat mystical, and it is. That's because the Christian faith is by nature somewhat mystical. Jesus spoke to His disciples about His oneness with them and about the Holy Spirit coming to speak to them (see John 14:16-20; 17:22-23); Paul wrote about encountering Jesus on a road to Damascus and of receiving inexpressible revelations in the third heaven (see 2 Corinthians 12:1-4); and Scripture in general is filled with many who encountered God and heard His voice. Clearly, the Bible describes a mystical relationship between Jesus and those who believe in Him. These readings are daily steps toward experiencing that relationship in deeper, more powerful ways.

January 1

Apart from me you can do nothing.

JOHN 15:5

The Presence is everything in the Christian life. Maybe that seems like an overstatement. Surely obedience is important, along with bearing fruit, being loving and compassionate, praying, growing in faith, overcoming obstacles, dealing with relationship issues, and so much more. That's why so many books are published and so many sermons preached about these things. Christian living is a vast array of disciplines, attitudes, and activities, and we have to know how to approach them. Right?

But think about it. What happens to your attitude when you have a palpable sense of God's Presence around you? How fruitful does your prayer life become? How strong does your faith grow? What obstacle seems large when you're aware that God is in the room? How hard is it to obey when He is present to empower you? How hard do you have to try to bear fruit if He is spilling out from within you? What relationship issues remain unyielding when His power overwhelms? The truth is that His Presence working within us is the key to everything, and without Him we can do nothing.

That's why cultivating both an awareness and an ongoing experience of His Presence is vital. When God shows up, miracles happen. Life comes out of death, beauty comes out of ashes, dancing takes the place of mourning, futility gives way to fruitfulness, confusion is replaced by order, and obstacles bow to His will. Even the hard side of His Presence—the convicting and correcting truth we don't want to hear—eventually gives life. When God is at work in and around us, everything changes.

Zealously, relentlessly, passionately pursue God's Presence. Every endeavor in the Christian life is futile without that. But with it, everything is possible.

Jesus, I need You—Your Spirit, Your life—in me and around me. I'm not content just to know about You or to believe the right things. I want to experience Your Presence. I know You want that too. Please, Lord, let me sense You always.

January 2

Where will my resting place be?
ISAIAH 66:1, NIV

In context, it comes across as a rhetorical question, a divine scoff at the idea that God might need a human-built home. But we know the heart behind creation, the desire of a God who *does* choose resting places for Himself. His Presence once filled a Tabernacle, then a Temple, and then the flesh of His own people. Scripture insists on a mind-boggling reality: not only did God incarnate Himself in Jesus, He continues to do so in us.

It seems to be a radical contradiction of Scripture, then, that so many of us lament the "distance" of God as often as we do. Sometimes He seems close, but for people who are meant to be inhabited by the holy Presence, we too often have to wonder where He is. His nearness becomes for us a mere theological principle rather than an experience. Why?

One reason may be that some of us fear closeness—what will God disapprove of or require of us when we encounter Him? We can be awfully insecure about His intentions. But the more common reason is that we don't pursue His Presence as zealously as we pursue other things in life. We are distracted by lesser goals and forget what's available to us. In other words, we don't have a strong sense of His Presence because we don't ask for it.

Spend some time today asking. Offer yourself as a resting place for Him to enjoy. God did not create you and then redeem you in order to keep His distance. He designed you for an intimacy deeper than you can imagine. Whatever your relationship with Him has been like recently, He is inviting you more deeply into that intimacy. Take Him up on the offer. Ask Him to come as close as He wants to.

Lord, let me be Your resting place. I offer myself to You and invite You to remove anything that stands in the way. Come close to me—as close as You desire.

You will show me the way of life, granting me the
joy of your presence.

PSALM 16:11

God's Presence evokes a variety of responses in Scripture. Some people are terrified in His Presence, others freeze in awe and wonder, and some marvel that they didn't recognize Him until after He left. Sometimes He appears with clouds and thunder; other times He shows Himself subtly and selectively. Regardless, there's one response we rarely see in a God-encounter in the Bible: joy.

Why is that? Probably because His appearances are sudden events, and the first response to the trauma of seeing Him can range from panic to guilt to awe to zeal. But for those who spend extended time with Him—Moses in the Tabernacle, David in his crises, or the disciples with Jesus—the alarm wears off and the relationship deepens. The result, David tells us in Psalm 16, is joy.

Even today, many believers dread really getting up close and personal with God. That's because they don't know who He is. They haven't grasped mercy or understood His goodness. They don't know He wants us to experience His pleasure forever, or that one of His primary purposes for us is to experience His joy (John 17:13). Few of us realize that He wants to delight us. His goal is that our hearts would overflow when we're with Him.

Father, help me ignore the teachers who emphasize
the obligation of serving You more than the
pleasure of knowing You. Help me embrace the
truth that You are zealous about my joy, and show
me how to experience it in Your Presence.

January 4

He has given us great and precious promises.
These are the promises that enable you
to share his divine nature.

2 PETER 1:4

What would happen if we asked God—not just occasionally but as a persistent, daily, even moment-by-moment request—to allow us to host His Presence? What if we sought to become a living, breathing, tangible demonstration of His person? Is that a realistic hope?

It seems like a bold, even arrogant request, but any lesser request falls short of our design and His stated purposes. God has promised that we will share in His divine nature and has given us His Spirit to make it happen. He apparently is more zealous to be present within us and among us than we are to experience His Presence. He seeks us more than we seek Him.

Why is that? It's a greater honor and privilege for us to host the living God than for Him to get close to a flawed, common human being. We should be the more enthusiastic seekers in the relationship. But God created us for this purpose: to inhabit us, to relate to us intimately, to *be* with us. That's why He created humanity. Love desires to share. God wants to share Himself.

Let Him. Don't just issue a casual invitation for Him to be present in your life. He doesn't normally respond well to casual invitations. His love is too intense for someone with halfhearted intentions. Instead, choose to relentlessly seek Him. Then give Him time. He will begin to fulfill His desire and yours.

Spirit, fill me continually. Please be present within
me. I want to experience You more than I do. Daily
increase the evidence of Your Presence in my life.
Make Your home in me so I can become a tangible
demonstration of who You are.

Come close to God . . .
JAMES 4:8

Have you ever looked at a blade of grass, a spider's web, or a waterfall as an expression of God's creativity? Have you seen nature's seasons and trends not for what they are in themselves but for what they reveal of the heart that made them? Have you ever just stopped and noticed the divine dream unfolding around you? All of these—observing creation, listening for whispers of God's voice or trying to put your finger on His pulse, absorbing the marvels of His world—are means to become more aware of His Presence. When we notice these things, and especially when they spark a conversation with Him, we are drawing close to God.

There are two major aspects in experiencing God's Presence: increasing our awareness of Him, and His approach to us. The first is our responsibility, the second His. Both are expressed in James 4:8, where we are told to draw close to God and are assured that He will draw close to us. But it's harder than it seems.

We let busyness distract us from experiencing God. Our daily routines and to-do lists are His rivals for our attention, and we often let them win. He can work in ways that drive us to seek Him, but He would rather that we come to Him because we want to than because He told us to or gave us few other options. Drawing close is meant to be an act of love. And love, if it's real, is always voluntary.

Your side of the "Presence equation" is to draw near to God. In every way you can imagine, do that. Then see how He responds to you.

Father, I want to notice You—everything about
You. I want to stop and notice any evidence
of Your work, Your voice, and Your Presence that
I can find. As I observe You, please make Yourself
even more observable. And draw me close.

January 6

. . . and God will come close to you.

JAMES 4:8

It's a familiar refrain: "If God seems far away, who moved?" The implication is that He's always there, and we're the ones who created the distance. And while that's true in terms of His omnipresence—He's everywhere all the time—it isn't necessarily true with regard to His *available* or *manifest* Presence. In experience, He's closer to us at some times than He is at others. And it isn't always because we drifted in the opposite direction.

We can make ourselves more aware of the ways God is moving and working all around us, but we can also attract Him to move toward us. As potential marriage partners instinctively know the rules of attraction, we can know what appeals to Him and invite Him into deeper intimacy. We don't earn His favor or His Presence—that's not even an option—but relational closeness isn't a matter of "earning" anyway. It's a matter of desire, commitment, and level of interaction. When we know the attitudes that warm God's heart, we can clothe ourselves in them. And when we draw close to Him, He draws close to us.

Notice what appeals to God: faith, humility, hunger for Him, honesty and authenticity, obedience from the heart, and many more attitudes you can find in Scripture. Granted, fallen human beings can't manufacture spiritual characteristics without His help. But we are clearly told to put on the right attitudes, so we bear a certain responsibility and initiative to do so. Seek Him in such ways, and you will find Him seeking you out too.

Lord, I know we can't come to You unless You draw us. But You also don't come to us unless we draw near to You. However that mutual attraction works, I want more of it. Please come close.

January 7

We know that the Son of God has come, and he has given us understanding so that we can know the true God.

1 JOHN 5:20

"What comes into our minds when we think about God is the most important thing about us," wrote A. W. Tozer, and he was right. The way we see God profoundly shapes who we are. If we see Him as a dictator, we'll be servile. If we see Him as an indulgent uncle, we'll live indulgently. If we think He's a vocal speaker, we'll listen; but if we think He's silent and obscure, we'll shut our ears to the possibility of hearing Him. If we believe Jesus is coming soon, we'll prepare. But is He coming to rapture us away to heaven, or are we meeting Him in the sky as He comes to earth to establish His Kingdom? Our answer affects the nature of our mission. Our confidence in Him, the way we talk to Him, the things we expect of Him—everything is shaped by our vision.

That's also true of how we see ourselves. If we see ourselves as sinners who can never get things right, we'll live up to that vision. If we see ourselves as new creatures of faithfulness and authority, we'll live up to that vision instead. The way we view God, ourselves, the world, and the future determines our outlook, moods, morals, relationships, and experiences. It's absolutely vital to pay attention to how we see.

Have extreme confidence in God. Look at His plan for the world through hope-colored lenses. Understand the calling and authority He has given you. Insist on seeing truth, letting His Spirit give you His eyes. Look for His Presence with the expectation of sensing it because you know He's a God who comes to His people. In every area of life, develop your vision. You may be surprised by what you see.

Lord, let me see You, myself, other people, the world, the future—all things—the way they really are. Radically shape me from within according to truth.

January 8

*They will call him Immanuel, which
means "God is with us."*

MATTHEW 1:23

Our imagination is a tricky thing when it leads us off on tangents into unreal fantasies or wishful thinking. But God gave us the ability to imagine for a reason. Our minds don't always conjure up fiction. The imagination is a God-given blessing when it helps us picture what is true. So imagine this: Jesus is in the room.

Are you aware of that? The same feet that walked the dusty roads of Galilee are walking with you on this day in the twenty-first century. The same Spirit who hovered over the deep at the foundation of the world is breathing into you right now. The Father is looking into every corner of your heart at this very moment and is not discouraged about you. Jesus is sitting next to you with love in His heart and a welcoming smile on His face. The Spirit is hovering over you and welling up within you. You are accompanied by the divine Three-in-One as you read this, and He will be with you in anything you face today. The eternal One inhabits every passing moment of your life.

Think about these things. Let them sink in. Picture the Jesus of the Gospels by your side wherever you go. Take a few deep breaths and envision the Spirit rushing in and pouring out of you. Know that you are surrounded by the Father's love. God called His Son "Immanuel" for a reason: His desire is to be *with* you. Not against you, not observing you from a distance, not just with people in general or theoretically omnipresent. Not just in the big picture of your life but right now in the details. He is with you in every way.

*Jesus, help me see what is already true—that You are here
with me right now, that You are a constant companion
throughout every minute of my days. Please remind me to
remind myself often that You are in the room.*

January 9

Since [God] did not spare even his own Son
but gave him up for us all, won't he also
give us everything else?

ROMANS 8:32

God makes extravagant promises about our prayers. He assures us that if we ask anything according to His will, He answers. He tells us that if we believe, we will receive. He urges us to keep asking, keep seeking, and keep knocking. And He always encourages faith.

Still, we are reluctant to believe with certainty that He would respond in a tangible way to our request for His Presence. Sure, we know He's there and always will be; He promised us that, and we believe it. But *tangibly* there? *Palpably* present? *Practically* at our side? No, we're much more comfortable with theology than experience. We tend to accept the truth without expecting His touch. We don't want to ask too much.

We forget that there is no such thing as "too much" with God. He has already given us the most enormous gift He could give; every other request we have pales in comparison. God sacrificed His own Son in order to pursue intimacy with us. Why would He make such a huge sacrifice and then withhold the very kind of relationship that sacrifice was meant to secure? When we pray a prayer for more relational closeness, we don't have to tack an "if it be Your will" on the end of it. It's His will already. It's His purpose for creating us. This is a prayer we can *know* He will answer.

Yes, you were born to ask such things. You were designed not just to know *about* God but to know *Him*—experientially. You were created to connect with Him, heart to heart, spirit to Spirit, face-to-face. When you pray for closeness, you are praying according to His desires as well as yours. How will He not give you what you ask for?

Lord, I know it's a bold request, but I can't settle for less
than this. I want to feel You, to sense Your Presence, to know
without a doubt that I am being held in Your arms. Please
touch me in a way that lets me feel connected to You.

When Christ appears . . . we will be like him,
for we will see him as he really is.

1 JOHN 3:2

Before a worship service, I had been discouraged, burdened, and pessimistic. During the worship time, I began to sense Jesus' Presence and feel hopeful and lighthearted. For that brief time, I felt that I could have faith for anything and do anything He called me to do, no matter how impossible. And then a few hours afterward, I began to feel discouraged, burdened, and pessimistic again. What was the difference? Before, during, and after, I was spiritually affected by the climate around me.

John told us that when Jesus comes back, seeing Him will transform us. It's a someday promise, but it has smaller, more immediate implications. Apparently, the more clearly we see Him, the more like Him we become. Surrounded by joy, hope, and the Presence, we get glimpses of who He really is as well as who we really are. But when we unplug from that environment, we can completely lose sight of any cause for hopefulness. When He is near, we are changed to be like Him. And when He isn't—or at least when we aren't experiencing His nearness—we are affected by the world around us or the fears within us.

Which is the true you? Most people think a spiritual experience is a nice high but an exception to normal life. But actually, our new identity comes out when we're with Him, and the rest is an aberration that's passing away and one day will be gone forever. If the Presence will define who we are on the last day, as John says, then it already has the power to define us now. Hang on to those moments of faith and power. That's His Presence drawing your true self out.

Jesus, I know I'll be like You when I see You as You
are. But as I come into Your Presence now, let me see
You more clearly and be transformed. You bring out
the best in me, and I embrace as my true self the
person I become when I am with You.

January 11

Be sure of this: I am with you always,
even to the end of the age.

MATTHEW 28:20

Close your eyes (after you've finished reading this, of course). Picture Jesus sitting in front of you—His eyes looking gently into yours, His smile as encouraging and patient as you need it to be, His posture calm and unassuming. Hold this image on the screen of your mind as long as you'd like to. Then open your eyes and ask yourself, Was that an escape from reality or an escape into it?

That's just my imagination, you might think. *It wasn't real.* But consider this question: When are you closer to reality—when you're holding a picture of Jesus' Presence in your mind, or when you are going about your day, forgetting that He is with you? Never mind whether you got the details of His face right; that isn't the point. The point is that when you picture Him with you, you're holding on to biblical truth. And when you're busy and bogged down in the details of life without consciously thinking about Him, you've forgotten what's true. Your sanctified "imagination" is more in touch with reality than your preoccupied mind is.

You'll find that if you do this enough—if you get familiar enough with this Jesus—He will probably speak to you at some point. Those words, if consistent with Scripture, can be very real too. Sure, you'll want to measure them against His written Word and avoid making major decisions based solely on the voice you hear, but you can certainly hear His encouragement and love anytime you need to. He has promised to speak (John 16:13), and He has promised to be with you to the end of the age. Assuming and envisioning the truth of these words is the privilege of any child of His.

Thank you, Jesus, for being with me. Help me see
You more clearly, hear You more certainly, and trust
You more fully—in every moment of my life.

January 12

Just as the heavens are higher than the earth,
so my ways are higher than your ways and my
thoughts higher than your thoughts.

ISAIAH 55:9

"I know you seek understanding, but your normal ways of thinking won't work in My Presence and in My Kingdom. You have already noticed many paradoxes—that the first will be last, that you must serve in order to be great, that the humble will be exalted, that you must give in order to receive, that you must die in order to live. My people forget these often, even though they are specifically stated in My Word. But there are many more that are forgotten, sometimes even hardly noticed.

"One is that you must believe in order to see. Your world tells you the opposite: that you must see in order to believe. But that isn't faith. My ways always emphasize seeing the Kingdom with spiritual eyes before you see it with physical eyes. Take care what you believe; only then will you have the experience you seek.

"Another paradox is related. You expect to be delighted in Me when your desires are fulfilled—when I answer your prayers and satisfy your heart. But it works the other way around. Your desires will be fulfilled when you delight in Me. In My Kingdom your internal reality shapes your outward experience. The world teaches you to move in the opposite direction, thinking that your outward experience shapes your internal fulfillment. Don't fall for that lie. Be fulfilled—in Me, in your delights, in your belief—and watch your outer life change. Come to Me on these terms—always in ways that are higher than yours."

Father, help me change the way I think. I know this
is the heart of repentance—a change of mind to be
able to see with Your eyes. Please help me delight in
You and believe what I don't yet see.

January 13

Christ lives within you. . . . The Spirit of God,
who raised Jesus from the dead, lives in you.

ROMANS 8:10-11

Imagine standing face-to-face with Jesus, enjoying a conversation about life and all its challenges. He looks into your eyes, and you sense His perfect knowledge of your innermost thoughts, feelings, and desires. You look into His eyes and see His deep love and acceptance of you. Then, in this moment of intimacy, you see Him step closer toward you, so close it looks like He's about to knock you down. But instead of a collision, He steps right into you. He turns around so that He's looking out of your eyes, He stretches His hands down into your hands, and you begin to feel His heartbeat. The Son of God is inside. He has clothed Himself with you.

This is a true picture. Jesus does dwell within us. His Spirit has made His home in our spirits. At times, Scripture tells us that we are "in Him"—we are the ones clothed in Christ, looking through His eyes and being sheltered by His Spirit. But other verses tell us that He is in us, that He lives His life through the bodies and souls He has redeemed. His Presence is more than "in the room." We are the room He is in.

Learn to live with this picture in mind. This is part of how we retrain ourselves to see truth. Our vision shapes who we are, and if we don't envision the indwelling Christ, we don't allow Him to live through us. In fact, we often live as though He isn't even near. Develop the awareness that Jesus is looking through your eyes, guiding your feet, ministering through your mouth and hands, and sharing His heartbeat with you. And the power and Presence will increasingly become part of your experience.

Jesus, step into me and live through me as fully as You want
to. Let me truly be Your hands, feet, eyes, and mouth.

January 14

*It is God who works in you both to will
and to do for His good pleasure.*

PHILIPPIANS 2:13, NKJV

I went through a season in life in which I tried to crucify every desire that entered my heart. I would "take up my cross daily" and insist that my life be "all of Him and none of me." The problem was that if He was in me, and I was crucifying everything in me, then I was attempting to crucify Him. His desires couldn't flourish in me.

If we are filled with the Spirit's Presence, then He is stirring up many of our dreams and desires. Paul assures us that God is at work in us both to will and to work for God's pleasure. That means that He shapes our desires. When we soak in Him and become saturated with His will, His dreams are imparted to us. He sculpts our hearts and minds and gives us pictures of our future. When we try to crucify all our desires, we might be crucifying the very seeds of inspiration He planted in us. We might undermine His purposes.

Sure, we have to be discerning. Not every whim that pops up within us comes from God. But many of our deep and lasting visions and dreams are birthed by His Spirit. Because they are internal, we think they originated with "self." But if we look at them carefully, we'll often see how well they fit God's purposes and His design for us. As with Hannah, who desired a child, God can fulfill a personal dream and change the history of a nation. He uses our need for fulfillment to accomplish His purposes.

Lift your desires to God. Pour out your heart to Him. Ask Him to fulfill the dreams He has planted within you. When His Presence has planted them there, He will cultivate them until they bear fruit.

*Lord, I want only Your will, but You have put
Your will within me. Let me dream with You
and see those dreams fulfilled.*

January 15

Place me like a seal over your heart, like a seal on your arm. For love is as strong as death, its jealousy as enduring as the grave. Love flashes like fire, the brightest kind of flame. Many waters cannot quench love, nor can rivers drown it.

SONG OF SONGS 8:6-7

Presence and passion go together. We can discern from Scripture that God created human beings in order to share His love. And we can also discern that His love must be startlingly intense to have made the sacrifices He made to fulfill it. It therefore follows that His desire for presence is motivated by His passion—a kind of zeal we can barely begin to experience.

The love expressed in the Song of Songs is a taste of God's passion. Yes, it's the expression of two human beings, but God didn't create a love—or anything, for that matter—that didn't come out of His own heart or that He couldn't experience. If He created the capacity for those made in His image to feel this intensity of love, it couldn't have been foreign to Him. And because the Song is in many respects a picture of the divine romance between God and His people, it becomes a remarkable expression of the motives behind God's relentless pursuit of us. Nothing can quench His love.

These verses express the heartbeat of the One who desires our presence, and this heartbeat is stronger than anything we can imagine. His love flashes like fire, burns fiercely, and overcomes death. If we ever thought God's Presence was a casual matter, we were mistaken. God has an unyielding desire to be with us and to make His Presence known to those who seek Him. And those who reflect the intensity and relentlessness of this infinite heart, at least in some finite measure, will connect with their heart's true home.

Lord, Your passion is the driving force behind the universe. I want to experience it, to connect with Your heart, and to know the strength of Your Presence.

January 16

Let the peace of Christ rule in your hearts.
COLOSSIANS 3:15, NIV

I could feel myself spiraling downward and still seemed unable to stop the momentum. Fear, hopelessness, and bitter thoughts swirled inside my head. I fought hard to remind myself of truth, but then my thoughts would slip back into negative assumptions because they seemed truer. I was stuck—until I appealed to Jesus out loud, lifted up my voice in worship, and contended for truth with audible words. In a little while, the downward spiral was broken.

Those murky thoughts are not a sign of the Presence. Being mired in despair, fear, and bitterness is evidence of not being filled with God's thoughts. The Spirit doesn't bring us those "gifts." In fact, He dispels them. When the peace of Christ is ruling in our hearts, attitudes like anxiety and discouragement can't remain. They are contrary to the culture of His Kingdom. The Presence gives us peace, assurance, and strength.

How do you get that peace, assurance, and strength when negative thoughts swirl around in your head? How do you experience the signs of His Presence when you're stuck in something else? Acknowledging that your thoughts don't reflect the culture of the Kingdom is a start, but it helps to use your voice. Call out the name of the King or sing a worship song to Him, even when worship is the furthest thing from your mind. Invoke the Presence of Jesus, and the darkness begins to flee. There's a reason this passage about "the peace of Christ" goes on to suggest hymns and psalms and spiritual songs. Vocalizing truth and worship invites God's Presence, and His Presence changes the atmosphere.

Jesus, may Your peace rule in my heart. When my thoughts spiral down, pull me up. Hear me call, answer my appeals, accept my praise. And let Your Presence change my heart.

January 17

The angel showed me a river with the water of life, clear as crystal, flowing from the throne of God and of the Lamb.

REVELATION 22:1

The human heart longs for utopia—some Shangri-la or Fountain of Youth that makes everything "right" again. Somewhere deep inside is an impulse hungering for a place where wounds are healed, conflict is resolved, pressures cease, desires are fulfilled, and death doesn't hang over our heads. The vestiges of Eden remain in our hearts; we know the world isn't as it should be. We want something—or someone—to make it right.

The theologically correct solution, from a Christian's point of view, is that the Son of God will return and make all things new. And, in fact, He is already renewing those who believe in Him. But the re-genesis we look for, the gleaming paradise hidden in our longings, hasn't fully appeared. We saw glimpses of it in Jesus' earthly ministry—love, healings, promises, restoration; we see it in various lives and ministries today; and we see a picture of it at the end of Revelation. There's one thing in common in all such pictures: His Presence. Wherever He manifests Himself openly, perfection begins to emerge.

Every time we encounter the living Lord in our everyday lives, we are to some degree renewed. Restoration, healing, fulfillment, peace, and freedom all begin to spring up within us. He Himself *is* the utopia we long for. He doesn't make everything smooth for us, obviously, because His process begins on the inside and works its way out. But that's the difference between Him and the utopias of our imagination: we envision them beginning in our outward circumstances and then impacting our inward state of being. Jesus gets to the root of the problem—our own hearts—and uses them as a starting point for transforming the world. And in the end, we will see perfection and completion in all its fullness.

Lord, breathe Your new life into me—every part of my being—as I sit in Your Presence.

January 18

*On each side of the river grew a tree of life,
bearing twelve crops of fruit, with a fresh
crop each month. The leaves were used for
medicine to heal the nations.*

REVELATION 22:2

In God's Presence, we receive everything we need—even more than that, actually, because God is generous and doesn't stop with needs. He is a fulfiller by nature, not just for us personally but for the nations of the world. His Kingdom is comprehensive. Though it begins in the human heart, it will spread outward to impact governments, schools, media, economies, and more. God is intent on giving an inheritance of nations to His Son and His people (Psalm 2:8).

The images of Revelation 22 point to a God who fulfills His plan and His people in every way. So why don't we see more fulfillment? Why don't His plans work out in our lives as quickly or thoroughly as we would like? They will—He has promised—but there's a purpose in the process between promise and fulfillment. When we come to Him, God gives us everything we need and fulfills our longings over time. But there's a gap, and it's always designed to draw us closer to Him. Instant fulfillment—on a personal or national scale, or anything in between—satisfies our desires but does little for the relationship. When our longings continually drive us to Him, our hearts bond with His heart and we learn His ways. The result is a fulfillment greater than we had originally dreamed.

Trust God's promises, but also trust His processes. The delays in your life are specifically orchestrated to deepen your relationship with Him. The processes lead to fulfillment: He either gives us what we seek, shows that He *is* what we seek, or so overwhelms us with better things that what we once sought becomes irrelevant to us. Regardless, our hearts are eventually satisfied in Him.

*Lord, fulfill me. I feel no guilt in asking that, no
sense of selfishness. It's Your desire too. Please draw
me closer to You and satisfy my heart.*

January 19

You can make this choice by loving the LORD your God, obeying him, and committing yourself firmly to him. This is the key to your life.

DEUTERONOMY 30:20

What are you preoccupied with? Chances are, at any given moment your mind is focused on a singular issue, interest, or need, and everything else becomes peripheral. Maybe that preoccupation is the biggest item on your to-do list, the biggest problem you face, or the biggest desire in your heart. Whatever it is, it takes up a lot of mental space. Our brains have limited focus.

Our preoccupations usually don't line up with Scripture. The Word continually points us back to worship or praise or some other Kingdom focus, but instead we're distracted by competing demands about careers and relationships and personal plans for the future. In themselves, these things aren't wrong. But we have a way of making them disproportionately large. And our one true focus—God—seems to get pushed out of the way to make room.

Why aren't we more preoccupied with Him? Why don't we wake up each day with one pressing question: how can I love Him well? Why aren't we more intentional about caring for the heart of the Father? Other concerns can drain energy from our primary purpose. Unless we fulfill our primary purpose, none of the rest falls into place or ultimately satisfies us. But if we do fulfill that purpose—if we choose to love God not just in theory but in the largest spaces of our hearts and minds—He becomes more practically and powerfully present in us and with us. He watches over our concerns when we watch over His.

Choose to love and adore Him as your primary preoccupation, and see what He does with the other concerns of your life. He will fight battles, win victories, and resolve issues for those who are focused on Him.

Lord, show me how You want to be loved. Help me know how to care for Your heart and adore You well. Fill my thoughts with Yourself above all else.

January 20

None of them shall teach his neighbor, and
none his brother, saying, "Know the LORD,"
for all shall know Me, from the least of
them to the greatest of them.

HEBREWS 8:11, NKJV

Experiencing God's Presence, hearing His voice, and sensing His touch are often criticized for being too subjective. Many prefer to keep their relationship with God in the realm of the purely objective, where no misunderstandings can occur and no cults can be spawned. But while an insistence on objectivity is certainly helpful in defining the tenets of one's faith, it's also a very effective way to quench a relationship. Warmth and intimacy are never the product of definitions.

Think about it. What meaningful human relationship isn't subjective? A marriage may be established objectively, but its depth certainly isn't. A marriage without feelings, intuition, instincts, and a history of subjective interpretation isn't much of a relationship. Neither does a friendship have any quality without its intangibles and abstract aspects. Any relationship that is more than a formality is by nature a subjective experience. And the last thing we want with God is a formality.

Don't define your doctrine subjectively, but don't be afraid to relate to God that way. The Bible is full of subjective experiences with Him. A religion can be taught, but a relationship has to be developed—moment by moment, person to person. The writer of Hebrews, quoting Jeremiah, assures us that everyone can know the Lord personally—not just know *about* Him, but know Him relationally. That involves a wide range of spiritual seeing, hearing, and sensing. God means to be experienced. He rewards those who know that and who diligently seek Him.

Lord, You promise that I can know You—not
just theoretically, but through the experience of a
genuine relationship. I want that. My prayer is
that You would become more and more real to me
as I turn my thoughts toward You.

January 21

*Anyone who wants to come to him must
believe that God exists . . .*

HEBREWS 11:6

It seems so basic. Anyone who wants to seek God must believe He actually exists. But since most people—and probably all of those in the original readership of the letter to the Hebrews—have believed God exists, the statement hardly seems necessary. Add that the statement is made to those who want to come to God, and it seems even stranger. Those who come to God wouldn't be coming if they didn't believe in His existence.

But the statement may be more insightful than we assume. For all our belief in God, many of us have lived as practical atheists—people for whom God is a rock-solid concept in our minds but who has no practical relevance to our daily lives. Many think about God, pray to Him sometimes, and assume He expects good moral behavior, but His Spirit doesn't enter into their moment-by-moment decisions, they don't hear or even listen for His voice, and they don't live in His strength rather than their own. So though God exists, He doesn't exist in any way that's meaningful to them. And that doesn't lead to any kind of meaningful experience with Him.

The first foundational truth in experiencing God's Presence in a real way is to believe that He exists in practical terms—as an accessible, relatable personality. That's the first step, but it's so simple that we often forget it. God drifts to the back of our minds, and before we know it, He's an idea, a quiet piece of background music to our lives. We have to continually bring Him back to the forefront—the object of our worship and the Person we relate to constantly. When we do, we begin an adventure into His very real Presence.

*Lord, I not only believe You exist, I believe You
want to be an integral part of every minute of
my life. Let me not forget like many do; give me
reminders of Your Presence moment by moment.*

. . . and that he rewards those who
sincerely seek him.

HEBREWS 11:6

Deists believe that "the supreme Architect" created the world and left it alone. Like a master clockmaker, He carefully crafted the universe and wound it up. Now it's running on its own, no intervention necessary. No miracles, no special revelations. God may be watching from a distance, they say, but He isn't active in our affairs. He's simply there.

The writer of Hebrews has told us that those who come to God must believe that He is, but that isn't enough. We also have to believe that He rewards those who sincerely seek Him—that pursuing Him makes a difference in how He responds to us. If we simply believe God is there, watching, or that we have to twist His arm to notice us or bless us, then we aren't perceiving Him well. According to His own Word, He longs to bless us, to have compassion on us, to answer our prayers, and to enter into a deep relationship with us. He invites us to seek Him zealously and faithfully. And He assures us that when we do, He rewards.

If you really want to know and experience God more fully, you'll have to approach Him with the expectation that He rewards those who seek Him. If you think He *might* respond, you'll interpret any delays or hiddenness as reluctance on His part. If you think He only responds to those who live up to His standards, you'll interpret any delays or hiddenness as a sign of failure on your part. But if you assume—by faith—that He is eager to respond to your pursuit of Him, you'll begin to interpret all of life as a conversation with Him. And your awareness of His Presence will increase dramatically.

Father, I know You enjoy my pursuit of You and
are zealous in pursuit of me, too. Please reward me
with Your Presence quickly and clearly enough that
I don't get discouraged but am inspired to press
even further into You.

January 23

It was by faith that . . .
HEBREWS 11:7

Hebrews 11 is a landmark chapter in Scripture—the Hall of Fame of faith, as many call it. It describes the experiences of those who heard God, believed Him, and followed Him into His purposes. Verses 4, 5, 7, 8, and 11 begin with "it was by faith that . . ." and are followed by the heroic exploits of those who believed. Repeatedly, this chapter and Scripture as a whole affirm that we aren't just called to believe in God's existence and seek to know Him, we are invited into a working partnership with Him. We become, as Paul called it, His co-workers (2 Corinthians 6:1, NIV). We join Him in His mission.

This was true even in the Garden, where God told Adam and Eve that they were to subdue the earth He had created. We see it in Isaiah, where God looked around for people to intercede (59:16) and where He urged His watchmen to pray ceaselessly for Him to do what He already said He wanted to do (62:6). God created human beings to know Him and love Him, but the relationship includes quite a few joint efforts. We are bound to Him not only for salvation but also for working with Him and, ultimately, reigning with Him.

God's goal for your faith is not just salvation. It's a deep and lasting partnership in which He accomplishes His purposes through you. He is powerful enough to do anything He wants without anyone's help, but power isn't the issue. This God of relationship doesn't often work in this world independently. He wants to work with you and through you. It's His way of ensuring that His Presence is known and experienced by those He loves. And it's a vital way in which you come to know Him.

Father, I realize that if I don't partner with You by
faith to accomplish Your purposes, I can't experience
You as fully as You want. Please lead me by faith
into great exploits for Your Kingdom.

January 24

All these people died still believing what God had promised them. They did not receive what was promised, but they saw it all from a distance and welcomed it.

HEBREWS 11:13

All the heroes of faith we look up to—all those famous characters we assume stand head and shoulders above us—are people who did not receive all of God's promise. Abraham, who received a promised son, didn't step fully into God's complete purpose for humanity. Neither did Enoch, who was taken to heaven without dying because his relationship with God was so close. Neither did Noah or Jacob or Joseph. God accomplished amazing things through them and wrote His story with them so we could probe for deep, eternal truths. But they didn't see the Kingdom come. They didn't experience His Spirit dwelling within them. They didn't enjoy His constant Presence. They lived in a time when things were still developing.

We live under a better covenant. That's the point the writer of Hebrews is making. Not only can we know God exists, receive His rewards for seeking Him, and partner with Him on His mission; the relationship we can have with Him now is qualitatively better than the relationship these heroes of faith had with Him. Jesus has raised us into an entirely new creation. We can know God more completely than they did.

God gave these men and women of faith some glimpses of the ultimate goal—an eternal dwelling where His Presence is the centerpiece and where we will dwell with them. So when you pursue His Presence today, you are pursuing His ultimate goal for you. You don't have to add "if it's Your will" to that prayer. It is. He has already said so and has pointed us to an eternal city filled with His Presence. The longing within you is like a homing device that always leads you to Him. Follow it without reservation.

Lord, it's hard to believe that I can experience You more fully than Abraham, Jacob, and Joseph did, but You say so. Please help me never fall short of that goal.

January 25

God had something better in mind for us.

HEBREWS 11:40

If we were designed for a deeper relationship with God than the Old Testament heroes of faith enjoyed, why do most of us have a hard time experiencing it? Perhaps it's because we rationalize God's overtures toward us as random or coincidence. Or maybe we just assume we can never live up to their example. But beyond the question of *why* is *what*. What kind of relationship can we have with God that they couldn't? How can we know Him more fully? The answer is sprinkled throughout the New Testament: we can be filled with God's Spirit, joined to Jesus in complete unity, inhabited and sustained by His very life. What Abraham, Jacob, Joseph, and others experienced externally has been planted within us. The Kingdom—and the King—are within.

Think about the implications of verses like Galatians 2:20, which informs us we no longer live but Christ lives within us. Or John 17:21-23, in which Jesus prays that we, Jesus, and the Father would be joined together in "perfect unity" as one. This is far greater than seeking God, knowing Him, and partnering with Him. It's an organic union that makes us inseparably joined with His Spirit. That's a far better thing than the Old Testament experience. The Presence isn't just for the eternal city. It's for now.

That should motivate us to pursue God even more zealously than we already do. We can have greater, fuller, more adventurous experiences with Him than many of the great people of Scripture did. They are examples for us, not exceptions, and the New Testament invites us to go deeper—to experience His Presence more fully and concretely and consistently. Don't miss that opportunity. Don't become complacent where you are. God is always inviting you to go further with Him.

Father, how can this be? I don't fully understand our union, but I want to experience it more completely. This is Your desire and mine, so I know You'll answer when I ask You to show me the depths of this truth.

January 26

*I will bless those who have humble
and contrite hearts.*

ISAIAH 66:2

God is drawn to humility. We can understand that; we're the same way. Most of us have a negative reaction to those who are proud, and we enjoy the company of the humble. So it's no surprise that God—who made us in His image—exhibits the same attraction to those who are selfless and unassuming. It's the way He meant us to be.

God deeply desires intimacy with us, but it has to be an intimacy of integrity. A relationship based on false assumptions isn't a real relationship, and pride is a false assumption. It's an overestimation of our own abilities or resources. It's a sense of independence from the One who made us who we are and gives us everything we have. The arrogant keep God at arm's length.

If we want God to manifest His Presence in our lives, we have to position ourselves to receive it. That requires a lot of humility, a sense of dependence, and an awareness of need. God comes to us as the source of life on the condition that we know we need His life in us. He comes to fill us only when we know we're empty. He comes to meet our needs only when we realize how deep they are. He comes as our strength on the condition that we know our weakness. Pride blinds us to these realities; humility accepts them wholeheartedly.

Position yourself to encounter God by embracing your desperation for Him. Let complete honesty with yourself produce humility, even if such honesty is uncomfortable. Know that letting down all walls and being completely vulnerable opens you up to His life-giving Presence. Only empty vessels are ready to be filled.

*Father, I come to You as an empty well. I bring
nothing but space for You. Fill me with Yourself.*

January 27

The Spirit said to him, "Simon, three men are looking for you. So get up and go downstairs. Do not hesitate to go with them, for I have sent them."

ACTS 10:19-20, NIV

God spoke to Cornelius through an angel, telling him to send for Simon Peter. Meanwhile, Peter saw a vision from God, telling him to receive the men sent from Cornelius and to go with them. This divine setup was an invitation to participate in God's mission to the Gentiles, but it would never have happened if God hadn't broken through some of Peter's assumptions. Peter had to be made sensitive to the Spirit's movement in a new direction.

One of the best ways to experience God's Presence is to notice what He's doing. When we notice His movements in people's lives and are sensitive to whatever role He might want us to play, we can align ourselves with His work. We then experience His direction and His power as we partner with Him. We join with His Spirit to accomplish His mission. We step into the Presence for a purpose.

Watch how God is working on people's hearts. Ask the Spirit to alert you to His purposes in drawing them to Himself. Notice the crises they are going through, the questions they are wrestling with, and the ways God is setting them up to encounter Him. Be available to encourage them, build them up, and point them to Him. If you notice the ways He is present in their lives and join Him there, He becomes more present in your life. The more closely you align with His plans, the more powerfully you experience Him.

Holy Spirit, make me sensitive to what You're doing, not only in my life but also in the people around me. Open doors for me to step into the flow of Your work. Give me wisdom and restraint not to get in the way, but help me see Your invitation when You offer it. Please give me the privilege of seeing Your Presence change lives.

January 28

We are the temple of the living God.

2 CORINTHIANS 6:16

When Moses built the Tabernacle and Solomon built the Temple, the glory of God filled those holy places so dramatically that observers were in awe and could hardly function or even stand up straight. In places that were dedicated to Him, set apart for His dwelling, cleansed from anything that represented impurity, and anointed with symbols of His Presence and power, He came. He wanted to dwell with His people.

He still does, and the relationship is much more intimate now. He doesn't just dwell *with* His people, He dwells *in* us. Most of us know that—in our heads. But what does that look like at a heart level? With what level of awareness do we live in that truth each day? How conscious are we of the Presence? That we have to keep reminding ourselves that the Spirit lives within us is revealing. We need to find a way to instinctively and naturally let the Presence flow out of us. And in order to do that, we need to be filled and saturated to the point of overflowing.

Try this exercise: Sit with your eyes closed and imagine the Spirit blowing around you like a gentle breeze. As He swirls up, over, and around, touching every inch of you, imagine the intensity of the wind increasing. Let it grow stronger. Then envision the rushing wind blowing *through* you—penetrating your skin and swirling up and around inside of you. As He does, picture every corner of your body, soul, and spirit being cleansed. You are glowing from within, smoldering with the glory of God. That glory will intensify, flowing up and out of you when needed. Savor that awareness as long as you can. It's a true picture. Let it sink in. Then live fully aware of this power at work within you.

Spirit, rush through me, cleanse me, blow the dirt and dust out of every corner, and fill me with Your glory. Let me live according to this truth.

January 29

When you go through deep waters, I will be with you. When you go through rivers of difficulty, you will not drown. When you walk through the fire of oppression, you will not be burned up; the flames will not consume you.

ISAIAH 43:2

"You may have noticed that I haven't kept you from the deep waters, the rivers of difficulty, or the fire of oppression. I'm capable of doing so, yet I've chosen not to. I've allowed you to experience situations that compel you to depend on Me, to learn about My Presence, and to believe in My goodness in spite of what you see. I'm honored when you insist—to the world, to your friends, to the adversary himself—that I'm loving and good. Your affirmations of My character are highly valued in heaven.

"Even so, I don't leave you in the waters and fires. I assure you that My Presence is with you in the midst of them, and I promise that you will pass through them unharmed. You will experience trials in this world, but you will not be overcome by them. You worry because you feel as if I'm watching from a distance, and the more you think so, the more you question My love and compassion for you. But I'm present at all times. The dangers you go through are carefully measured. Evil is rampant in this world, but I put limits around it. Your trials may seem overwhelming, but I would never let them crush you. I can't. I'm the God of promise, and I always keep My word.

"You never need to wonder if I've forsaken you. You've placed your trust in Me, and I never violate your trust. In your crises, remember My Presence. Know that I'm there. And be assured that you will pass through them unharmed."

Father, help me hang on to Your promise, even when I can't see or sense Your Presence. Give me the strength and faith to pass through my trials in triumph.

*"My thoughts are nothing like your thoughts,"
says the LORD. "And my ways are far beyond
anything you could imagine."*

ISAIAH 55:8

God issues an invitation to His people in Isaiah 55—an invitation for the thirsty and hungry to come drink and eat at no cost and an invitation for those who need mercy to receive it freely. Apparently the opportunity is surprisingly generous; the Lord has to assure them that He doesn't think like they do. And it's true: He is often assumed to be more unyielding than He is. He is more lavish than we think.

That's a constant discrepancy between those who see imperfectly and the God who is perfect: "People don't understand My desires. I'm viewed through the wrong lenses, unsympathetic ones. My people have been so immersed in falsehoods and distorted perspectives that they have become sympathetic to mistaken views of Me. But I want you to see through My eyes. I want you to have My mind, and I've assured you that you can. You need to understand My heart for you.

"Don't underestimate the treasure I've put within you and the magnificence of the new creation I've made you into. Yes, I know your history, and I know all the flaws in your heart right now, but why focus on that? How does looking down on yourself reflect My glory? Haven't you realized that I'm much more glorified by turning creatures of dust into children of God than by all your talk about being 'only human'? Your thoughts about yourself are not My thoughts about you, and neither are your thoughts about Me the same as My thoughts about Me. You haven't even begun to grasp My extravagance. But you will. If you let Me, I will show you more of Myself and reveal more of My thoughts. They are better than you think."

*Lord, impart Your thoughts to me. Give me Your eyes so
I can see how You see. I don't want to view You through
the wrong lenses. I want to know Your goodness fully.*

January 31

*Wherever the Spirit of the Lord is,
there is freedom.*
2 CORINTHIANS 3:17

One of the most beautiful by-products of the Presence of the Lord is freedom. The reason it's so beautiful is that so many people have been enslaved. All of us start out in that condition as captives of a fallen world and the sin that plagues us, but many of us continue in that condition as believers. Why? Because we address our former captivity with relentless attempts at developing new behavior patterns. New behavior is part of the gospel, of course, but not as the result of a religious system or even "biblical" principles to which we try to conform. External constraints can never free us from sin; they can only clean up our appearance. Real freedom comes when we are transformed from within, actually experience a new nature, and then act "naturally."

Many Christians don't experience freedom because they don't know what kind of freedom the Spirit gives. Not only does the gospel free us from sin, it also frees us from anything that defines our relationship with God as something other than a relationship with Him. From systems of belief or behavior rather than living interaction with Him. From laws about righteousness rather than the righteousness that results from His Presence in us. From the dictates of a constrained heart rather than a transformed heart. Anything less than this is bondage.

Refuse to be bound by sin, by religious systems, or by false principles of "spiritual" behavior, even if those principles are derived from parts of the Bible. The Bible tells us what a new creation looks like, but it also tells us that the only way to become new is by God's supernatural power working within us, not by standards imposed from outside of us. The only "obedience" now required of us is obedience to the impulses and movements of the Spirit Himself. When we follow Him freely, we freely become who we were meant to be.

*Holy Spirit, You are my only law because You are
my life. Thank You for setting me free!*

February 1

"Who can know the Lᴏʀᴅ's thoughts? Who knows enough to teach him?" But we understand these things, for we have the mind of Christ.

1 CORINTHIANS 2:16

Paul has been writing about spiritual wisdom—*God's* wisdom, the "deep secrets" of His heart (v. 10). No one can know God's thoughts except God's Spirit, Paul says, but God has given us His Spirit. Therefore we can know His thoughts.

Does Paul simply mean we can know God's thoughts as they are revealed in the New Testament? No, he is writing to people long before a "new testament" was ever conceived or compiled. He means that the Spirit within us can plant within us the very mind of God. We have supernatural access to divine wisdom.

Why would God allow us open access to His thinking? Listen to His voice: "When you have the mind of Christ, as I've promised, you will see through My eyes. Then you will know what My mission and My purposes are, and you will therefore know what *your* mission and purposes are. See through My eyes, and you won't have to wrestle with My will for your life. You'll go where My Spirit leads, and when in doubt, you'll be sensitive to My redirection. Remember how I redirected Paul to Macedonia as he traveled through Asia. I just had to guide him more specifically, but he was already moving because he had My heart. Live according to the heart I've given you, and I will redirect you when necessary.

"My Presence leads you like the cloud of glory and the pillar of fire led Israel through the wilderness, but now from within, not from outside of you. Know that the cloud and fire are inside you. Trust in My guidance. Once you see through My eyes, you'll simply go and do according to what you see."

Lord, I want to see as You see and act according to Your vision within me. I'm tired of trying to decipher Your will. Please plant Your thoughts within me and move me as You desire.

February 2

Love never gives up, never loses faith,
is always hopeful, and endures
through every circumstance.

1 CORINTHIANS 13:7

You have moments—those times when God seems to be against you, when everything seems "off" and He seems far, far away. And you let Him know about it too, don't you? Maybe you don't voice accusations out loud, but you think about how He wouldn't let certain things happen if He were really good. You point out that He could have intervened differently if He wanted to. You assume He has let you down.

It's okay. Most of us have those thoughts. In our honest moments in the midst of a trial, we fear that we are out of sync with God—or worse, that He might be out of sorts with us. The mind can go to a lot of bad places when we feel distant from God. That's when we can develop imperceptible grudges that last decades and keep us from fully trusting Him. Those are opportune moments for bitterness toward God to seep into our souls.

What's the solution? No matter what you're going through, determine to look at God through love-colored lenses, which are far more accurate than our natural perceptions. Apply the well-known truths of 1 Corinthians 13 not only to others but also to God. We are called above all else to love Him, after all, and if love is patient, then we can choose not to be impatient with Him. If love bears all things, then we can choose to bear all things. If love always hopes and always perseveres . . . well, you get the picture. If we love God, we can look past our trials and troubles to see God's heart of love somewhere behind them. When we do, the distance we feel between us and Him begins to disappear.

Father, I know You are with me and for me. I choose,
even against my natural perceptions, to show my love
for You by being patient, trusting, and hopeful, and by
persevering in whatever I face today.

February 3

I tell you the truth, the Son can do nothing by himself. He does only what he sees the Father doing. Whatever the Father does, the Son also does.

JOHN 5:19

A lot of people read the Bible to answer the question, "What should I do?" Their primary focus in their relationship with God is on behavior. But while doing the right things is important, it isn't primary. The main purpose of any genuine relationship of love and friendship is not doing but knowing. Actions flow from intimacy, not vice versa.

We see that in Jesus' words, if we look closely enough. First, He does nothing by Himself. That means His intimacy with the Father has developed before His actions. He has to know the Father in order to say that. But He also says He does only what He sees the Father doing—which means before any behavioral response, He sees. He knows and sees, then He does. That's how relationships work.

Jesus never said, "I figure out what to do by reading Scripture and obeying what it says." His "doing" is relational from beginning to end. Does Scripture play a part in that? Absolutely. But the issue on Jesus' heart isn't deciphering what the Word instructs; it's knowing the One who spoke the Word to begin with.

What question is on your heart as you read the Bible? What are you trying to find out? Your answer makes a huge difference not only in how you live your life but also in how well you get to know God. Many of us default to "instruction mode" when we read Scripture because we don't have the interest or the know-how to pursue real intimacy with Him. We don't see what He's doing, so we dig out the principles in the Word and rely on them as His instructions. That's religion, not relationship, and God wants to get much more personal than that.

Lord, I can't settle for just "reading the instructions." Please show me who You are so I can recognize what You are doing. I want intimacy with You, whatever it costs.

February 4

The Father loves the Son and shows him
everything he is doing.

JOHN 5:20

As Jesus continues to explain His modus operandi for doing the Father's will, He further ties it to their relationship. This is no read-it-then-do-it approach. It's the outflow of intimacy between Him and the Father. Jesus is able to do what He sees His Father doing because the Father loves the Son and shows Him what He is doing. Though many Christians pursue a Master-servant relationship with the Lord, that isn't what Jesus models for us. And that isn't the kind of relationship that cultivates a sense of His Presence.

Read the Bible with this question in mind: "What's on your heart, Lord?" Intimacy and a sense of Presence develop in that kind of approach. Relationships are about spending time with someone—not in order to hear instructions but to get to know likes and dislikes and priorities and values. The point is for our hearts to grow together with God's. When we approach God on those terms—with a genuine interest in knowing *Him*—we begin to hear His voice and sense His Presence. He shows us what He is doing. Then we, like Jesus, can do what we see the Father doing.

What's your agenda when you come to God? Is it only to get instructions so you can do the right things? Or is it to soak in His Presence, cultivate intimacy, and absorb His heart's desires? One approach develops a strong Master-servant relationship, and the other develops a strong Father-child or Friend-friend relationship. According to Jesus' example, God's ultimate goal for us is the latter. And that's how we more deeply experience Him.

Above all else, Father, I want to experience Your
love. And I want everything else—every act
of service, every decision about priorities, every
relationship—to flow out of that love.

One thing I ask from the LORD, this only do I seek: that I may dwell in the house of the LORD all the days of my life, to gaze on the beauty of the LORD and to seek him in his temple.

PSALM 27:4, NIV

For many, the Christian life is a series of how-to principles. How to pray, how to share our faith, how to study the Bible, how to discover our spiritual gifts . . . and on and on. We seek formulas. Why? Because it's hard to have a relationship with an invisible God. Formulas are easier. If we can just find the key, crack the code, or take the steps that will get us from point A to point B in any given area of life, we'll be the people we were meant to be. That's the path of discipleship. So we think.

Though it's a well-worn path, it leads to futility. God is not a formula or a series of steps. He's a Person who enjoys relationship. He doesn't draw near to those who learn the principles or "get it right." He draws near to those who have a heart connection with Him. When we invest ourselves in His interests, He is much more inclined to invest Himself in ours.

Psalm 27:4 gives us a relational paradigm—not a how-to formula but a heart attitude—that cultivates God's Presence. David wants to be in the house of the Lord "to gaze" and "to seek." The first is worship—adoration of the King. The second is prayer—pleading His will. And the order is important. Love comes first, then asking. That's how healthy relationships function.

Don't rush into God's Presence with a list of requests and then marvel that your prayer formula doesn't accomplish much. Relationships are more than lists. Invest in His heart and see how He responds.

Lord, I want first and foremost to gaze at You. To behold You. To take the cares of Your heart into my own. Only then can I seek Your direction and Your gifts.

February 6

When the cool evening breezes were blowing,
the man and his wife heard the LORD God
walking about in the garden. So they hid from
the LORD God among the trees.

GENESIS 3:8

Imagine a place where God's Presence is obvious, where He can be sensed and experienced. In this place, there's nothing to keep you from knowing Him. No shame, no guilt, no fear—nothing. You are free to be completely yourself, knowing that He's fine with exactly who you are. You experience Him fully.

That's how it was in Eden. But when our first parents disobeyed God, that sense of Presence was lost. They were afraid and embarrassed to be around Him. Designed for an intimate relationship with their Creator, they wanted only to hide.

Ever since then, we've felt distant from God. We don't see or hear Him like the first human beings did. We feel ashamed and just assume God doesn't want to be close to us. And we question whether we can trust Him: "I know He loves others, but does He really love me?" "Does He even *like* me? Or am I on His bad side today?" "I know His plans for me are good—by *His* definition—but will I like them?" Our questions come because of the distance we feel. We can't see His smile or feel His love or hear the warmth of His voice. We mistrust an invisible God.

God wants an extremely deep, very personal relationship with us. We believe—at least theologically—that everything standing between us and Him was removed through Jesus' sacrifice. But do we really *live* as though nothing stands between us? Not often. Our instinct is often still to hide. Yet Scripture is clear: the relationship is restored. Nothing can hinder it but unbelief. So what's the key to experiencing His Presence? Believing. Know that He is there and live as though it's true.

Father, I believe that there's nothing between You and
me, and I choose to base my life on that fact. I have
nothing to hide from You. I come to You as I am—and
pray that You would come to me as You are.

You will keep in perfect peace all who trust in you, all whose thoughts are fixed on you!

ISAIAH 26:3

Your attention is a precious commodity, and myriad voices are vying for it. Your to-do list screams at you. The circumstances that pop up unexpectedly demand an immediate reaction. The people in your life are probably a little more polite about getting your attention, but they still expect a response. And the to-do list, the urgent circumstances, and the people you live and work with all have important concerns. You have God-given responsibilities with all of them. But their cumulative voices can be relentless. Meanwhile, you're sometimes just looking for a moment to breathe.

It's impossible to remain aware of God consistently when we're under such assaults. We have to prioritize, placing Him at the top of our list even at the expense of other worthy goals. If we want to have any awareness of His closeness, any sense of His Presence, any hint of His voice, we have to clear the clutter out of our minds, sit with Him, and be still. There's no other way.

This is where we find out the depth of our desire for God. Would we simply like to experience Him? Or are we desperate for Him? The way we prioritize our time reveals a lot. If knowing Him is more urgent to us than the voices that demand our attention, we'll make room for Him and eventually experience Him deeply. If not, we won't.

We have to determine to make hard choices and then brace for the assault against them. That doesn't mean we neglect our loved ones and responsibilities, but we do have to remember which relationship is our life. Seeking God's Presence and fixing our thoughts on Him takes time, but it's vital. And it speaks peace to every other voice that seeks our attention.

Lord, I fix my thoughts on You. I choose to spend time sitting in Your Presence each day, to turn my heart toward You in brief in-between moments, and to expect You to step into my circumstances and relationships.

February 8

You are holy, enthroned in the praises of Israel.

PSALM 22:3, NKJV

God inhabits praise. Actually, God inhabits our hearts and all circumstances we devote to Him, but He is especially active in our worship. When our hearts are turned toward Him in adoration, He feels at home in them. This is what He designed us for.

Why is God so drawn to worship? Not because He's an egomaniac but because it's an accurate perception of who He is and a celebration of the relationship we have with Him. It's the clearest picture of heaven that we can reflect on earth.

Think about it. How do words of affirmation sound to you? How much do you enjoy compliments for a job well done or a life well lived? You, who were made in God's image, thrive on appreciation from others. It only makes sense that the God who patterned us after Himself has the same feelings of joy when He is appreciated.

When we realize this and choose to praise God more intentionally, our first attempts often feel contrived. An inner voice may tell us we are just praising Him out of a sense of obligation or in order to experience His benefits. Ignore that voice. So what if worship takes practice—if we have to press through some awkward moments? All relationships have those moments. Choose to worship anyway. Pick an attribute of God and compliment Him for it. Tell Him you love how He created this world or the tenderness He was able to put in the human heart, which surely reflects His own. Admire Him. We usually have no trouble talking about the skills, talents, and admirable characteristics of other human beings; we can do the same with God. And when we do, He inhabits us, our words, and our hearts in often dramatic ways.

Father, I love how You are drawn to words of affirmation. I love that You desire my heart and my attention. I want to fulfill Your desires, knowing that Your Presence will fulfill mine.

February 9

Go! Let it be done just as you believed it would.

MATTHEW 8:13, NIV

There is a sense in which we experience God the way we expect to. In a parable about a master who had given his servants some money to invest, two servants were comfortable enough with the master to take some risks. One saw him as "a hard man" (Matthew 25:24, NIV). And though all three had the same master, they each experienced him exactly according to their expectations.

It's the same way with God. If we perceive Him as a hard master, we probably experience a hard master. If we understand His grace, we experience grace. It isn't that God's character varies; He's unchanging. But our faith determines our experience of Him.

This is a hugely important truth in whether we experience God's Presence. If we ask Him to make His Presence felt but think the answer to that prayer is a long shot, we aren't very likely to be aware of His touch. But if we pray fully confident that He will answer, we'll encounter Him.

Do you really believe God's Presence is meant to be experienced—that it's more than theoretical? Do you seek with the expectation that you'll find? Do you ask for a tangible touch with the knowledge that He wants to give it? Look within when you ask, seek, and knock. What you expect in your heart will largely determine what you get in your experience.

God gave us a Bible full of examples of real encounters with Him, of hearing His voice and seeing His works, and we have to agree with these standards. The relationship is based on faith, to be sure, but the experience of it is meant to be concrete. Not to believe we can experience Him in real, tangible ways is to disagree with Him. If He promised we would know Him, not just know about Him—and He did—then we can.

Lord, I believe. I expect You to make Yourself more real to me each day. And I wait with eager anticipation for You to do so.

February 10

*I pray that the eyes of your heart may be
enlightened in order that you may know the
hope to which he has called you, the riches of his
glorious inheritance in his holy people, and his
incomparably great power for us who believe.*

EPHESIANS 1:18-19, NIV

Your heart has eyes. In fact, you have a whole range of spiritual senses that correspond to your physical senses. According to God's Word, you can "hear" His voice (John 10:3, NKJV), you can "taste and see" that He is good (Psalm 34:8), you can experience His "touch" (Luke 4:40), and you can carry the "aroma" of Christ (2 Corinthians 2:15, NIV). Scripture and history are full of examples of people who have encountered Him with these spiritual senses. Such perceptions are much more than figurative encounters; they are real—as real as the seeing, hearing, feeling, tasting, and smelling we do with our natural senses. God has always invited us not into a system of beliefs but into a range of experiences.

But our spiritual senses have become dulled. Perhaps it's because we've been well trained by materialist philosophies and believed the lie that we can trust only empirical data—as if any relationship could be measured by empirical data. Or maybe it's because we just haven't cultivated our capacity to perceive. Either way, we're missing out on our primary means of communing with God. Our senses need to be awakened.

How do we do that? Ask God to awaken them. Use them often. Reject any fear of making mistakes—all growing children make mistakes in how they perceive things. Over time, we learn. Like Paul, we can pray for ourselves and others that the "eyes" of the heart—as well as the ears, hands, and other means of spiritual perception—would be enlightened so we can know Him and receive whatever He has prepared for us (Ephesians 2:10). Eventually, we experience Him in ways that are more real than anything our physical world can give us.

*Breathe into my senses, Spirit. Let me commune
with You with spiritual sights, sounds, touch, tastes,
and smells. Drive me into a deeper reality than my
physical nature has ever known.*

February 11

*Surely the LORD is in this place, and I
wasn't even aware of it!*

GENESIS 28:16

Jacob had fled his home and slept under the stars on a stone pillow. As far as he knew, he was in a very ordinary place. But ordinary places become extraordinary when God shows up. During the night, Jacob had a dream in which he saw a stairway leading into heaven and angels going up and down it. At the top of the staircase was the Lord Himself.

Jacob woke up with a new understanding of his location and renewed assurance of God's promises. Portals to heaven don't occur often, and when they do, the place seems sacred. Jacob went to sleep one night without a clue that God was unusually present, and he woke up the next morning in awe of His Presence. Neither the place nor the person had changed; the only difference was an encounter with God.

That's why we seek encounters. Jacob hadn't sought—and God does sometimes choose to encounter those who haven't expected to see Him—but the invitation in Scripture is to pursue God's Presence wholeheartedly. An if-it-happens-it-happens approach is rarely rewarded; God honors those who single-mindedly seek Him.

We can never assume that God is absent from the ordinary places of our lives. Neither can we assume that long seasons of "ordinary" are a sign that God doesn't want to meet with us. Just beyond our vision, He watches and waits.

Know that wherever you go, you are on potentially sacred ground. An encounter with God will make it so. Ask for that. Open your eyes. Expect divine visitations. The God who seeks a relationship will find ways to make Himself known to those who look for Him.

*Lord, I'm looking for You. Open my eyes
to see. Let me encounter You in the ordinary
and extraordinary places of my life. Help me
be prepared to recognize Your Presence at any
moment of any day.*

February 12

This is the secret: Christ lives in you. This gives you assurance of sharing his glory.

COLOSSIANS 1:27

The New Testament contains quite a few verses that we often "believe" without really believing. One of them is that the same Jesus who walked this planet two millennia ago is actually alive in us, moving and working through us now. It's a great theological principle that slips from our consciousness quickly and easily, in part because it's such a mystery. We're more comfortable with concrete, practical reality, not invisible realms we can only access by diving into spiritual depths. We affirm the principle of the mystical union between Jesus and us while shying away from the actual experience of it.

There's a cost to not consciously and constantly embracing "Christ in you, the hope of glory" (NIV). We miss His Presence. Pastor and scholar A. W. Pink agreed: "One grand reason why we have so little of His sacred Presence with us, and His power and influence manifested among us may be laid to the account of neglecting to preach supernatural, spiritual truth, and the mysteries of the everlasting Gospel." When we dwell on this mystery and let it sink in, we experience it more. When we don't, we don't.

Our only hope of truly knowing the glory God has given us—the beauty and weight of His goodness—is in becoming aware that Jesus is in us without fear of the supernatural or mystical aspects of this truth. The actual Being who walked dusty roads with His disciples, unveiled His glory on a mountain, and did miracles that stunned those around Him is in those who believe. Right now. And though it's always true, we only experience it when we know it and believe it. It's our responsibility and privilege to know and believe it well.

Jesus, You really are in me. I know that. But I want to know it in actual experience every day—to see the evidence of You in me and to know the hope of glory. Please display this mystery in me.

February 13

We have this treasure in jars of clay to show that this all-surpassing power is from God and not from us.

2 CORINTHIANS 4:7, NIV

The safety video on an airplane reminds us that if the oxygen masks fall from the overhead compartments, parents should put on their own masks first before helping their children. It seems selfish, doesn't it? A parent taking care of his or her own needs before trying to save the life of the child sitting in the next seat? That goes against our instincts. But the reason for the me-first approach is obvious: if the parent passes out, there is no one to help the child.

Some of us tend to pour out our lives for others without taking care of ourselves. Though God has called us to be carriers of His Presence into this world, we often go into the world without having cultivated the Presence. We neglect the flame within us, and the result is a host of burned-out God-carriers who have only normal human capabilities to offer. But the world is already full of normal human capabilities. It needs more of God's nature. It needs people who can impart God's peace, speak His truth, access divine strategies, and carry His power. And in order for that to happen, we have to cultivate His Presence within us.

Pouring out for those around you is a vital part of the calling God has placed within you, but if you aren't pouring out the life of God, you're pouring out yourself. That's admirable, but it isn't enough. You're a vessel that contains God, a priceless treasure in high demand. One of the greatest mission efforts you can ever make is to cultivate the Presence within yourself. Only then can you offer Jesus to the world.

Jesus, it's amazing that I can embody You—that this jar of clay carries such a priceless treasure. But Your Word says it's true, and I don't want to waste one bit of the treasure. Stir up Your Presence in me so I can carry You into a world hungry for what You offer.

February 14

*O Lord, you have examined my heart
and know everything about me.*

PSALM 139:1

There are no compartments of life that are beyond God's view. Every thought, every nuance, every hint of a whisper in our souls is an open book to Him. At first this might be alarming; we have corners of our souls we'd prefer to hide. But when we get past our shyness from divine eyes, we realize an amazing truth: the God who knows everything about us does not withdraw because of anything He sees.

The desire to be accepted is universal. That's why we hide aspects of ourselves even from those close to us—we fear rejection. But we have an even deeper desire to be intimately known and still accepted in spite of what's known. That's why we are drawn to those who know our faults and choose to be with us anyway. They instantly become candidates for our intimacy needs because they are safe.

God is safe. He isn't safe in the sense that He leaves everything intact—He'll change the parts of us that need to be changed, if we let Him—but we don't need to fear rejection from Him. He went to great lengths to bridge the gap that was created by the rebellion in Eden. There's no way a few common (or even uncommon) human flaws would compel Him to leave the gap intact. Those compartments we think are utterly depraved do not deter Him. He knows us—and loves us—deeply.

You probably know—theologically—that God knows everything about you. But has your total transparency before Him completely sunk in? Do you realize that He is gazing into your heart even at this moment? That you, at your core, are fully, completely known? You've been stripped of all facades, and it's okay. Rest in the fact that you have been thoroughly examined—and the Examiner has stayed.

*God, You see everything about me. You hear
my thoughts, know my needs, and see my
sins, and still You stay. Thank you.*

February 15

You see me when I travel and when I rest at home. You know everything I do. You know what I am going to say even before I say it, LORD.

PSALM 139:3-4

Where was God? That's the question we often ask when we find ourselves in a predicament—even a self-inflicted one. We expect a certain amount of protection from danger in our circumstances and our relationships. When our path has taken excruciating turns and we end up in extreme hardship or pain, we wonder why we weren't better protected. Even when we know the blame is ours, we wish, for the sake of ourselves and others, that we had been spared from our own decisions.

The good news is that God was present in every twist and turn we made. He knew them ahead of time. If He gave a promise or a calling and we think we blew it, we can remind ourselves that He already accounted for our missteps when He promised or called. Our faults were considered in advance, and He chose, called, and promised anyway. He who sees both the beginning and end simultaneously did not make a mistake.

Consider Joseph, the favored son of Jacob, whose God-given dreams landed him in slavery and prison. Over many long years, he had limitless opportunities to second-guess himself, his family, and his God. Yet God had already seen the process up front. His calling proved true. Nothing could thwart it.

Nothing, apart from unbelief and rebellion, can thwart your calling either. The God who is so intimately present in your life that He knows every thought—ahead of time—will get you where you need to be. No matter how many wrong turns you think you've taken, He knows where you are and where you're going. You are not outside of His path or His process. Pursue Him, and He will determine your path.

Lord, You know my past, my present, and my future. Am I on the right track? Have I missed Your plan? You have always known I would be right here, right now. And I trust You will continue to lead me forward.

February 16

*You made all the delicate, inner parts of my body
and knit me together in my mother's womb.*

PSALM 139:13

Think about the care and concern that went into the intricacies of your design. Your organs were crafted cell by cell; your hair color was written into your DNA; your facial features, your size, and your personality tendencies were slowly and carefully woven together by an unseen hand. Even the features you wish you could change are somehow part of His purposes. You were not a random growth of cells. The cells were guided and governed by an amazingly intelligent Being.

Even so, a lot of people think God prefers to remain aloof from the human beings He spent so much effort to design. They emphasize that He is high and holy and we aren't, and therefore we must respect the gap between us and Him. Though it's true that He is high and holy, and that we would fall on our faces in terror if He showed us too much of Himself, He desires a close and tender relationship with us. His purpose in creation was not to surround Himself with subjects; it was to share Himself with kindred hearts. And He has done everything He can to make it possible for our hearts to connect with Him.

Spend some time thinking about every piece of intelligence and care that went into designing you and all of your attributes. Consider what purpose must have motivated such a designer. Ask yourself why a Creator would develop such intricacies and plan such capacities in His creatures that they would be able to feel deep emotions, think inspired thoughts, and ponder profound mysteries. Is it simply to follow commands? No, it's to experience God Himself. Never lose sight of this purpose. It's why you were "fearfully and wonderfully made" (Psalm 139:14, NIV).

*Father, You have made me for Yourself. I want
You to enjoy me, and I want to find my
fulfillment in You. Please draw me closer so I
can experience You in the depths of my being.*

February 17

How precious are your thoughts about me, O God. They cannot be numbered! I can't even count them; they outnumber the grains of sand! And when I wake up, you are still with me!

PSALM 139:17-18

God is in every detail of the universe—every atom of every planet and every star, every quark and lepton within every atom, even every particle no one has discovered yet. Even though He is infinitely enormous, not a single piece of information escapes His notice. He created it all and is involved in every minor movement, every nuance, every shift and shudder within His creation. And His awareness is personal; He is involved in every aspect of *you*—every cell of your body, every atom within every cell, every subatomic particle within every atom. He knows and cares about *everything*.

That this God committed to be our Immanuel, "God with us," tells us a lot about His heart. His desire is to be present within every corner of our lives. And though that means He is near to us, that He holds our hand and walks with us through each day like a human being would, it's more than that. He is *in* us, closer than we can imagine. He is aware of every breath, every heartbeat, every impulse we have. He is in the tiniest details of every aspect of our existence.

Continue to ask God to help you be aware of His Presence every moment of every day. This isn't a onetime request. Be relentless in it. Try to think about His nearness as often as you can. Whenever you feel alone, know that He is in the room with you and that He loves you deeply. Just as He knows your every breath and heartbeat, He wants you to feel His breath and His heartbeat too.

God of majesty and mystery, reveal Yourself to me more deeply. Let me feel Your closeness—Your every breath and heartbeat. Remind me constantly that You are here.

February 18

Search me, O God, and know my heart; test me and know my anxious thoughts. Point out anything in me that offends you, and lead me along the path of everlasting life.

PSALM 139:23-24

These verses used to scare me. Why would I want to be searched? I know what's in there. I have a hunch about the things that offend Him. But the prayer is a desire to be entirely God's possession—for Him to have free rein in a human heart. And once prayed, it can produce some surprising results. Some of the things that I thought would offend Him didn't; and some of the thoughts I assumed were fine turned out not to be. That's good information to know. Therefore, this is a good prayer to pray.

Notice the invitation in this psalm. God is welcome in this heart. After acknowledging the intensely detailed and comprehensive knowledge of God—and that God already knows every thought—the psalmist asks God to search His thoughts. This isn't a request for God to find out information He doesn't already have; He already has it all. It's an invitation for God to put His finger on what needs to stay and what needs to go. It's an invitation to prompt change.

A lot of people have an implicit leave-me-alone or please-don't-hurt-me attitude in their relationship with God, a desire to sweep the painful stuff under the rug. But we invite the Spirit's holy intrusion because it really isn't an intrusion. It's a benefit of the relationship. We want things to be right between us and God, and we want Him to let us know when they aren't. That's how good relationships work and intimacy develops. There's honesty and transparency—on both sides. As we open ourselves more to God, He opens Himself more to us. Transparency is the only way to reach deeper depths.

Yes, Lord—search me. Put Your finger on whatever doesn't please You. If there's anything that creates a rift between us, I want it gone. Please let me know what You see and help me change it.

February 19

*I will give you a new heart, and I will put
a new spirit in you.*

EZEKIEL 36:26

We often approach God with a sense of futility. With motives as mixed as ours, how can we expect Him to give us the blessings promised to the whole-hearted? With faith as weak as ours, how can we expect Him to reward us with answers? With tempers or cravings or agendas as strong as ours, how can we expect Him to hear us without our sins getting in the way? The standards seem so high for that flourishing, superspiritual, ask-and-receive relationship experienced by so many great saints. We never seem to measure up, and we know it.

The greatest blessing of the gospel of grace is that God gives us all we need for life and godliness. If conditions are required of us to receive from Him—like faith or desire, for example—He fills in where our hearts are lacking. In the verse above, God spoke through Ezekiel to people who were in exile. They would need to seek God in order to be restored, but they weren't in a seeking mood. That's okay—God was going to give them a heart to seek Him and know Him. Their restoration was conditional, but God would give them the means to meet the condition. Ultimately, their only requirement was to not rebel against what He was doing in them and with them.

Paul wrote that God is at work in us shaping our desires and our actions (Philippians 2:13). He is not only the intended end of our search, He is the means to the end. Yes, our approach to Him would be futile—*if* we were approaching Him with our own resources, our self-produced faith, our own stirred-up desires, and so on. But we aren't. We approach Him with a heart that He has given us. And that heart is designed to measure up.

*Father, I need that kind of heart—the kind You
give. Fill me with Your desires, Your faith, and
anything else that pleases You.*

February 20

*He had compassion on them because they
were like sheep without a shepherd.*

MARK 6:34

Many people think feelings have nothing to do with discipleship—that we study God's Word and apply it, nothing more. But Jesus was moved with compassion on many occasions, felt anger toward hypocrisy and greed, wept over Jerusalem and those grieving at Lazarus's tomb, and offered up prayers with loud crying and tears (Hebrews 5:7). This incarnation of God, the exact representation of the Father, had deep feelings. Part of being Christlike means being emotional.

God calls us to feel His feelings, to be in sync with His heartbeat. And one of the clearest expressions of His heart is His compassion. When we are feeling compassion, we are feeling like God. And when we are in His Presence, His love will be stirred up in us. The more love we have, the more we sense the Presence. And the more we sense the Presence, the more love we have. Our communion with God grows tighter when we begin to feel like Him.

If you've felt distant from God, perhaps this is why. Most Christian teaching emphasizes knowing God's Word and applying it. If our minds aren't aligned with God, we conform them to the image of Christ. If our behavior isn't aligned with Him, we conform it to the image of Christ. But if our feelings aren't aligned with Him, we say feelings don't matter anyway. And that's discipleship with only two-thirds of the soul. It isn't enough.

Make it a high priority to synchronize your heart with God's emotions. He has them—lots of them. If we don't feel the way He feels, we aren't as Christlike as we think we are. Cultivate your heart, and your mind and actions will follow. You will grow into His Presence in ways you never have before.

*Lord, I want to feel Your emotions. You promised a
new heart; please put Your feelings within me. In
every relationship I have, let me be moved with
compassion just as Jesus was.*

February 21

*The L*ORD *said, "Shall I hide from Abraham*
what I am about to do?"

GENESIS 18:17, NIV

For years, I pleaded my agenda with God—the one big thing I wanted Him to do. I believed it sprang from desires He had planted within me and was therefore part of His plan. But it wasn't the whole plan. His agenda was bigger. And until I lifted my eyes and saw the big picture of what He was doing—and learned to pray more specifically and purposefully with His agenda in mind—my relationship with Him was a struggle. My prayers were answered sporadically and in parts. I experienced a few of His favors without really experiencing Him.

We experience God's Presence by catching a vision for what He is doing and getting in on it. That doesn't mean our desires and dreams are irrelevant; they are often designed to fit His larger purpose. But when our focus is simply on our part of the plan or our own fulfillment in it, our vision is too small and we aren't near enough to God. When we lift our eyes to embrace His mission in the world, taking our primary focus off our own part in the plan and putting it on the totality of what His heart desires, the Presence powerfully increases. And the beauty of this relationship is that He then begins to fulfill our portion more readily. When we embrace the desires of His heart, He more zealously embraces ours.

God showed Abraham what He was about to do, and He often does the same with all who have entered a friendship with Him. When we enter His confidence by taking up His vision, prayers are answered quicker and more powerfully, and our experience of the Presence increases dramatically. Wherever our hearts align with His, He's there.

Lord, show me what You are about to do. I lift my
eyes up to a vision bigger than myself and my own
concerns. I trust You to fulfill my portion of Your
plan when I invest myself in the whole.

February 22

The LORD delights in his people.

PSALM 149:4

God has passions and delights. Many view Him as staid and immovable, but that isn't a scriptural perspective. Nothing in His Word indicates that He's beyond the swells of emotion. And His emotions are dramatically affected by His love for those He calls His own. He takes pleasure in, delights in, and calls His people the apple of His eye (Zechariah 2:8, NIV). He delights in His own works. We serve a God who enjoys pleasure.

Many of us don't live with a sense of wonder and delight. We may get along with many of God's people, but we find it hard to take great pleasure in them. We may be consumed with passions, but they often aren't the same passions He has. That puts us out of sync with Him.

God's Spirit will cultivate all sorts of wonders and delights in our own hearts. It's impossible to live with a deep sense of His Presence and be listless and apathetic in our own experience. God and boredom don't go together. He experiences pleasures Himself and inspires them in others. He takes us on adventures and fills our hearts with wonders. That doesn't mean we never face hardship or difficulty, but it does mean we never face *only* hardship and difficulty. In His Presence, we experience unexpectedly good things.

If you feel stagnant, bored, listless, or indifferent, ask for His Spirit to fill you with wonder. Pray for a season of refreshing. Take time to notice the miracles around you. Most of all, sit in His Presence and receive the feelings of His heart. Be aware of what He delights in. Let His passions rub off on you. If you ask and believe, He will impart His sense of excitement and pleasure to you.

Father, I want to know Your pleasures—not just to know what they are, but to experience them with You. Help me notice Your delights, and impart Your heart to me. Fill my life with the wonders of Your Kingdom.

February 23

Imagine your soul mate, the person with whom you've had the deepest heart connection in your life, is with someone else. Instead of taking long walks, having long talks, and spending romantic evenings with your true love, your mind is filled with visions of your true love loving another. It gnaws at your heart, doesn't it? Jealousy is a brutally painful feeling. Yet this is how God says He feels when His people give their love to others.

Can God really feel jealous? Isn't jealousy among the attitudes of the flesh? It's true that it made Paul's list of unholy fruit of a sinful nature (Galatians 5:19-21); jealousy can be misplaced, selfish, and destructive. But there's also a kind of jealousy that's a necessary aspect of true love. If someone in a supposedly exclusive relationship of intimate love didn't care if the other person strayed, his or her love wouldn't be very strong. Holy jealousy is part of holy love.

Scripture says God's name is Jealous (Exodus 34:14), and Paul said he was jealous with the jealousy of God Himself (2 Corinthians 11:2). That means at least two things for us: (1) God is passionate about receiving our exclusive devotion; and (2) when His Presence shapes our hearts, we'll feel His jealousy for His people and long for others to worship Him. Holy jealousy will rise up within us when love meant for Him is diverted to less worthy objects. We'll be passionate about true worship.

Let God's jealousy impact you deeply. Know that He is zealous for your love and for the love of others. Give Him your heart exclusively, and pray that others would do the same. Give Him all the affection He so earnestly desires.

*Lord, it's hard for me to understand Your jealousy
for human beings—and specifically for me—but I
never want You to have a reason to feel that way
because of me. I give You all of my love.*

February 24

The LORD takes pleasure in all he has made!
PSALM 104:31

When you try to picture God's face, what expression does He have? Many people see Him as serious, others as angry, and still others as emotionless. Movies about Jesus often depict Him as humorless and expressionless, constantly staring into the distance and speaking in a breathy, weighty voice. I've known few people who, in their minds' eye, see God or Jesus smiling.

Considering how often Scripture speaks of God's joy, that's surprising. God's people are repeatedly encouraged to rejoice, and we are told that the joy of the Lord is our strength. God takes pleasure in what He does, delights in His people, and rejoices when those who were lost come into His Kingdom. C. S. Lewis said that joy is the serious business of heaven, and he was right. The climate of the Kingdom isn't primarily an all-work-no-play attitude. It's gladness. Pure, unbridled joy.

Sadly, few Christians live in a way that reflects the joyful environment of heaven. Some know they should and try to act joyful in all circumstances, but in trying to convince themselves of their joy, they convince few others. But true joy springs up from within, not because we *should* be joyful but because we *are*. A heart that truly grasps the nature of God—that actually senses Him smiling—is a heart that begins to overflow with joy.

Spending time in God's Presence cultivates all the feelings of His heart, but it especially cultivates joy. You may go through difficult situations that don't exactly put a smile on your face, but know even in those times that joy is the environment of heaven. And God wants that environment to pervade your soul. Soak in His Presence, feel His goodness, see His smile. And be joyful.

Lord, let me sense the pleasure in Your heart and "see"
Your smile. Even in my most stressful, anxious times,
impart Your joy to me. Change my perceptions and help
me know You as a happy, delighted God.

February 25

How I have been grieved by their adulterous hearts, which have turned away from me.

EZEKIEL 6:9, NIV

If God is love, as His Word declares, then He experiences grief. That's because it's impossible to love in a broken world without some kind of heartache being involved in the process. In a perfect environment, where love is never violated or rejected, grief doesn't come with the territory. Among fallen human beings it's inevitable. And God has chosen to love fallen human beings.

Jesus, the image of God, wept over Jerusalem (Luke 19:41–44). Its people didn't know the heart of the God who had repeatedly come to them through prophets and this Messiah. Paul said it's possible to grieve the Holy Spirit (Ephesians 4:30). And here in Ezekiel, the Father declares clearly that He is grieved by hearts that turn away from Him. All three members of the Trinity are capable of grief, and in His Presence, we will sometimes feel it.

That's not abnormal in this world. If we have God's heart within us, we'll know the pain of rejection and betrayal. We'll sense the loss of the original goodness of creation and the wounds of straying from God's plans. We won't experience those things without hope—the Spirit of God within us knows all about redemption and the glories of heaven and the age to come—but we'll know the ache of unreturned love now. Our God is not unaffected by rejection, and neither are we. It hurts.

When you experience grief, let it serve as a glimpse into God's heart. Say to Him, "Oh, so *this* is how you feel when I reject you." Let it be a bonding moment between you and your loving Father. Know that those who mourn will be comforted. And all grief will be wiped away.

Father, grief is hard. How does it feel in an infinite heart? I couldn't handle that. I'm sorry for the pain You feel. May You never have cause to grieve over me. And may Your grief—our grief—over others bind us together and draw them to You.

February 26

I am filled with the LORD's fury.
JEREMIAH 6:11

The Presence of God in Jeremiah prompted fury. The Presence in Ezekiel stirred up anger and bitterness (Ezekiel 3:14). The Presence in Jesus provoked anger at harsh judgments and a volatile reaction to religious exploitation (Mark 3:5; John 2:14–16). In every case, the servant reflected the heart of the Father. Apparently the passion of God isn't always comfortable.

We tend to think being godly involves only positive, peaceful emotions, but God gets angry at injustice, hypocrisy, and anything that harms His people. That anger isn't sinful, obviously; God is without sin. In fact, true love demands it. Passion *for* someone implies passion *against* anything that hurts that someone. That means that if we experience God's Presence and sense His heartbeat, we'll be bothered by the same things that bother Him. We'll develop a godly anger at anything that violates His Kingdom.

Don't direct that anger at people—God loves even the most wounded, misguided, distorted souls—but don't render your godly anger impotent by calling it sin. Anything that contradicts God's Kingdom or His character should become the subject of our prayers. We are invited to exercise spiritual authority over all manner of darkness and even exhibit a certain hostility toward the spirits behind that darkness. The Presence of the Lord often prompts the fury of the Lord, and there's nothing ungodly about it.

In your prayers, take aim at anything that doesn't look like the Kingdom. You already have a list of what you pray for; also have one of what you're praying against. Instead of people, target ideas and actions and unholy agendas. Like the prophets and the Messiah Himself, be angry without sinning. Let the Presence synchronize you with Him—and whatever His heart feels.

Lord, fill me with Your feelings, regardless of what they are. Help me love what You love, hate what You hate, rejoice over Your joys, and be angry at whatever angers You. Shape my heart and let my prayers and actions flow from what You've put within me.

*Then the LORD said, "You feel sorry
about the plant. . . . Shouldn't I feel sorry
for such a great city?"*
JONAH 4:10-11

Someone was spreading slanderous suggestions about me, and there was nothing I could do about it. Well, I could have spent a lot of time and effort refuting the lies, but that rarely accomplishes much. Engaging in such debates only draws the defender down to the accuser's level. All I could do was watch the lies spread, noticing who would believe them and who knew the real me instead. It was painful. And then it dawned on me: this must be how God feels about the adversary's attempts to cast shadows on His goodness. My painful experience turned into a point of fellowship with God's heart.

In fact, God gives us many ways to connect with His heart through our own experiences. He gave Jonah an object lesson with a vine in order to make a point about His own compassion. When we hold a newborn baby, we experience unconditional love for someone who has done absolutely nothing to earn it. When we feel jealous for someone's love, we know how God feels about those who love lesser gods. When someone offends us, we get a taste of what God overcomes in forgiving our sins. In the joy of a wedding, we connect with the joy of the coming marriage of the Bridegroom and His bride. When we give a gift that isn't appreciated, we can relate to the disappointment of the Giver whose gifts are routinely ignored. Practically any experience in life can turn into a connecting point with God's heart.

Notice how you feel in each of your experiences in life, and ask yourself if there's a divine parallel. Better yet, ask the Spirit to tune your heart to moments of revelation like that. Realize that nearly every feeling and attitude you have—other than fear, despair, and bitterness, which God doesn't have—can unveil insights into His heart. You'll find that His fellowship with you is closer than you think.

*Lord, let my heart connect with Yours. Show me
how my feelings reflect Your feelings, and draw me
closer with each new insight.*

February 28

"You must love the LORD your God with all your heart, all your soul, and all your mind." This is the first and greatest commandment.

MATTHEW 22:37-38

If loving God is not our highest priority in life, we're missing our purpose. No other dream or desire or search for significance will satisfy. To love and be loved by Him are paramount.

But how do we love Him well? Is it a feeling of affection? Worship services and songs? Simply obeying Him? All are part of the upward flow of love, but they aren't enough. It's possible to feel affection for Him without any sense of commitment, to attend worship services and sing songs without feeling any affection, to obey without love. Jesus said those who love Him will obey Him, but not everyone who obeys Him loves Him. In fact, this is why obedience is such an enigma in Scripture. In those who loved God, it was heaven on earth. In the religious hypocrites of Jesus' day, it was nauseating. The motive made all the difference. Obedience isn't the key; obedience that flows out of love is.

In order to love God well, think of how you show love to any other person. It involves deep affection, being attentive, developing the same passions, and taking that person's words seriously. However you show heartfelt love to others, apply that to God. Cultivate affection. Stoke your feelings. Pay attention to His every move. Notice His desires and interests. Spend time talking to Him. Care for His heart. Whatever He says, take it seriously. Follow His instructions, not because you have to but because you're passionate about pleasing Him. And if anything gets in the way of your loving Him, see it as an intruder on your highest priority. Every day you love Him well is a day you have fulfilled your purpose in life.

Lord, I want to love You with all of my being—my emotions, my thoughts, my words, my will, my actions—everything. Help me maintain this desire as my highest priority. And help me to love You well.

March 1

The time is coming—indeed it's here now—
when true worshipers will worship the Father
in spirit and in truth. The Father is looking for
those who will worship him that way.

JOHN 4:23

I've heard it argued—usually by incognito skeptics and critics in online conversations—that the "you" in God's calling and promises is almost always plural and that it refers to the group as a whole rather than the individuals within the group. In other words, God has related in Scripture to Israel and the church but not one-to-one with people. Individuals can experience Him indirectly and impersonally by getting in on God's plan for His people as a whole. But an intimate, personal relationship with Him isn't scriptural.

What complete nonsense. Groups can't have a heart-to-heart, face-to-face relationship. Only individual people can do that. That's why we were made in God's image—to relate to Him. In Scripture, we see Him coming to comfort Hagar in the desert, appealing through Paul on behalf of a slave named Onesimus, or, as in the verse above, tenderly reaching out to an outcast woman at a well. It's true that God has a big-picture plan for Israel, other nations, and His church, but the God who made His universe out of amazingly intricate atoms and cell structures certainly has His eye on each of us as individual people. He is an intensely intimate God.

If you wonder sometimes if God is interested in connecting with others but not with you or if He's interested in the big picture but not the details of your life, remember Jesus' one-on-one interactions with a woman at a well, with lepers and outcasts, with disciples whom He loved, and more. Jesus, the exact representation of God, got personal with people. And He is always passionate about those who will come to Him in spirit and in truth.

Lord, You are the God of macro-universes and
micro-organisms, and You have chosen to relate
specifically to me. You do care about the details of
my life and want to meet me in them, so I present
them to You as a place for us to connect.

March 2

I have loved you, my people, with an everlasting love. With unfailing love I have drawn you to myself.

JEREMIAH 31:3

The boy finally mustered up his nerve and asked the object of his affection on a date—sort of. "You, um, wouldn't want to go out by any chance . . . would you?" It's the right question, but expressed in a way that reveals an underlying assumption that a yes is extremely unlikely. And with that kind of approach it probably is.

Yet that's how we often approach God. "You, um, wouldn't want to actually show me Your Presence by any chance . . . would You?" "You're probably not going to do anything unusual when I pray today . . . are You?" "I *could* wait in Your Presence some more . . . I mean, if it matters." We know God wants us to spend time with Him—for our sake. But we often assume that on His end, He's a take-it-or-leave-it God, the kind who might say, "You missed your time with Me today, didn't you? Oh well, that's your loss." We suspect He doesn't miss our presence.

But He does. The heart of God shows up in this passage. No one could say, "I have loved you with an everlasting love," and then be casual about whether we are into the relationship. This love cannot have a take-it-or-leave-it attitude. It *must* have a response in order to be satisfied.

In order to experience God's Presence, we have to believe He wants us—that He desires our affection and feels some sense of loss when we don't give it to Him. The idea that God is too big or too satisfied to be touched or moved by us is unbiblical and a contradiction to the heart of "unfailing love." Know that He enjoys you and wants to spend time with you. A lot of it.

Father, it's hard for me to imagine Your missing me or desiring me. But according to Your revealed heart, You do. I can come to You confidently because You want me to.

March 3

[Hannah] made this vow: "O Lord of Heaven's Armies, if you will look upon my sorrow and answer my prayer and give me a son, then I will give him back to you."

1 SAMUEL 1:11

I prayed fervently and persistently for God to fulfill a deep desire. Over time the pleas grew deeper and more desperate, and the desire grew larger in my own mind. In fact, it grew so large that I eventually realized it had become almost as important to me as God was. I had been desperately praying for God to fulfill my love for something that would rival Him in my heart.

We do that often, though usually so subtly that we hardly notice. We treat God as our Cyrano de Bergerac, who was put in the painful position of helping another man win the heart of someone Cyrano himself loved deeply. We ask God for those objects of our affection, forgetting that He desires to be an even greater object of our affection. We provoke His jealousy in our prayers for His blessings. God then has to choose between either watching our heart delight in His gift rather than the Giver or disappointing us by not giving us our heart's delight at all. In His mercy, He often gives anyway, but our joy in our treasures often overshadows our joy in Him.

There's a way around this dilemma, of course. It's to always treasure God over and above the things we ask of Him. But that's easier said than done, considering our common misperceptions of His goodness and glory. Hannah was able to maintain her priorities by offering the gift, her child Samuel, back to God. And in a sense, that's what we have to do with every request we plead. The God who loves us passionately offers us extravagant blessings, as long as we love Him more extravagantly than them all.

Lord, please forgive me for exalting my requests above You. I want You to fulfill my desires, but not more than I want to fulfill Your desires. My greatest affections belong to You—always.

March 4

*Don't worry about anything; instead, pray
about everything. Tell God what you need, and
thank him for all he has done. Then you will
experience God's peace, which exceeds anything
we can understand. His peace will guard your
hearts and minds as you live in Christ Jesus.*

PHILIPPIANS 4:6-7

During one of many long nights in a hospital waiting room, I pleaded with God to speak. To come near. To make His Presence known. To somehow, in some way, bridge the huge gap between my sense of alienation and His touch. The more I focused on the need, the farther away He seemed. The overwhelming need dwarfed His promises and Presence.

One of the greatest enemies of the Presence is worry. The more we focus on a problem, crisis, or need, the larger that problem, crisis, or need becomes in our own hearts and minds. Our attention has a magnifying effect: when we're preoccupied with something, it grows. And the result is anything but peace.

Paul advises us to shift our focus from the problem to the Provider. Instead of worrying about circumstances, we should turn our attention to God in prayer and gratitude. If we do this, he tells us, we will experience God's peace. Why? For one thing, God is drawn to those who know they need Him. But beyond that, our shift in perspective reverses the dynamic. If what we focus on seems to grow larger, then it makes plenty of sense to change our focus from the problem to God. When we magnify Him in our thoughts, our circumstances become relatively minor. The result is the peace that passes understanding.

Choose your focus. If you are preoccupied with worry over a problem, the problem will seem huge. But if you shift your focus to God, His ability, His compassion, and His willingness to answer prayer, He will seem big and the problem will seem small. And you will experience peace.

*Lord, I want the peace that is too wonderful for
understanding. I give my circumstances to You and focus
entirely on Your wisdom, power, and love.*

March 5

I will meditate on your majestic, glorious splendor and your wonderful miracles.

PSALM 145:5

No matter how intent we are on focusing on God, the events of any given day seem to undermine our focus. Most of us don't live in a monastery or a cabin in the woods and exist solely to commune with Him consciously. We have schedules. Distractions. Fires to put out. People to answer to. And a cacophony of voices vying for our attention. Focusing on God doesn't come naturally.

That's why we need to practice paying attention to Him—what Brother Lawrence and many others have called "practicing the Presence of God." We have to take moments—seize them forcefully—to consciously turn our attention back toward Him. We have to *make* ourselves think of Him until it becomes natural, until we are constantly aware of His Presence.

How can we do that? Think of all the times we wait for something—in line at the store, on hold to talk with someone, or any other downtime when thoughts wander. Open a conversation with God in those moments. At the beginning of a meeting or even in the middle of a conversation with someone, breathe a quick, silent prayer inviting God into the room. Ask Him to fill your words with His Presence or to work through circumstances. The result can turn a casual conversation into a major advance in a relationship or a new direction in goals. It can leverage a crisis situation for His glory. The course of a day—or a lifetime—can be radically shifted by inviting Him into the details of any given moment.

Try that today. Every few minutes invite Him into whatever is happening in you and around you. He can invisibly but powerfully change the environment with His peace and Presence, and your days can take on a whole new meaning.

Lord, I invite You into this moment right now—and the next, and the next. Please help me keep my thoughts fixed on You, Your goodness, and Your power.

March 6

You have visited me in the night.

PSALM 17:3, NKJV

Few people carefully guard the way they go to sleep at night. Perhaps they watch depressing news or talk-show gossip, or maybe they lie down anxious and stressed about the coming day. Most of us put our head on the pillow with unresolved issues in our hearts or our relationships. And all of these things simmer within us as we sleep.

God offers to minister to us throughout the night. While we sleep, His Spirit within us doesn't. He can do transforming work, addressing deep heart issues beneath the surface of our consciousness. He can shape our vision and our desires, heal the wounds we acquired during the day, implant solutions to problems, and do battle on our behalf in the depths of our souls. He gives counsel in hidden recesses, even when we aren't aware of it (Job 33:14-18; Psalm 16:7). He can influence our thoughts and fill our dreams with His purposes.

Perhaps that's why the calendar in God's Word counts days from sundown to sundown. The victories of the night come before the victories of the day—not only in the rhythm of our lives but also as a picture of human history and salvation. Life begins with seeds before manifesting in fruit. This is God's pattern.

Be careful how you go to sleep. Ask the Lord for much more than "your soul to keep." Fellowship affectionately with God in the forefront of your heart as you doze off. Invite the Spirit into your night hours. Pray for Him to do deep, internal work on your thoughts, dreams, vision, desires, wounds, attitudes, and battles. His nightly ministry will affect how you wake up and enhance your ability to carry a sense of His Presence throughout the day.

Lord, visit me in the night hours. Let me fellowship with You in my last waking moments, and continue to fellowship with me as I sleep. Minister to me and transform me from within. And remind me of Your Presence as soon as I awake.

*Let me hear of your unfailing love each
morning, for I am trusting you.*

PSALM 143:8

For many of us, every morning is a battle. Between the time the alarm clock rings and when our feet hit the floor, our thoughts can spiral downward. Today's to-do list and potential hurdles combine with leftover fatigue from yesterday, all seeming to conspire to overwhelm us and beat us down. In a few very short minutes, our attitude can shift drastically from neutral to negative.

Though the morning battle is real for many, it isn't unwinnable. The key is to turn the downward spiral into upward momentum, and the best way to do that is by inviting Jesus into your internal conversation as soon as you wake up. Before thinking about to-do lists, potential hurdles, lingering problems from the day before, or anything else, have a conversation with Him—not about issues, but just for the pleasure of His company. Enjoy the fellowship. Lie still in the Presence. Utter some words of worship and gratitude. Listen to His words of affection and encouragement. Let Him shape your internal environment before you get up to face your external world. Make Him the priority of your day.

When you do that, the day can take on a whole different tone. And the tone of a day can have lasting impact. Decisions are made in a different light, long-term relationships are strengthened rather than weakened, ideas and innovation come much more easily, and obstacles lose their power. Winning the morning battle day after day can radically impact a lifetime.

Whatever it takes, invite Jesus into your morning. Before your feet hit the floor, enjoy His Presence. The earlier you make Him the center of your day, the more profoundly He will shape it.

*Jesus, I know my attitude needs an adjustment
every morning. I invite You to adjust it—to hold
me, fill me with Your Presence, and transform me.
You are more important than any issues I'll face
on any given day—and fully able to handle them.*

Look! I stand at the door and knock. If you hear
my voice and open the door, I will come in, and
we will share a meal together as friends.

REVELATION 3:20

Jesus stands at the door and knocks. That's a great image to use in an evangelistic presentation—and it's undoubtedly true—but that's not the context of the verse. No, the words of Jesus to the church at Laodicea appeal to the congregation to stop shutting Him out. They have been indifferent to Him, and their lukewarmness is nauseating to God. They have been having their feasts, specifically the Lord's Supper, without His Presence. They are a church going through the motions but not filled and empowered with the Presence of the living Lord. This "body of Christ" is behaving as though it is lifeless.

That can easily happen to our congregations too. We go through the motions and "do church" by habit rather than by the Living One spontaneously moving in and through us. We have programs and policies that take on a life of their own, slowly marginalizing the Jesus who birthed the church to begin with. If we aren't careful, the church becomes an impersonal organization rather than a living organism.

Guard your fellowship zealously—not to keep it in its patterns and habits but to keep it responsive to each breath of the Spirit. The picture of Jesus standing outside of His own church is tragic. Not only does that disappoint Him, it leaves His people without their source of life. Any fellowship that isn't experiencing supernatural fruit is missing Jesus. Without the Presence, it's nothing more than a club or committee. With Him, it's a living temple of God Himself.

Jesus, I open the door to You and invite You into
the fellowship of those I worship with. We need
You. Without Your Presence, we have no reason
to exist. Please enter in, eat with us, and let us
enjoy Your friendship and life.

Love the LORD, all you godly ones!

PSALM 31:23

My son could tell something heavy was on my heart, so he asked what was wrong and listened to my response like he cared. Because he did. And I found my heart drawn to him in that moment in an unusual way.

Sons and daughters aren't used to being in that position with their fathers, but there comes a time in the maturing process when a child realizes that parents have feelings, concerns, and dreams—that they aren't just counselors or dictators or managers of the household. And how a child responds to that awareness has a lot to do with how the relationship develops. Children who have a genuine concern for the heart of a parent find the relationship deepening dramatically.

Our highest purpose is to "love the Lord." Scripture identifies that as the greatest commandment. And that love has reached a new level of maturity when we learn to care for the heart of the Father. What are His goals and dreams for His world? What is His mission? What grieves Him? What gives Him joy? When we notice these things and then open up conversations with Him not just about our needs but about His heart, the relationship deepens. Intensely.

God is drawn to those who care for Him—who treat the relationship as a two-way interaction and invest in it as such. His Presence comes to those people in unusual ways. He lets them in on His secrets (see Amos 3:7, NKJV). When we mature to the level of seeking His heart because we genuinely care for what's in it, He draws close.

Lord, I love You. I want to know what's on Your heart. I want to hear Your plans, dream Your dreams with You, and enter into Your vision. Please show me the things that concern You and that give You joy.

March 10

[Speak] to one another with psalms, hymns, and songs from the Spirit. Sing and make music from your heart to the Lord, always giving thanks to God the Father for everything, in the name of our Lord Jesus Christ.

EPHESIANS 5:19-20, NIV

Brother Lawrence was a low-ranking monk who spent most of his time washing the monastery's pots and pans and repairing the sandals of other monks. He could have been a miserable man if he allowed his mind to dwell on the drudgery of his work, but he chose another attitude. He made a conscious decision to see every act of service, every act of engagement with others, and the physical world around him as moments inhabited by God's Presence. He determined to let gratitude and worship flow from him constantly. As a result, he was so filled with and surrounded by the Presence that people went out of their way to seek his wisdom and enjoy his company.

One of the most important keys to Brother Lawrence's experience of God's Presence was gratitude. He learned to give thanks even for the pots that needed scrubbing. He began to see all of life as a gift and to interact with God as the Giver. God rushed to meet him in that attitude, and Lawrence became known for his Presence-saturated life.

Always give thanks to God for everything. Don't fake gratitude for painful circumstances, but at least know that God is with you in them and that everything in life, even the hard stuff, will result in a good outcome. It's all stacked in your favor. He works everything into good for those who love Him. That's worth your gratitude. A heart that can see that and respond with thanks is a heart that God rushes to fill. And that turns every chore, every relationship, every moment into an encounter with Him.

Father, thank You for everything You are doing in my life. Thank You for all Your gifts, including life itself. Help me develop a heart of deep and lasting gratitude in all situations.

*As the deer longs for streams of water, so I
long for you, O God.*

PSALM 42:1

Ask a hundred Christians if they are grateful to have a relationship with God, and most or all will say yes. Ask them if that relationship is perfect and complete, and virtually all will say no. Why? Because even though we are glad to know Him, we never know Him enough. There's always more. When it comes to God, we can't be satisfied with the status quo.

That's good. God isn't satisfied with the status quo in our lives either. He wants us to be grateful, but He doesn't want us to be fully content. Though He enjoys pursuing us, He enjoys even more the time we pursue Him. When a heart longs for Him and does something about it, He is pleased. A holy discontentment is good.

Some people wonder if it's okay to ask God to show up, to speak, to move powerfully—as though seeking an experience undermines faith. While it's possible to seek experience as a substitute for faith, there's nothing wrong with seeking it for the right reasons. We should *want* to encounter God and zealously pursue Him. Faith that He is there and wants a relationship with us should be seen as an invitation to come closer. If we treat it that way, we will be rewarded with closeness. If we don't, we won't.

Never be reluctant to ask God for more of Himself—more tastes to see that He is good, more words to guide and encourage, more awareness of what He is doing. Be grateful for what He has already given, and don't be motivated by a lack of faith that needs visual evidence to be appeased. But do pursue more relational experiences. Deep down, every soul longs for Him, including yours. Treat the longing as an invitation engraved on your heart, and ask Him to satisfy you more and more.

*Lord, I'm not ashamed to seek experiences with You.
I love our relationship, but I'm not content with it
remaining as is. Put a fire in me for more of You.*

March 12

Ask me and I will tell you remarkable secrets
you do not know about things to come.
JEREMIAH 33:3

Usually we approach God with words, most often in the form of requests. And He loves to receive them. But the relationship is meant to be more diverse than that. If we seek His voice, we will be able to hear it.

The possibility of hearing God's voice with reasonable certainty troubles many Christians. Some are worried that it undermines Scripture (which, by the way, gives example after example of people hearing God's voice), while others are convinced they can't hear Him speak. In most cases, those who haven't heard Him haven't asked questions with an expectation that He will answer them. And most haven't sat in His Presence for extended periods of time and focused their minds on Him.

Both practices—asking with expectation and waiting for His voice—are prerequisites for hearing Him consistently. As in any relationship, hearing occurs only when we listen. Answers come only when we ask for them. He speaks to those who tune their hearing to Him.

Hear Him speaking now: "Come, sit in My Presence. Ask Me questions. Quietly wait and see what answers rise up from My Spirit within you. I am 'the Word': how could I be silent with those I love? I want a deep relationship with you, and all relationships involve communication. Listen for My voice, and I will speak."

Ask God questions and sit quietly in His Presence, waiting for answers. See what thoughts rise up within you. You may be surprised by how profound "you" have become—and you'll know He has whispered in the depths of your spirit.

> *Father, I want to hear You. I'm asking You to speak in a way I can understand. I know I may make mistakes and mishear You sometimes, but I trust You to gently correct me and teach me. I need to know Your voice.*

If any of you wants to be my follower,
you must turn from your selfish ways,
take up your cross, and follow me.

MARK 8:34

Do we really want to be with Jesus and experience His Presence? He tells us the cost—we have to pick up our cross and follow Him. Although many people interpret this as a call to suffering and a prophecy of hardship, a deeper meaning lies under it. Jesus' words may imply suffering and hardship, but that isn't His only purpose. His purpose is primarily to call us to a choice between our own lordship and His.

We can't really worship Jesus and experience His Presence until we let go of ourselves. Jesus was clear that no one can serve two masters. He said so in the context of money, but the truth applies to all relationships. Though our desires and His often overlap and our agendas and His often align, we have to choose which drives the other. In this relationship between human and divine, one has to take the lead. And it needs to be Him.

Some people try to crucify their personality along with all their gifts and desires, as though God wants the relationship to be all of Him and none of us. But if God wanted that, why did He create us to begin with? He already experienced having "none of us." No, it's our self-direction and search for self-fulfillment that need to go to the Cross. We can't follow Him or know His Presence until they do. But if we're able to let go—to allow our agendas to bow to His—we can know Him deeply and experience Him fully. He picks up those who have let go. And He fills the empty spaces of those who give Him room.

Jesus, I want to follow You fully, and I
know that means I need to let go of being
preoccupied with myself. Help me fully focus
on You and Your Kingdom—to be totally
preoccupied with Your purposes. Let me
experience You to the degree I follow You.

March 14

"Now pick up the other arrows and strike them against the ground." So the king picked them up and struck the ground three times. But the man of God was angry with him. "You should have struck the ground five or six times!" he exclaimed. "Then you would have beaten Aram until it was entirely destroyed. Now you will be victorious only three times."

2 KINGS 13:18-19

Elisha foretold victory over Israel's enemy and instructed the king to perform a prophetic act. The king did so, striking his arrows against the ground three times. But the paltry effort angered Elisha. Why not five or six? Perhaps more? The king had been too tentative in his assumptions about God's promise. He didn't understand how thoroughly God wanted to intervene.

Scripture urges us to be unassuming and modest in our relationships with others, but God invites us to be bold and assertive in our requests of Him. That's because He is able to do abundantly beyond what we can ask or think, and He wants to. He draws us into a relationship of extravagance—the kind that says, like Jacob, "I will not let you go unless you bless me" (Genesis 32:26). Those who come to God with childlike faith must believe that He doesn't give reluctantly or offer just barely enough, but that He is a wealth of resources waiting to pour out Himself and His blessings on those who ask. He always has more than we need.

This ought to encourage us. We come tentatively with small prayers, when really we are invited to pray bigger. We have to push past appearances—not only outward appearances but even our subtle assumptions and negative experiences in the spiritual realm—and be bold at His throne. We need to pray Kingdom prayers with an awareness of the vastness of the vision of His Kingdom. The size of our prayers will determine the size of our victories.

Lord, give me big visions and then boldness to pray for them in faith. May I never settle for small victories when I could have asked for bigger ones.

March 15

Do not bring sorrow to God's Holy Spirit.

EPHESIANS 4:30

The Holy Spirit is bold like a lion. He came with loud noise like a rushing wind at Pentecost. He inspired Peter to stand up that same day and preach to thousands of people. He moved Paul to speak decisive words to opponents of the gospel. He can change the environment in an instant. He is not afraid to make a scene or go against the flow.

He can, however, be sensitive to the sins of His people. He is, after all, the *Holy* Spirit, and He withdraws His Presence from unholy thoughts, words, and actions. He is aware of them, of course, and He never exactly leaves. But He flows freely through those who have acknowledged their offenses and presented themselves for cleansing. He works through those who don't force their own agenda but step into the flow of His. He works most powerfully when we give Him free rein in our lives. And He doesn't when we offend Him and don't notice.

Learn to notice. Ask to be made sensitive to Him. Be so familiar with His Presence that you are immediately aware when He withdraws it. Be so well acquainted with things being right with Him that you notice when something's wrong. Give Him permission to notify you when you've offended Him. It may seem strange to "give Him permission," but Scripture makes it clear that we can harden our hearts toward God. Invite Him to soften yours.

Spirit, I need to be extremely close to You, not just sort of close or somewhat aware of Your Presence. Please make me sensitive. I give You blanket permission to let me know emphatically when I've offended You, and I commit to making whatever adjustments I need to make when You do.

Keep on asking, and you will receive what you ask for. Keep on seeking, and you will find. Keep on knocking, and the door will be opened to you.

LUKE 11:9

God's best rewards go to those who are persistent. A Gentile woman pressed through Jesus' off-putting comments and the disciples' contempt, and Jesus blessed her for her great faith (Matthew 15:21-28). A hemorrhaging woman pressed through her own insecurities, a lot of social stigma, and a thick crowd, and Jesus healed her (Mark 5:25-34). Zacchaeus pressed through his own ethical and physical shortcomings and a crowd to get to see Jesus, and Jesus changed his life forever (Luke 19:1-10). God seems to be drawn to those who don't give up.

That's why Jesus' words about prayer, both here and in two parables about persistence (see Luke 11:5-10; 18:1-8), imply continuing appeals. With God, requests are often not a onetime transaction. They are a door into deeper relationship, and only those who will press through initial appearances or obstacles will receive what He offers.

When we seek a stronger sense of God's Presence, we have to ask. James told his readers that they did not have because they did not ask (James 4:2). The key to experiencing God in more tangible ways is to ask repeatedly and persistently—to press through the crowded circumstances of our lives, the negative voices in our own minds, and the theological expectations of those who think we're wasting our time.

This is Jesus' invitation. "Ask Me. Seek My face. Knock on the doors of heaven. I stand ready to open up to you. Pray and don't lose heart."

Jesus, I accept Your invitation. I want to prove to You that I desire Your Presence enough to keep going, to persist against disappointments and a lack of apparent results. I choose to press through contradictions until I experience You more fully.

March 17

The woman left her water jar beside the well and ran back to the village, telling everyone, "Come and see a man who told me everything I ever did! Could he possibly be the Messiah?" So the people came streaming from the village to see him.

JOHN 4:28-30

The woman waited until noon to get water at the well. Maybe that's when it was most convenient, but it's more likely that she waited until then to avoid the stares. Her reputation made her an outcast. She could avoid more people by going in the middle of the day.

But one stranger was there, a traveler who broke society's rules to speak to her. And when He spoke, He seemed to know all about her—even details that no one could have known. Even though she had sinned, He spoke to her gently and didn't embarrass her. He knew her heart.

Jesus knew all about the woman at the well because God, who knows every detail of our lives, told Him. The God who examines our hearts and knows everything about us (Psalm 139:1) had read her life like a book. He knows every moment of our lives and every thought we've ever had. God told Jeremiah that He knew all about him before he was even born (Jeremiah 1:5). Jesus told His disciples that God had numbered the hairs on their heads (Matthew 10:30). When God came to Hagar in the desert, she realized she had seen "the God who sees me" (Genesis 16:13). Over and over again in Scripture, God made it clear that He was intimately involved in people's lives and knew them deeply.

Put your finger on your neck or wrist and find your pulse. Think about the fact that God already knew the frequency, strength, and rhythm of every one of your heartbeats many, many years ago. Amazing, isn't it? Everything about you—even your flaws and struggles—is lovingly governed by Him.

Father, You know every detail about me and still choose to be in a close relationship with me. I don't want that choice to be wasted by my neglect. Please let me experience You to the fullest.

March 18

*These people honor me with their lips, but
their hearts are far from me.*

MARK 7:6

My doctrine was as straight as an arrow. My understanding of Christian theology was deep and rich. I taught Scripture faithfully. My application of spiritual truth was blameless. My prayers were in line with God's revealed will.
And I was as miserable as a person can be—for years.

It's possible for us to specifically define doctrine and theology, get all our
beliefs in line with Scripture, do all the right things, and still be unfulfilled
and far from God's heart. Paul expressed the same condition in Philippians 3,
where he described his Jewish heritage and his keeping of the law. And while
he zealously held wrong beliefs, he didn't say the answer was simply to adopt
the right beliefs. It was to *know* Jesus—personally. Right doctrine and beliefs
are essential, but they aren't enough. We were designed for more than knowing and doing the truth. We were created for adventures, creativity, warmth,
and wonder. And that comes only through interaction with Him at a deeply
personal level.

That's why many Christians are living as faithfully as they know how
and still feel distant from God. They have an understanding of Jesus and His
Word without any encounters or personal interaction with Him. No adventure, no sense of wonder, no joy. They hold to a system of beliefs rather than
a Person. And that can never be ultimately satisfying.

In every aspect of your life—thoughts, prayers, actions, everything—
choose Jesus above Christianity. Always opt for the personal over the
propositional or the practical. Seek His touch before His truth. All are important—vital, in fact—but your emphasis can make the difference between
experiencing His life and feeling dead. If you feel cold, barren, or weary, seek
the abundance of His Presence and personality.

*Jesus, I want adventures with You. I want the
warmth of Your Presence, and I want to wonder
at things I have no hope of ever understanding. I
don't need to figure it all out; I need You.*

*He is the Holy Spirit, who leads into all truth.
The world cannot receive him, because it isn't
looking for him and doesn't recognize him.
But you know him, because he lives with
you now and later will be in you.*

JOHN 14:17

Knowing He was about to be executed, Jesus spent His last evening with the disciples, focusing on some last vital instructions. Woven throughout the discussion was a promise to send His Spirit to be with them. "I will ask the Father, and he will give you another Advocate, who will never leave you. . . . He will teach you everything and will remind you of everything I have told you" (John 14:16, 26). "He will guide you into all truth. He will not speak on his own but will tell you what he has heard. He will tell you about the future" (John 16:13). But in the middle of these promises, one statement in particular describes the nature of our relationship with this Spirit: "He lives with you now and later will be in you" (John 14:17).

We learn a lot about the Spirit from those few statements. It's as if He takes us by the hand and leads us wherever we need to go and teaches us whatever we need to know. But it's more than that. He isn't only *with* us, He's *in* us. He speaks to us, strengthens us, leads us, and changes us from within. At a very deep level, He becomes our life.

Think about what that means. The most powerful being in the universe is living inside your flesh-and-blood body. The wisest being in the universe inhabits your brain. The most loving being in the universe is inside your heart. He is there—relentlessly, passionately there. And when we know that, think about it, and trust in that truth, we begin to experience Him more and more.

*Spirit, I invite You to make Your home inside me.
Let me sense You there. I believe I can experience
Your power, wisdom, and love as I trust in You.*

Do not come any closer.

EXODUS 3:5

Why would a God who desires a close relationship with those made in His image tell one of His servants not to come any closer? Is it because in this introductory meeting between God and Moses at a burning bush, closeness would have been dangerous? Because a human being next to a holy God is a perilous combination? Perhaps, but that doesn't explain why God invited this same Moses up to the top of Sinai to experience His intense Presence later—even while warning every other Israelite to stay away or else suffer death. Nothing happened between the burning bush and Sinai to remove Moses' sin. The sacrificial system hadn't been instituted yet, Moses expressed no great confession and repentance, God made no declarations of forgiveness. In one event, Moses couldn't come close. Some time later, he could. Why?

Perhaps, like Abraham, Moses had demonstrated the kind of faith in God that can be counted as righteousness. At the burning bush, he was living in exile and unacquainted with God's ways. By the time he reached Sinai, he had followed God into Pharaoh's courts, through ten plagues, through the complaints of his own people, and through the parted waters of the sea. He had grown in the relationship to the point that he could enter the cloud of glory on the mountain and the other people couldn't. He was allowed to *come* close to God because he had *grown* close to God.

We are given the same opportunity. We are allowed to experience more of God's Presence if we choose to grow into it. The more we follow Him in faith, the more we are invited into the depths of communion with Him. All relationships grow deeper with mutual investment. When we invest in God in response to His investment in us, He gives us the privilege of greater access to Him.

Lord, when I am on holy ground, I want the privilege of coming closer. Please help me grow in our relationship to the point that You invite me into the cloud of Your glory.

March 21

I will be with you.

EXODUS 3:12

God gave a God-sized assignment to Moses, a human being. If He had given a human-sized assignment, Moses wouldn't have needed God to go with him. But with the monumental task of delivering Israel from Egypt, Moses was suddenly thrust into a desperate situation—exactly the kind that sends us begging for God's Presence. From the point of view of a God who desires relationship, this is a perfect setup.

God performs perfect setups in our lives too. He puts us in situations that are destined to fail or blow up in our faces unless He intervenes. He calls us to accomplish things that no human being can accomplish without heavy doses of divine assistance. He provokes desperation. Why? So we can call out to Him and He can assure us that He is with us. In the process, we grow closer to Him and He strengthens our ability to lean on Him.

The good news is that God gives us the same promise He gave Moses: "I will be with you." That doesn't answer our question of how He will assist us—Moses' question about the process of delivering Israel remained unanswered—but it does assure us that we will have all we need to do what He calls us to do. We'll have Him. And we can trust that He is enough.

Hear His promise to you: "I will be with you. I *will*—in every situation—be with you. Your trials are not designed to discourage or defeat you; they are designed to provoke a cry in your heart for me. I fully intend to be with you and give you everything you need to move forward. My Presence makes all the difference in every circumstance you face."

Lord, I'm not ashamed to confess my desperate need to You. I simply cannot do what You've called me to do in life without Your intervention. Please show me what it means—in practical terms—for You to be with me in my circumstances.

March 22

Then Moses climbed the mountain
to appear before God.

EXODUS 19:3

Moses has made demands in Pharaoh's courts, declared plagues upon the country, suffered harsh criticism and complaints from his own people, and stood at the brink of humiliating slaughter at the edge of the Red Sea. And God has been with him, showing up most dramatically in the uncomfortable pinch between the sea and a pursuing army. Now, on the safe side of the sea, God beckons him up the mountain to witness the cloud of glory, the thundering voice, smoke and fire, and a long and loud horn blast from close range. The people below will die if they get too close. Moses won't. God has invited him.

We see a model of the human-divine relationship in this picture. God invites, we come up, He comes down, and we experience Him in the very disorienting environment of His Presence. This God who often hides Himself chooses to reveal Himself to those who will respond to Him. Most people never experience lightning and thunder like Moses did, but God has ways of making His Presence known.

How much of this relationship is our "going up," and how much is His "coming down"? Both are essential. We can ascend many mountains without ever meeting Him, and He can approach many people who never notice Him. We have our part, and He has His. We accept the invitation and start up the mountain; He comes on His terms and meets us as He chooses. When those bilateral efforts coincide, we encounter Him. But the mystery as to when and how that happens is deep.

Determine to accept any whisper of an invitation to go up and meet God. Err on the side of readiness. It's always better to seek Him in all seasons than to not seek Him when He wants to be found.

Lord, I want to respond every time I sense Your
invitation, even when my senses might be mistaken. If
there's a hint of a possibility of a deep encounter with
You, I choose to act on that hint. And I know that
sooner or later, You will make Your Presence known.

*On the morning of the third day, thunder
roared and lightning flashed, and a dense
cloud came down on the mountain. There
was a long, loud blast from a ram's horn,
and all the people trembled. Moses led them
out from the camp to meet with God, and
they stood at the foot of the mountain.*

EXODUS 19:16-17

From the creation of the world, as long as Mount Sinai had existed, God was there. We know because God is always everywhere. He was at Sinai when Israel's descendants became captives in Egypt, He was there when Moses was presiding over plagues in Egypt, and He is there right now. But on the morning of the third day after newly freed Israelites prepared to meet with God, He was at this mountain *differently*.

This is a graphic picture of the distinction between God's general Presence and His manifest Presence. If the Israelites at the base of the mountain had been aware of the possibilities and so inclined, they could have looked up to the heavens at night and seen them pouring out knowledge of God (Psalm 19:1-2); or they could have listened for the "gentle whisper" of the Lord (1 Kings 19:12). Those are some of our options when we want to become more aware of God's Presence. But there are times when He is *more* present, when He manifests Himself uniquely, when He becomes more obvious than nature's designs or a whispering voice. Sometimes God shows up.

We long for both kinds of experiences—the subtle awareness of an invisible God and the in-your-face encounters with a manifest God. And there's nothing in Scripture limiting us to one or the other. Only our past experience tells us the first is more likely and therefore all we should expect. The Bible gives us every reason to pursue—boldly—encounters with the God of thunder and lightning.

*God of power, I want to experience You in
every way. Break me out of my expectations
and show me Your glory—even today.*

> *Warn the people not to break through the*
> *boundaries to see the LORD, or they will die.*
> *Even the priests who regularly come near to the*
> *LORD must purify themselves so that the LORD*
> *does not break out and destroy them.*

EXODUS 19:21-22

God's Presence can be dangerous. It wasn't so at creation, when those made in His image enjoyed His company openly and freely. But the Fall created a rift, and we know how our knowledge of God has been hidden and confused since then. Sin separated us from Him and even from life. So it's no surprise that a host of Israelites who were only beginning to be reacquainted with God's ways and who were still demonstrating disbelief and grumbling at every turn could not get close to holy fire without being burned.

But Moses' faith responses to God, however faltering, afforded him the privilege of coming closer. God apparently credited Moses' responses to him as righteousness, just as He did with Abraham and continues to do with us. But we must remember the gap that ought to exist between unredeemed human beings and a God who is wholly other. His purity cannot fellowship with impurity that has never been dealt with. That's why He instituted a sacrifice system on Sinai, and that's why *we* must believe in Jesus' sacrifice, the offering to which Sinai's commands pointed. We can never take His Presence for granted.

Meditate on the gigantic gap between a holy God and sinful humanity—the enormous gorge that could not be bridged by any natural means. Only a supernatural intervention could bring us close to God. Without it, we would be forever lost. With it, we can come to His throne boldly.

> *Thank You, Lord, for bridging the vast distance between*
> *us. If You hadn't, I would be hopelessly alienated and*
> *alone forever. You've opened the door into Your life-giving*
> *Presence. From the bottom of my heart, thank You.*

March 25

They said to Moses, "You speak to us, and we will listen. But don't let God speak directly to us, or we will die!"

EXODUS 20:19

The Israelites had just been delivered through an "impassable" sea, they had drunk water from a rock and eaten bread from heaven, and they had won a fierce battle through supernatural intervention. But their comfort level with this God was low. They knew their frailty, they knew His power, and the contrast was scary.

Like many of us, however, Israel would be awed by this God on some occasions and treat Him with contempt on others. They feared His voice and hurled accusations against His works. They honored Him sometimes but took Him for granted more often. Their relationship with God was a volatile experience.

Many of us can relate to that. If we've pursued closeness with Him with any seriousness, we've known some ups and downs. We've experienced that on-again, off-again pattern common to many friendships. But in this particular relationship, which we absolutely have to have, the stakes are so high that we have to press on. We have to remember who we are, remember who He is, and seek His Presence—even when we're apathetic, even when we're busy, and even when He scares us.

We can handle the weight of God's Presence only in limited measures, and that's okay. He will increase our capacity for Him over time. It's true that the weight of glory could be crushing, but He chooses not to crush us with it. He gives Himself to us in increments we can handle, even though they stretch us.

Take what He offers of Himself. Ask for even more. Don't make the mistake the Israelites made and shy away. Pursue Him, even recklessly. He honors such desire with a greater measure of Himself.

Lord, I know the only claim I have to this relationship is based on Your promise, not what I've earned. But I come on Your terms and will take what You offer. Please, even if it overwhelms me, let me see more of You.

March 26

*See, I am sending an angel before you to protect
you on your journey and lead you safely to the
place I have prepared for you.*

EXODUS 23:20

God knows how to get people from point A to point B. We forget that
sometimes. Even though we know He is technically "there," we may feel like
we're traveling alone. And to be honest, we often wonder if we're going to
get where we need to go.

God goes with us. That's a promise He gave to Moses and that He gives
to us. But His Presence alone—His angelic help, His Spirit within us, and
His sovereignty over our situation—only takes care of our outward circumstances. *Knowing* His Presence takes care of our inward turmoil. We get the
benefits of His Presence whether we sense it or not, but our awareness that
He is with us—guiding us, dealing with our obstacles, and governing our
steps—makes a tremendous difference in how we handle the process. Those
who aren't certain of His Presence make it to their destination as nervous
wrecks. Those who are certain make it there in peace.

Trust and follow God, and you will get to where you need to go. That's
a given. But if you don't experience His being with you in each moment, the
journey will be more painful than it needs to be. It's possible to go through a
difficult process in peace, knowing and trusting that God is taking each step
with you. He offers reassurance along the way that you are on the right track
and gives comfort when the track hurts. Know that he is with you today and
every day. And He is clearing the way before you.

*Father, You have not abandoned me, and You never
will. I know that and trust You to be with me in
every step of my journey, even the painful ones. Please
open my eyes to the ways You guide my path.*

*The glory of the L ORD settled down on
Mount Sinai, and the cloud covered it for
six days. On the seventh day the L ORD
called to Moses from inside the cloud.*

EXODUS 24:16

Moses ascended high on Mount Sinai. God descended to its peak. And for
six days, the two maintained their positions. The cloud of glory hovered, and
to the people at the foot of the mountain, it appeared to be a consuming fire.
This same God whose fire blazed away on a bush but did not consume it was
now, from all appearances, devouring the top of a mountain. And Moses, the
man who had spoken with this God, was not running in fear. In fact, for six
full days, he stood poised to go even closer.

On the seventh day, God called. And Moses not only entered this terrifying cloud of glory, he stayed in it forty days and nights. He received
dramatic, landmark revelation in it as God gave commands and instructions
and unveiled His heart for His people. The desires of this God were laid bare:
He seeks a relationship with His people and wants their exclusive love. He
expects His people to be ethical and pure like He is. He cherishes His people
and wants to bless them. These were the matters weighing on the heart of the
"consuming fire."

What do we miss when we are too intimidated to go deeper into God?
We miss the unveiling of what's on His heart. In His Presence, divine desires
are revealed. His purposes and missions are set forth. His expectations become clear. The extent of His love is expressed. If we don't enter the cloud
of glory, we don't experience these priceless treasures. But if we do, eternal
blessings open up before us.

*Lord, I want to see and hear what's on Your heart.
Share Your desires and dreams with me. Show me what
You treasure. Lead me into Your cloud of glory.*

March 28

Have the people of Israel build me a holy sanctuary so I can live among them.

EXODUS 25:8

God gave Moses extensive details for His dwelling place, not because He's unreasonably demanding but because these details had a much larger purpose. The designs for Israel's worship reflected heavenly realities. The Tabernacle and all its articles of worship were "only a copy, a shadow" of the real place of worship in heaven (Hebrews 8:5). It was a visible expression of the invisible throne room. God gave Moses a picture to help translate one realm of reality into another. And the copy, the shadow, had to be accurate.

That tells us a lot about the nature and purposes of God. He wants to dwell with us, for one thing; He desires closeness. But it also tells us that He wants us to know the environment of heaven. He shared with us a picture of where He has lived for all of eternity so we could experience a taste of eternity now. In showing us His "natural habitat," He has invited us to explore that environment and make ourselves at home in it. His description of heavenly realities was an intensely relational move.

Other places in Scripture give us glimpses of those heavenly realities—the visions of Isaiah, Daniel, and Ezekiel, as well as the heavenly scenes of Revelation 4 and following. These are invitations to imagine what God's environment is like. Some people read them and think, "I can't comprehend that," so they stop trying. Others step into the pictures and try to hear the sounds, smell the smells, see the sights, and more. That pleases God. Such pictures are not given in order to frustrate; they are given in order to share the experience. If you let your thoughts run wild in the pictures of His Presence, your sense of His Presence will increase.

Lord, inspire my vision to see Your throne room and all Your dwelling places, both in heavenly and material realms. Wherever You choose to dwell, I want to see You there.

I will meet with you there and talk to you from above the atonement cover between the gold cherubim that hover over the Ark of the Covenant.

EXODUS 25:22

When we realize that the Tabernacle and all its articles of worship were a reflection of heavenly realities, we can begin to understand how the images and symbols apply to us. We can know that when God said He would meet and speak with Moses from above the atonement cover of the Ark, He was giving a picture of the basis of our relationship with Him. He meets us at the place of atonement.

For us, in this post-Tabernacle era, that means He meets us in our relationship with Jesus, where sins are covered and communion with a holy God can deepen unhindered. Between the cherubim—the angelic beings who surround His throne and who gaze at the divine blood that was spilled—the holy Presence pursues us. This is where we respond to Him. Outside of this place, we can't know Him. We can know *of* Him, and we may be able to hear His voice sometimes, but we can't know Him in that experiential, face-to-face interaction that defines relationships and makes them rich. Only at the covering can we draw close.

That's why God seems so distant when we try to relate to Him with a strong sense of guilt and shame. We assume a rift where there is no rift, an offense where there is no offense, a grudge where there is no grudge. Everything that would hinder a relationship with Him has been covered. He has chosen to be blind to that which separates us. And He refuses to interact with us in deeply meaningful ways when we don't fully believe that. But when we realize what atonement has accomplished—and completely count on His favor—He freely meets us there.

Lord, I choose to fully believe that I am covered—that my offenses no longer exist and that I am in holy fellowship with You as Your child. In this freedom from all that separates us, please make Yourself known to me.

March 30

Place the Bread of the Presence on the table
to remain before me at all times.

EXODUS 25:30

The twelve loaves of bread set on the table in the Holy Place were called "the Bread of the Presence"—literally, "the bread of the face." The priests would set the loaves out once a week, and they would remain in His Presence until the next week, when a new set of loaves would be set out to sit in His Presence. At all times, bread would remain where God dwelled.

It's interesting that the Hebrew word for "face" is always written in plural form. Perhaps this linguistic quirk isn't significant, but when dealing with words of revelation, minor details can have major implications. And it makes sense that "face" would imply some variety: (1) in reference to a God of Trinity, three Persons are involved; and (2) with any person, we can encounter multiple "faces." In God's Presence, we can experience His face of compassion, His face of forgiveness, His face of strength and power, His warrior face, His healing face, and so on. He invites us to experience His various attributes in the circumstances of our lives. Sometimes we need to see one side of Him, sometimes another. In His Presence, we encounter over time a wide range of who He is.

Seek in your time with God today not just an encounter with Him in general but an encounter with a specific "face"—one of His many attributes that fits your various needs. Understand that He wants to show you many facets of His personality. Expect to be drawn into His compassion or mercy on one occasion and His jealousy or zeal on another. Know that His Presence applies to any situation you might find yourself in and any need you could possibly have. Whatever you're going through today, there's an aspect of Himself that He wants to reveal in it.

Father, Son, and Spirit, please let me know the
many sides of who You are. Let me see the face
of Your glory that I most need to see today.

March 31

The lampstand will stand in the Tabernacle, in front of the inner curtain that shields the Ark of the Covenant. Aaron and his sons must keep the lamps burning in the LORD's presence all night.

EXODUS 27:21

Day and night. That's how the flames of the Presence were to burn. The light in the Holy Place—seven lamps on a golden lampstand, each filled with oil by priests constantly on call—would glow continually, without fail.

Scripture calls several things "light": the revealed Word, the Temple, Jerusalem, and the Messiah. But the Messiah, in addition to calling Himself the light of the world (John 8:12 and 9:5), also called His people the light of the world (Matthew 5:14). Not only do He and the Spirit continually shine in the Father's Presence, so do we. Continually filled with the oil of the Spirit, we stand in the Holy Place as flames before God. We are fueled by Him and spent on Him simultaneously.

Both processes—being fueled by Him and being spent on Him—are integral to experiencing His Presence. When we are simply fueled by Him, we taste of His power but can't keep it flowing. We have to pour out in order to keep being filled up. But if we are simply spent on Him, we burn out quickly. In neither case are we effective for Him, nor do we benefit from Him for long. If we are to know Him, enjoy His Presence, and bear His fruit, we have to both receive from Him and give to Him. That's the only way this relationship can work.

Continually receive from God—unashamedly and without apology. And continually burn for Him—again, unashamedly and without apology. That's how lights in His Presence are meant to shine.

Spirit, flow into me and fill me abundantly and continually. And Father, let me burn for You abundantly and continually. Let me shine as fully as You designed me to do.

April 1

I will meet the people of Israel there, in the place made holy by my glorious presence.

EXODUS 29:43

The Tabernacle was a meeting place, a designated rendezvous between God and His people. We know it wasn't the final dwelling place of God on earth; His Presence fills us in deeper and fuller ways today. But for that era, His Presence was a concrete experience for those who would come to that specific place. Compared to captivity in Egypt and God's apparent absence in that era, this was deep intimacy.

But compared to what's available to us today, the Tabernacle experience was a sporadic encounter. For people like Moses and Joshua it was more, but average Israelites only got to witness God's relationship with their leaders and hear of divine conversations secondhand. They saw God's Presence without entering into it personally. In fact, on one occasion they pleaded with Moses to converse with God for them; they were afraid and wanted to keep Him at arm's length. They considered a personal encounter with God to be too intense.

We have the same option. Do we want to enter into God's Presence personally or let others—either past characters of Scripture or present spiritual adventurers—encounter Him on our behalf? Many people unconsciously choose distance because a personal encounter with God might be too intense. A face-to-face experience comes with high accountability and a strong sense of mission. One option is easier, the other more rewarding.

Choose intensity. The Tabernacle—in this case your body and your community of believers—will be set apart and made sacred by the glorious Presence. Meeting with God may be challenging, but it's much better than the alternative. Never neglect the privilege of Presence that has been offered.

Lord, I don't want to miss a single opportunity to experience You in any area of life. Open my eyes to holy moments and places of divine rendezvous.

April 2

Blend the spices together and sprinkle them with salt to produce a pure and holy incense. Grind some of the mixture into a very fine powder and put it in front of the Ark of the Covenant, where I will meet with you in the Tabernacle. You must treat this incense as most holy.

EXODUS 30:35-36

The holy incense, *ketoret*, was a powerful substance, sacred to God and used in at least one instance to stop a plague (Numbers 16:46-50). Jewish oral law designated a precise compound of eleven ingredients that, if mixed improperly, could result in exile or even death for the mixer. It was never to be made for personal enjoyment. Handling the incense was a serious and sacred business.

Not all of the ingredients of *ketoret* are known for certain today, but some historians and rabbis believe they recently discovered an ancient stockpile of it in the caves of Qumran. When analyzed, it was found to contain at least eight of the eleven ingredients, and when burned, it produced a strong, pleasant aroma that would have overcome any stench of sacrifice in ancient temple rituals. (For testing it was burned not with fire but with acid, since by biblical law, burning it with fire apart from a temple or altar could have invoked immediate and deadly divine wrath.)

Incense often represents prayer in Scripture. If this is the case with *ketoret*, God has painted a powerful picture of what our prayers mean in heaven. They rise up from the holy place as an intensely pleasant aroma that overwhelms the unpleasant effects of sacrifice. They have the ability to please God and prevent plagues. They are not simply for personal enjoyment and pleasure but for a holy offering to God. He considers them sacred.

We should consider them sacred too. Our conversations with God are powerful and pleasing to Him, full of purpose and sacrifice. They should never be minimized or underestimated. God responds to the pleasing aroma of incense rightly offered.

Lord, forgive me for the times I've neglected prayer. Hear the requests I offer now. Remind me often of the power of having Your ear.

April 3

*Inside the Tent of Meeting, the Lord would speak to
Moses face to face, as one speaks to a friend.*

EXODUS 33:11

Before the Tabernacle had been assembled, Moses used to set up a tent outside the camp. He would go there to meet with God. All Israel would witness
the old man walking out to the meeting place; they would stand at their tents
and watch the cloud of glory hover over the tent. They knew the eternal God
was communing with a man with an extraordinary calling.

Scripture makes a remarkable statement about God—one we might
rebuke someone for making if we didn't know it was backed by divine inspiration. It says God spoke with Moses "as one speaks to a friend." Without compromising the majesty or holiness of God, Scripture humanizes His
relationship with a person. It makes no comment on Moses' unworthiness as
a fallen human being or God's unapproachable nature. It mentions no possibility of Moses dying in the Presence as the rest of Israel feared they would
do. It details no rituals or confessions Moses would have to make before con-
versing with God. It simply says they met together as friends.

That's our goal—to meet with God as a friend. We want to hear Him
speak to us with words we can understand, just as if we were having a cup of
coffee with someone and enjoying a transparent conversation. We crave the
intimacy and familiarity with God that Moses had.

How can we get it? If we respond to God as Moses did—if we are willing to follow Him anywhere, take enormous risks for Him, and endure the
drama and trials of someone who hears God's voice—we can meet with Him
as Moses did. We may or may not see a cloud of glory or hear an audible
voice as he did, but we can know Him confidently and deeply—as a friend.

*Lord, I want to know You like that, and I'm
willing to follow You as Moses did. Please lead me
into that kind of relationship with You.*

*The LORD replied, "I will personally go
with you, Moses, and I will give you rest—
everything will be fine for you."*

EXODUS 33:14

God can be really confusing. Listening for His direction isn't a matter of simply asking yes/no questions or hearing clear-cut oracles. When God speaks, He usually does so in a way that requires faith to believe it really is His voice and in a way that requires us to dig for the treasures of wisdom and guidance He has hidden for us. Finding His will for us in personal decisions can seem like a cosmic game of hide-and-seek, and usually as if He is having more fun in it than we are.

So we can relate to Moses' bold request for more information from God. "You have been telling me . . . but you haven't told me . . . if it is true . . . ," he pleads in Exodus 33:12-13. His plea is as well reasoned as any child's petition for parental permission: "Let me know your ways so I may understand you more fully and continue to enjoy your favor" (v. 13). How could God refuse? It's all about knowing Him better and doing the right things.

God's response is comforting. He actually answers the plea for more information. Moses has asked who will accompany him to the Promised Land, and God says He will personally do it. Not only that, His Presence along the way will provide rest and peace. "Everything will be fine for you," God reassures His servant. The Presence accomplishes everything Israel will need.

That's true for us, too. We spend a lot of time focusing on what we need, but if we prioritize His Presence, what we need won't be an issue. If He goes with us, it doesn't matter which problems arise. He is there to take care of them. And we can rest.

*Lord, You are all I need. It doesn't matter what I face
as long as You are with me. I choose to focus on You,
not on my need. Please help me do that always.*

April 5

Moses responded, "Then show me
your glorious presence."

EXODUS 33:18

It wasn't enough for Moses to know God's Presence was going with him. He wanted to *see* God's Presence—to experience His glory, to taste and see the goodness of the God who had been speaking to him. The promise of Presence wasn't encouraging enough, and the fact of Presence wasn't satisfying enough. Moses wanted an experience.

Think about who is asking the question. This is the servant of God who has seen a burning bush, watched ten plagues play out in front of him, walked through the parted waters of a sea, witnessed the provision of bread from heaven and water flowing from a rock, met with God face-to-face in a tent, and spent days in the cloud of glory at the top of a mountain surrounded by lightning, thunder, and heavenly trumpet blasts. Now, in the aftermath of an extremely reassuring promise of God's Presence, he asks to see God's glory. Apparently the drama of the Exodus hasn't been enough. Nor have the audible words and extravagance of God's revelation. He knows he has seen the things of God, not God Himself. And he isn't yet satisfied.

Perhaps we don't experience God today more than we do because we don't have such holy discontentment. Perhaps we're far too easily satisfied with the knowledge of God's Presence rather than the experience of it. Perhaps we settle for much less than we're offered. Regardless, Moses' request is a model for us. If we ask to see God's glory, He just might grant it.

Don't be content with where you are spiritually. Don't assume that the level of revelation you have right now or the experiences you've had with God are the norm. There's more. There's *always* more. Ask for it—persistently—and seek it with all your heart.

Lord, please let me see Your glorious Presence—
more and more every day.

April 6

*Whenever he went into the Tent of Meeting
to speak with the LORD, he would remove
the veil until he came out again. . . . So he
would put the veil over his face until he
returned to speak with the LORD.*

EXODUS 34:34-35

It sounds like the ultimate spiritual experience. Moses glowed because he had been in God's Presence, and the sight was a little unnerving to those around him. So he covered his face with a veil when speaking to the people, but uncovered it while meeting with God. For Moses, encountering God was a regular occurrence. For his fellow Israelites, it wasn't. Moses was the exception, not the norm.

But the New Testament points to a more widespread spiritual experience, a familiarity in encountering God. According to 2 Corinthians, the new covenant makes us "very bold" (3:12). We don't have to worry about glory fading. "All of us who have had that veil removed can see and reflect the glory of the Lord. And the Lord—who is the Spirit—makes us more and more like him as we are changed into his glorious image" (3:18). This is spoken of all who turn to God in faith. Deep experiences with God should be the norm, not the exception.

What does it mean to have an unveiled face? It means that (1) like Moses, we encounter God openly and honestly, with no separation between us because of sin or ignorance; and (2) unlike Moses, we are among plenty of other people who have experienced God like we have and plenty of people who need to, and we have nothing to hide from any of them. To whatever degree we soak in God's Presence, we become reflections of His glory. We become what we behold.

*Father, I want to become a reflection of You. I want to
glow with Your Presence and Your glory. Let me soak in
Your Presence and carry it with me into the world.*

April 7

*Then the cloud covered the Tabernacle, and the
glory of the L*ORD *filled the Tabernacle. Moses
could no longer enter the Tabernacle because the
cloud had settled down over it, and the glory of
the L*ORD *filled the Tabernacle.*

EXODUS 40:34-35

There are times when the glory of God's Presence fills us with energy and a
clear plan of action. We spend time with Him, experience His touch, and go
into the world with purpose. But when God chooses to overwhelm us—and
may those times always increase—His glory immobilizes us. There can be no
busyness or distractions when we are in utter awe. The fullness of His Presence commands complete attention—not as an obligation but because there
is no other choice. When He manifests Himself, we are silent and still.

Even Moses, who had encountered God in so many dramatic ways, was
unable to enter the Tabernacle when the cloud of glory filled it. Moses had
entered the cloud of glory on Sinai before; apparently this time it was thicker,
fuller, and more awesome than ever. God was making a statement: "I'm making a home among you, and I want your full attention."

God's desire remains the same. The prescribed place of meeting is different—it's richer and more personal now—but the zeal to dwell with us hasn't
changed. That's why we can't be content with a few God-moments here and
there or an occasional verse that gives us a lift or an insight. We need more.
We need depth and intensity and passion. We need intimate encounters every
day. We need the experience of God in us, overflowing and obvious. We need
to be immobilized in awe.

If your spiritual life is stagnant, ask for this. Even if it's thriving, ask for
this. God shows His glory to those who seek Him.

*Lord, I need a sense of awe. I need to walk in the
weight of Your glory. Show me Your majesty. Give
me a reason to be still and gaze at You.*

April 8

*Whenever the cloud lifted from the Tabernacle,
the people of Israel would set out on their
journey, following it. But if the cloud did not rise,
they remained where they were until it lifted.*

EXODUS 40:36-37

In explaining the new birth to Nicodemus, Jesus described life in God's Spirit. "The wind blows wherever it pleases. You hear its sound, but you cannot tell where it comes from or where it is going. So it is with everyone born of the Spirit" (John 3:8, NIV). In other words, the Spirit moves in ways that are unpredictable to natural human minds. He defies our reason. We can't figure Him out ahead of time. We have to watch and follow closely.

If that were not so, we could enjoy a pretty comfortable religion. We could figure out God's precepts and principles and then live by them independently rather than by relating to Him constantly. In fact, that's what vast numbers of Christians do. We tell people our faith is a relationship, not a religion, and then map out our doctrines and how-to steps for living the Christian life. In other words, we default back into religion. Meanwhile, the Spirit blows wherever He pleases. Only those who relate to Him closely can follow.

God didn't give Moses and the Israelites a system to follow either. He gave them a cloud by day and fire by night. They could have mapped out a strategy to get to the Promised Land if they wanted to, but it would not have given them victory over the enemies and obstacles in their way, and it wouldn't have relieved their fears. They had to have God, and they had to follow Him step by step.

So do we. Refuse to systematize the Christian life as though it's a set of principles and precepts. God often led people down strange, unexpected, and even contemptible paths in Scripture. Let Him lead you however He chooses. Keep your eyes on the cloud.

*Lord, forgive me for trying to predict Your
ways and presume on Your guidance. I turn
my attention to Your subtle leadings and
invite You to direct me however You choose.*

April 9

He is the one who mediates for us a far better covenant with God, based on better promises.

HEBREWS 8:6

Think of all the promises God gave to Moses and the Israelites: that He was leading them to a land of promise, that His Presence would go with them, that they would be blessed if they followed His will and obeyed His laws, that they would be victorious against their enemies and fruitful in their labor, and on and on. These promises were often conditional on their obedience, but they were extravagant nonetheless. And we have seen the mind-boggling ways Moses and those around him experienced God's Presence. God was doing a truly remarkable thing among His people.

Yet the writer of Hebrews twice—in 7:22 and here in 8:6—refers to our covenant in Jesus as a "better covenant." It's based on better promises. The God who cannot lie and who does not change His mind somehow fulfilled His covenant with Moses in the work of Christ, and He has grafted us into all the blessings His Son will receive. We receive a standing of righteousness, an inheritance of glory, free access to the throne room of God, and all the qualities of life our Savior secured for us and experiences Himself. It is truly an exchanged life; He took our death upon Himself and gave us His life in all its fullness. That's a better covenant.

It's amazing to consider that Moses' closeness to God and face-to-face encounters with His Presence have been surpassed by a better covenant with better promises. Yet that's what Scripture declares. We look at Moses and marvel, but God has offered us more. Jesus did not come simply to turn us back to the law; He came to put God's own Spirit and righteousness and desires and dreams within us. We dare not neglect what He has made available.

Lord, Moses experienced You in unimaginable ways, but You offer us an even deeper relationship with You. Let me experience more than Your written words; I want every benefit of the better covenant.

April 10

I have given them the glory that you gave
me, that they may be one as we are one—I
in them and you in me—so that they may
be brought to complete unity. Then the
world will know that you sent me and have
loved them even as you have loved me.

JOHN 17:22-23, NIV

On the night before His crucifixion, Jesus prayed an amazing prayer: that His followers would be "one" in the same way that He and the Father are one. How are He and the Father one? They are one in substance, one in purpose, one in personality . . . in other words, they are perfectly united, not as two parts of a whole but as the whole itself. They are, according to our understanding of the Trinity, the same Being.

Jesus' prayer is often interpreted as a plea that the disciples would be united with each other. And though that unity is certainly included in this prayer, His intent is much more than that. Jesus doesn't just pray for unity; He prays that we would be one *in the same way* that He and the Father are one. And He does not specify "one with each other." In fact, we can just as easily understand the request as meaning "one with Him." The picture is of Jesus' followers being drawn into the oneness that He and the Father share—the intense, unchangeable union between Him and the Father from all eternity. That's His desire for us.

Think about that. We can be one with Jesus *in the same way* that Jesus is one with the Father. And it only makes sense, doesn't it? The kind of love the Trinity has shared among its members is the kind of love that seeks to spill out toward others. It isn't exclusive. We have been invited into the deep fellowship of Father, Son, and Spirit as welcome participants of their love. Intimate, intense, passionate, inseparable, unending.

Jesus, this invitation is beyond my
understanding, but I want to step into it. I
want the kind of oneness with You that You
have with the Father—complete unity with
You, the Father, and Your Spirit.

April 11

*Don't you realize that your body is the
temple of the Holy Spirit, who lives in you
and was given to you by God?*

1 CORINTHIANS 6:19

Where does God dwell? We think of heavenly thrones with crowds of angelic
worshipers gathered round. Or of a long-ago Tabernacle in the wilderness or
Temple in Jerusalem. We may even think of the right answer, but often only
because we've been taught, not because our experience has made it obvious.
The Spirit of God lives within those who believe in Him and have received
Him.

Paul had to remind the Corinthians that the Spirit was within them; apparently that wasn't obvious to some of them, either. Many of them had worshiped the Jews' God, who had once visited a Tabernacle and a Temple; many
had worshiped in the Greek temples that honored gods without expecting
their presence. But the human body as a residence for the divine Spirit? That
wasn't expected.

Like many of us, the Corinthians had experienced the Spirit at work—
as One who utilized His people for service. But they forgot the deeper truth
that the Spirit lived in them constantly for the purpose of relationship—that
they might know God and be fully known by Him. The Greek gods used
their subjects but didn't particularly enjoy them. The Hebrew God was different. He came to share life.

The awesome, majestic God of the universe chooses to make His home
deep in the depths of your being. You have likely sensed Him often—perhaps
without even knowing it was Him. Ask Him to teach you which voice is
His, which impulses are His, which dreams and desires are given by Him. He
resides there not primarily to use you but to move you, empower you, and
enjoy you.

*Spirit, I know You're within me; please help
me recognize You. I want to know which
thoughts and dreams are Yours. And I want
to enjoy You as You enjoy me.*

April 12

Don't you realize that all of you together are the
temple of God and that the Spirit of God lives in you?

1 CORINTHIANS 3:16

The Presence of the Spirit within is not just an individual experience. God inhabits the community in a way that requires individuals to access Him there. He has faces we can't see unless we see them in each other. The fellowship of believers is an essential part of knowing God.

Why doesn't God give us as individuals everything we need in our relationship with Him? Because He absolutely refuses to put us in a position of independence and self-sufficiency. He created us not only to be dependent on Him but to be interdependent with others. That's why He distributes spiritual gifts among His people rather than equipping any one person with all of them. The body of Christ has many parts; He will not allow them to be in a position of functioning separately.

If you want a full experience of the Presence of God, spend plenty of time with other Christians. Benefit from their gifts. Listen to their experiences. Search for His face in theirs. Each person experiences His heart uniquely. The more we share in those experiences with others, the broader our own experience with Him becomes. God is present in a unique way in the collective body of His people.

Seek fellowship—at church services, in small groups, in spiritual friendships—as a means to experience God. If you think you can do without gatherings, think again. God attends our meetings. He is present at our tables. He shows Himself in a variety of ways through a variety of people, and only by encountering them can we encounter Him in those ways.

Spirit, I want to see You in the faces of others. I want to
connect with You through their gifts and experiences. Please
help me see the ultimate treasure—You—in them.

One of the disciples, the one Jesus loved dearly, was reclining against him, his head on his shoulder. Peter motioned to him to ask who Jesus might be talking about. So, being the closest, he said, "Master, who?"

JOHN 13:23-25, THE MESSAGE

Jesus and His disciples were sitting around a table sharing a meal together, the last meal before He was crucified. At one point, Jesus became visibly upset and said someone was going to betray Him. The disciples wondered who it might be, so Peter naturally asked the one closest to Him—John, who was leaning against Jesus with his head on the divine shoulder. "The one Jesus loved dearly" was close enough to hear Jesus' whispers.

This is the same John who would later fall at Jesus' feet as though dead (Revelation 1:17), but on this night he was leaning comfortably against his Friend. And those who assume that position hear divine secrets. It's a picture of God and His people drawing close in the kind of relationship we're all invited to have.

Imagine someone who knows you inside and out, who listens to your dreams and your pain, who is always pulling for you, and whose love for you and faithfulness to you will never change. He is the God of the tiniest details of your life, the God who lets you lean against Him, the One who sees into every corner of your heart and whispers in your ear. He's always inviting you closer, and everything He plans for your life is designed for that purpose—to bring you closer to Him.

Jesus, I accept that I am a disciple whom You love, and I choose to lean against You. Let me hear Your quiet voice in my ear. Share Your heart with me.

I no longer call you servants, because a servant does not know his master's business. Instead, I have called you friends, for everything that I learned from my Father I have made known to you.

JOHN 15:15, NIV

On the same evening John leaned against Jesus, Jesus invited all of His disciples into a deeper level of knowing Him. They had been taught servanthood and would still need to practice it; He had washed their feet as an object lesson in that attitude hours earlier. But they were to be more than servants. They were His friends.

The Bible describes our relationship with God in many ways: He is the Potter, we are the clay; He is the Shepherd, we are the sheep; He is the Master, we are the servants. And all of these are true. But those who really get close to God—anyone who accepts His open invitation—can have an even deeper relationship. Father to child, Friend to friend, or even Groom to bride. Those relationships are as close as people can get to each other, and that's how God pictures His greatest desire for us. He knows our hearts, and He wants us to know His.

It's hard to understand that the King of the universe who holds every galaxy in His hand also invites us into an up-close-and-personal relationship, but He does. So what do we do about that? Ask for it. Pursue it. Seek it with all our heart. Act as though the intimacy is already true, because it is. Keep our focus on that relationship above all others. When we do, God responds. He actually confides in us. He shares His secrets. The Son tells His followers what the Father is doing. God shows up in amazing—and very personal—ways.

Jesus, I accept Your friendship. I want to hear Your secrets. Open my ears to hear all the ways You confide in me, and show me how to respond when You do.

April 15

So be very careful to love the LORD your God.

JOSHUA 23:11

Many are familiar with "love languages"—the idea that each of us has a preferred mode of receiving love from others. Love languages include spending quality time together, physical touch, receiving gifts, acts of service, and words of affirmation. We understand the affections of others when they are expressed through one of these means.

What we often don't realize is that God has love languages too. He enjoys words of affirmation (praise), receiving gifts (offerings), acts of service (obedience), quality time (prayer/meditation), and even physical touch. The last in the list may be a little difficult for us to express—though Jesus surely enjoyed John's leaning against Him at the Last Supper, and the Father surely enjoys our savoring the physical gifts He gives us—but God receives love in much the same ways we do. He even tells us how to express love to Him. Scripture is full of instructions about how to give to Him, speak to Him, and serve Him. God has made His desires clear.

All of our expressions of love—praise, offerings, obedience, conversations with Him, and longings for sensory touches—are meant to be an overflow of our heart. When we turn God's instructions into nothing but a set of obligations, we undermine their purpose. They were all given first and foremost as ways to express our love. That's why the greatest commandment to love Him is above all others; it was meant to shape everything we do in our lives toward God. More than anything else, we were designed to adore Him. And our number one pursuit is to figure out how to love Him well.

*Lord, how can I love You well today? What time should
I set aside to spend with You? What service can I do?
What can I say that will touch Your heart? Help me
love You deeply and show it well.*

April 16

*He existed before anything else, and he
holds all creation together.*

COLOSSIANS 1:17

You would need about ten million hydrogen atoms to make a one-millimeter line out of them. But each atom is made up of many much smaller parts. The diameter of the proton is 100,000 times smaller than the diameter of the atom itself, and each electron rapidly racing around the proton is a thousand times smaller than that. The actual substance of an atom is so small that we can't imagine it. Yet Jesus, through whom all things were created, is somehow present in every tiny particle. In fact, He holds them all together.

And His involvement goes well beyond material substance. He knows the secrets of every heart (Psalm 44:21), as well as every motive behind them (1 Chronicles 28:9). He is aware of every sparrow that falls to the ground anywhere in the world (Matthew 10:29). He sees into the future, even naming a king more than a hundred years in advance (Cyrus in Isaiah 45:1-3). God knows every tiny speck of His creation—past, present, and future.

And He knows what will happen next in your life too. Every step on your path is laid out before His eyes. Fears and doubts rise up in your heart? He already has an answer for them. Obstacles stand against you? He has already seen them and has a solution for them. You feel pain or loneliness? He has been there all along and will be there with you in the future. You want to win victories in your life as you fulfill the destiny He has called you to? He has prepared the way for every one of them. In the impersonal pieces and processes of this world, as well as the personal aspects of your life, He is there.

*Jesus, thank You for holding together every
cell in my body and every atom in every cell.
You know me better than I know myself.
Help me remember the care and zeal with
which You watch over my life.*

April 17

Go down to the potter's shop, and I will
speak to you there.

JEREMIAH 18:2

"Are you *sure* it's okay to eat this? Do you *promise?*" the boy asked his mother. His allergies provoked anxiety at the sight of any new food, so he felt compelled to ask if it was safe—again and again and again. Just to be sure. So she answered—again. "I've already told you once. Saying it again won't make it any more true." And listening to this exchange, I immediately heard God's voice: "You keep asking me to confirm My promise to you. But I've already spoken. Saying it again won't make it any more true."

God gives us parables like that—a conversation, a turn of events, a scene from nature or everyday life—that remind us of His ways, His words, or His purposes. These parables reinforce what we know to be true from His Word, but they sink deeper into our hearts in a way that words on a printed page rarely do. They paint portraits of the Kingdom and the King. In our lives, as in Scripture, God's favorite language is pictures.

Pay attention to the parables in your life. This is how God often spoke to biblical prophets, it's how Jesus taught, and it's how God continues to teach us from Scripture. The metaphors of the Red Sea and Goliath and the mustard seed speak loudly, and this picturesque language of God continues to show us truth in our everyday lives. Just as the skies pour forth speech incessantly (Psalm 19:1-2), so God continuously uses His creation, people, and events to share the thoughts of His heart. If we notice, images begin to unfold all around us. And God shows up in dramatic ways—literally.

Lord, open my eyes, open my ears, and help
me understand Your language. Make me
a noticer of Your pictures. Let me see Your
thoughts and understand Your heart.

April 18

It is no longer I who live, but Christ lives in me.

GALATIANS 2:20

Scripture tells us that the Holy Spirit lives in us (John 14:17; 1 Corinthians 3:16). And that we can be filled with the fullness of God (Ephesians 3:19). And that Jesus is in us (John 14:20; Galatians 2:20; Colossians 1:27). In other words, every member of the Trinity is present in our being. That drives people who love precise doctrine crazy, but it's a truth that flows from the experience of the earliest Christians. Something had fundamentally changed within them, and they experienced divine life. This is how they—and even Jesus—expressed it.

In our quest to experience more of God's Presence, we aren't just after the God who lives *with* us. We're seeking the God who lives *in* us. And not just as a matter of doctrinal belief but as a practical and palpable Presence. When we think of the inner life, we are right to envision any member of the Trinity at any time: the Father on His throne, the Son in His earthly and heavenly ministry, and the Spirit blowing through us or flowing out of us. All the attributes of the Godhead are there: the majesty and mystery of the Father, the compassion and visible touch of Jesus, the comfort and counsel of the Spirit, and many more characteristics than one can list. We can never say we are lacking in resources. Even the faith and patience and wisdom of Jesus are ours for the asking. We are filled with immense power.

So why don't we experience such spiritual riches? Perhaps because we don't believe we can, or maybe because we don't understand the implications, or possibly even because we don't see results at first and give up the pursuit. Regardless, God puts within us a life we have not yet fully realized. But it becomes more real the more we seek, believe, and persist.

Jesus, I don't want to fall short of the potential You've put in me. Express Yourself fully through me and in me.

April 19

The heavens proclaim the glory of God. The skies display his craftsmanship.

PSALM 19:1

"Lord, let me see Your beauty," I asked. His response was clear: "I'm already showing it to you. I show you My tenderness all the time, but you don't recognize it because you're too suspicious of Me. I give you favors, and you think they are random circumstances or smaller blessings than they really are. I reveal My generosity toward you, but your fear causes you to think each step forward is a setup for failure or hardship. I reveal My heart, and you don't know how to interpret it."

We encounter God and hear His voice much more than we think we do. Creation is constantly pouring forth knowledge of Him, yet we wonder if we hear well. He assures us He is sovereign over all our circumstances, yet we marvel at "coincidences." He fills our lives with joys, yet we hold them tightly because we fear losing them. Our insecurities and doubts blind us to the beauty He constantly unveils.

God has designed creation, our circumstances, our relationships, and even our own hearts to reflect Him and speak of His goodness and beauty. Sure, we have to sift through some unbeautiful appearances to see Him, but the revelation is there. The problem is that we've trained ourselves to interpret things naturally, randomly, and impersonally. Our senses have been dulled to His overtures.

Awaken them. Open your eyes to every divine gesture. If you think He might be speaking to you, He probably is. If you've asked to see His beauty and His glory, the evidence of beauty and glory that follows isn't by chance; it's from Him. Accept the gift of His reminders that He is there.

Lord, I choose to see the signs of Your heart for what they are—not to dismiss them or assume they are coincidences. I accept the ways creation, my circumstances, my relationships, and even my own heart speak of You.

April 20

Everything else is worthless when compared with the infinite value of knowing Christ Jesus my Lord.

PHILIPPIANS 3:8

I had experienced God's touch and heard His voice, but several fellow Christians objected to experience as part of the Christian life. (I marvel at the absurdity of that objection now—isn't the Bible a vast collection of people's experiences with God?—but it's sadly commonplace and gave me some concern at the time.) And the tension mounted between what God was actually doing in my life and what people told me He would or would not do. There came a time when I had to decide whether to make a choice to follow Him or to follow the positions, traditions, and assumptions of human beings who saw the experiences of the Bible as exceptions, not examples. I chose Him. "Lord, I don't care what anyone else thinks. Maybe I'm wrong. Maybe I'll fall flat on my face. Maybe I'll be humiliated in the eyes of everyone I know. But I'm going after You—completely, recklessly, desperately. And I'll trust You to lead me, correct me, and establish me however You choose."

From that point forward, the Presence increased. I read the Bible through new lenses, and its people, stories, and truths became clearer and clearer. I received affirmation after affirmation: my choice was good, and many of my past assumptions were wrong. God was leading me in new, exciting, and entirely biblical ways.

God honors those who abandon themselves to Him—those who are willing to relinquish every restraint in order to follow His leading, who almost recklessly go after Him without fear of looking ridiculous or being criticized by those around them. He expects discernment, obviously, and He will correct those who are moving in wrong directions; but He also treasures those whose desire for Him refuses to be quenched by hyperanalytical self-examination. He shows Himself to eyes focused exclusively on Him.

Lord, I choose You. I'm tired of religious principles and precepts and traditions that make assumptions about what You will and will not do. I open myself to whatever You want to do in my life—anything at all, no matter how out-of-the-box— as long as it fits with Your character and purposes.

April 21

We confidently and joyfully look forward to sharing God's glory. . . . And this hope will not lead to disappointment.

ROMANS 5:2, 5

We are reluctant to admit it, but many of us hope for good from God while expecting disappointment. We would love to encounter Him, but we suspect the encounters may come in the guise of suffering—as though the only way we grow closer to Him is through pain and trials. We aren't sure we want to seek Him fully because we are afraid of the cost. Yet God calls us into an experience with Him with the promise that His Presence will bring us joy. Our expectations don't line up with His promise. And we have to decide which we believe.

Hope believes the best about God—that He doesn't just put us through trials but that He plans pleasures and joys for us too. He *uses* the difficulties in our lives, to be sure, but He doesn't sadistically arrange them. He desires to bless. That's His nature. When we hope in Him, we are acknowledging who He is.

Rejoice in God and mistrust any expectations that His promises will be broken, His plans will be thwarted, or His goodness will be veiled in our lives. Hope hears His heartbeat accurately and ignores any lies about His character. It's a concrete expectation of good—not wishful thinking, not optimism, but a firm knowledge of God's favor. And hope in Him, according to the Word, will not disappoint us. A life rooted in expectation of His goodness will always eventually be satisfied.

Lord, I place my hope in You. I trust that You are working on my behalf, no matter how difficult my circumstances become. Please fill me with hope—the kind that comes from Your Spirit and cannot disappoint. And help me live in that hope today.

April 22

Notice how God is both kind and severe.

ROMANS 11:22

Majesty and humility. Awe and intimacy. Judgment and mercy. These are the tensions and paradoxes in relating to a God who is both unimaginably infinite in power and unimaginably tender in His love. We see the extremes in someone like John, who leaned intimately against Jesus at the Last Supper (John 13:23, NKJV) but later "fell at his feet as though dead" in Revelation 1:17 (NIV). Do we fall on our faces in front of this God or crawl into His lap? Do we fear His judgments or listen to His love songs? Do we approach Him as humble servants or close friends? It's hard to know.

The truth is that we need to know both sides of God—to be in awe and to become deeply familiar with His tenderness. An emphasis on one or the other leads to a skewed view and an unbalanced relationship. There are times when His Presence will comfort us and other times when it will cause us to hit the floor in fear. And in any encounter with Him, we have to be prepared for either.

In either case, we need to know that His love is behind any experience we have with Him. If He invites us into a warm embrace, it's because of His love. If He corrects us firmly, it's because of His love. If He causes us to wait for Him—for a word, a touch, an answer to prayer—it's because of His love. But in the context of His love, we can experience Him in a variety of ways. Some bring us comfort; others make us tremble.

In your quest for deeper intimacy with God, don't make the mistake of taking Him for granted. Rest in His love, but do not become complacent in it. Enjoy His acceptance, but do not mistake it for blanket approval of your every impulse. Know the majesty of the God who is close.

Lord, let me never take You for granted or
presume upon Your grace. Grant me the
privilege of being in awe of You.

He is severe toward those who disobeyed,
but kind to you if you continue to
trust in his kindness.

ROMANS 11:22

Too many Christians feel as if they have fallen out of God's favor with every little sin or misstep, as though every lapse into a habitual weakness disqualifies them from His kindness and brings them face-to-face with His severity. We think of Moses' outburst that cost him entry into the Promised Land (Numbers 20:10-12) or Uzzah's casual attempt to stabilize the holy Ark that cost him his life (2 Samuel 6:6-7). It takes only a couple of high-profile events like this to give us the impression that God is a high-strung deity whose aversion to sin prompts capricious judgments. Somehow, we trust in the severity of God more than His kindness.

When we look at the overall picture of Scripture, we realize two important points: (1) Sin has been thoroughly dealt with. That doesn't mean it's irrelevant; we can certainly forfeit God's calling on our life if we are living in rebellion. But that's the case with stubborn disobedience, not failed attempts to follow Him well. If we keep pointing our hearts back in the right direction, He doesn't treat us severely. (2) The context of God's severity—in many passages, including this one—is usually related to unbelief. His anger is stirred up over continual faithlessness, mistrust, and assumptions that He is not present, active, or reliable in what He says. He is not harsh toward the frequent failures we make in spite of our best intentions. He is harsh toward a persistent unwillingness to believe Him and to trust His kindness.

That's comforting. We have a choice in how we experience God. If we trust in His kindness, we find Him to be kind. If we are always suspicious of His intentions, we find Him intolerant of our unbelief. Perfect behavior is not the key to experiencing His goodness. The key is knowing how good He really is.

Father, I trust Your kindness because You tell me You are kind.
I trust that You don't pressure me to perform perfectly—
Your grace is far greater than all my sins. I choose to come
to You confidently, believing in Your goodness.

April 24

*You have endowed him with eternal blessings
and given him the joy of your presence.*

PSALM 21:6

David knew what it was like to seek God for rescue, defense, victory, provision, direction, and more. But he also knew what it was like to sit or even sleep in God's Presence. He thirsted and panted and longed for God. He believed someone could taste and see that the Lord is good. His greatest desire was to live in the Lord's house, delight in His perfections, and meditate on His Word. David knew that God—though mighty to save, provide, guide, and heal—is primarily relational. He is a Being. He calls Himself "I Am." He *is* before He *does*.

Those made in His image need to be the same way. We are simply to be in His Presence before doing things for Him or seeking things from Him. Our words aren't even necessary for Him—He knows our thoughts already—and they often aren't necessary for us, either. Like sitting in a room and enjoying a loved one's silent companionship, we can sit with God and just *be*. There's joy simply in a sense of His Presence.

Hear His voice: "Spend time with Me today. I don't just mean have conversations with Me, though our conversations are good. I mean spend time just being with Me. Learn to exist, to move in the knowledge of My Presence. Many of the answers and changes you long for come with seeking My Presence rather than seeking the answers and changes themselves. When you prioritize Me, I move on your behalf much more readily. I desire good things for you. But above all, I want your heart."

Lord, my heart is Yours. I want Your benefits, but I want You even more. Fill me with the joy of Your Presence as I seek You above all else.

April 25

Oh, that we might know the LORD! Let us press on to know him. He will respond to us as surely as the arrival of dawn or the coming of rains in early spring.

HOSEA 6:3

When you are in love, you long to share who you are. You want your beloved to know your passions and your deep thoughts, admire your skills and talents, understand your pain, and work with you toward your goals. You may be reluctant at times to share parts of yourself because transparency makes you vulnerable to rejection. But ideally, in that deep-down place of dreaming, you want to be known and appreciated for who you are. That's why heart-to-heart, gaze-into-the-eyes romance is a relentless human longing. Everyone wants to connect.

God has the same desire. In fact, that's why He made people in His image—to be known and appreciated for who He is. He has shared His passions and His thoughts with us so we can know Him. He does praiseworthy things so we can praise His power and wisdom and works. He spoke His grief through the prophets so we could understand His pain in broken relationships. He called us into His mission so we could work with Him toward His goals. He has not been reluctant to share Himself with us, even though any transparency on His part exposes Him to our rejection. The risk of rejection is worth the love of His creation. This is why we were made. God, like us, wants to connect.

The promise of Hosea 6:3—and really of Scripture as a whole—is that if we choose to "press on to know him," God will respond to us with His availability and love. Press on in whatever way you can think of, knowing that God longs to share who He is. When your heart is pressing in to Him, His response will be as certain as the dawn.

Lord, I want to fully appreciate who You are. Show me more of Yourself. Draw me closer and let me gaze into You.

I am the bread of life. Whoever comes to me will never be hungry again. Whoever believes in me will never be thirsty.

JOHN 6:35

"I am your nourishment. Your body can't survive long without food, but your spirit can't survive long without Me. Those who have never known Me are not spiritually alive. Those who do know Me but who don't eat and drink My Spirit are malnourished and weak. I won't let them die—they are born of an eternal Spirit—but they can't flourish without Me. They walk through their days lifelessly.

"Many people believe that accepting Me as their Savior should cause them to never hunger or thirst again. But look around. How many people called by My name are hungry and thirsty? How many are satisfied with life? Numerous Christians are burdened with heavy issues, struggling with their relationships, frustrated and disappointed that their dreams are dying. It isn't because they aren't saved. It's because they aren't feeding on Me. They aren't filling their hearts—not just their minds, but their innermost selves—with My words and My thoughts. They may focus on the Bible—through whatever lenses they see it—but they aren't focused on Me, the Living One. They are saved without experiencing the joys of salvation.

"Don't be like that. I offered you abundant life, and I meant it. I came that your joy might be full. Do you want to experience the abundance of My life and the fullness of My joy? Do you want to overcome problems rather than be victimized by them? You'll face them, of course—everyone does. But I never mean for them to crush you. I never mean for your joy to be quenched. And I never mean for you to 'live' without life. Come and eat. Feed on Me. Fill yourself with the Bread of Life. You never need to hunger again."

Jesus, I'm tired of stale "bread"—the religious dictates that offer no joy. I want the real You. Personally. Feed me with Your life.

April 27

I am the light of the world. If you follow me,
you won't have to walk in darkness, because
you will have the light that leads to life.

JOHN 8:12

"I am your light. Yes, you live in a dark world. You walk among confused people who don't know their right from their left and can't even see the next step in front of them. You have many teachers who are blind but trying to impart light and sight to others. My light is in the world, of course; many of My people see and speak according to truth. But so many other voices confuse those who listen to them. You can't distinguish light apart from Me. I'm the only one who shines pure truth.

"You'll notice that I never told you to learn the truth and then follow what you know. I said to follow Me. There's a difference between walking in light and following a light. One is your environment, the other is your direction. If you learned truth, the absolutes I have spoken, and then followed them, you would become wise and principled. You would be living in the right environment, but you would then rely on living by methods and not by knowing Me. When faced with two wise options, you wouldn't know which one to take. When moving toward a wise goal, you wouldn't know when to advance and when to wait patiently. Wisdom and truth alone don't get you where you need to go. I want you to follow the light—Me—rather than just living in the light of My truth.

"Open your spirit to Me. I am your light. Be filled with Me and follow where I lead. You will still go through dark places, but you won't stumble in them. I will always shine light on the next step. Take it, and it will always lead you to life."

Jesus, help me recognize Your light. Fill me
with truth and guide my steps. Teach me to
live by the light of Your Presence.

April 28

I am the good shepherd; I know my own sheep, and they know me, just as my Father knows me and I know the Father. So I sacrifice my life for the sheep.

JOHN 10:14-15

"I am your shepherd. Few people in your society know what that really means; you aren't familiar with the life of a shepherd. But I want you to know that I sleep where you sleep. I lead you—even *drive* you—where you need to go. Unless you willfully reject Me, I make sure you don't stray too far from the path, though I let you wander freely within My pastures. When you get stuck in a ditch, I pull you out. When you fall into a ravine, I rescue you and heal your wounds. Without Me, you would wander aimlessly, scrounge for food wherever you happened upon it, and be vulnerable to predators all around you. You wouldn't survive. I spend My days and nights with you because it is My responsibility to care for you. You can't take care of yourself. You need Me.

"I like that arrangement. I enjoy shepherding. I develop a relationship with My sheep and teach you to recognize My voice above all others. You don't know the significance of all the places I take you or even why I take you there, but you can trust Me to guide you well. I may correct your course, but I don't punish you harshly. You're sheep, after all. If you understood—if you saw the landscape as I do—you would never stray. But you don't, and you can't—not from your perspective. I know your weaknesses and am patient with you, much more patient than you are with yourself.

"You need to understand that sheep don't worry about the future, obsess about their mistakes, or strategize their lives. And if you knew the heart of this Shepherd, you wouldn't either. Sheep follow. That's all I'm asking you to do."

Jesus, I know I can trust my Shepherd. You've proven that You will go to extremes to care for me. Help me follow You well.

April 29

I am the resurrection and the life. Anyone who
believes in me will live, even after dying.

JOHN 11:25

"I am the unquenchable life. I cannot die. When I come to live within you, you can't die either. You can *feel* lifeless, and you may fear death, but you will never know the worst of its sting. Those who believe in Me will live in Me.

"Think of how this frees you to live. Many of My earliest followers chose to care for and comfort people who were dying of plagues and had been isolated from their families. They could demonstrate My love because they didn't fear death. Their compassion changed the world. Martyrs have remained true to Me because they were not afraid of those who could kill the body. Their testimony rises up before My throne and lives forever. I have responded to their sacrifice with My power, and again the world is changed. You live in an age and a culture in which people obsessively pursue long, happy, fulfilling lives. Meanwhile, they obsessively fear death. That never allows room for fulfillment. It only enslaves.

"In My Presence in heaven, you will wonder why it took so long to get here and wish you had been here sooner. You will never want to go back into a dark world and fallen existence again. You will wish you could tell everyone in that dark world and fallen existence to stop worrying and live freely because their trials and sufferings are brief. So are the passing pleasures they seek. You will regret not living with a heavenly perspective during your physical life.

"Choose that perspective now. Let go. Live freely. Fear nothing. I am the resurrection and the life. Nothing—not even death—can quench the life that is in you."

Jesus, fill me with the awareness of unquenchable life.
Help me know the power of the resurrection that is mine
by Your Presence within me. Let me live fearlessly.

April 30

*I am the way, the truth, and the life. No one can
come to the Father except through me.*

JOHN 14:6

"I *am* the way, the truth, and the life. Many assume that means only that I
show you the way, teach you the truth, and give you life, but that's far too impersonal for Me. I am not just a path or a teaching or a key. I'm a Person. You
can't get what you need apart from firsthand encounters with Me. You have
to get close to Me and let Me get close to you. In fact, you have to invite Me
to enter the most private areas of your soul and live there. There is no other
access to the way, the truth, and the life.

"I am *your* way and *your* truth and *your* life. Yes, I am available to the
entire world—whoever is drawn to Me and responds—but I'm also individual to you. I know you inside and out. The religions of the world set you
on a course toward whatever promise they offer, but they don't take you by
the hand and lead you. They offer formulas but don't incarnate their truth
within you. They give you tools to learn, tell you to be disciplined, and
promise you rewards for diligence. That's not a light burden or an easy yoke.
It's not My way.

"It grieves Me when My people follow the techniques of the world to
become 'holy' or to find fulfillment. They forget that I'm a Person and that
I'm individually available to each of them. Don't let it be that way with you.
Always be on guard against lapsing from living in Me into following religious
practices. If you feel that you haven't done enough or reached high enough
to experience My fullest blessings, you've forgotten My truth. Stop striving
and *know* Me. I'm not just *what* you need, I'm *who* you need."

*Jesus, You are my life—and the only way to God. Fill
me with Yourself and take me where You want to go.*

May 1

I am the true grapevine, and my Father is the gardener. . . . You are the branches.

JOHN 15:1, 5

"I am the true vine. Isaiah once told a parable about Israel being a vineyard and My Father being disappointed in the fruit, but I want you to know that I am the true Israel. I came to represent everyone My Father has ever called to be His own. Everything He wanted His people to be, I am. You never have to worry about fruitlessness if you let Me live in you.

"That's what branches do: they sit on the vine. Did you really think you had to strain and strive to eke out some semblance of fruit? What would your efforts accomplish that My Father needs? Yes, He appreciates the heart behind your effort, but He appreciates even more your awareness that without Me, you can do nothing. When you rest in Me and let Me live in you, fruitfulness will happen. I will spill out of you and affect those around you. I call you to *be* before I ever urge you to *do*. Whatever it takes, you must learn to be in Me and let Me be in you.

"I don't want you to ask me how to do that. Any words I can say about 'how' will cause you to shift into self-effort to make it happen. What I'm telling you instead is simple but difficult. Though it isn't complicated, it goes against the human nature you have been steeped in since birth. I want you to meditate on Me by faith to envision My life flowing through your legs and out of your feet, through your arms and out of your hands, through your heart, into your head, and out of your mouth. Hold that image in your mind. Then go live. That's it. Trust Me and see. I am the life that flows through you."

Jesus, tune me to Your flow. Fill my mind and heart with a picture of Your life within me. And please bear much fruit for Your glory.

May 2

Suddenly, there was a sound from heaven like the roaring of a mighty windstorm, and it filled the house where they were sitting.

ACTS 2:2

How many millennia had God waited for this moment? How intently were the angels focused on this event? The Spirit who had moved and hovered over the waters at the dawn of creation, whose breath had sparked the first life in creatures of dust, and who had worked and moved among God's people throughout their history, was now coming to inhabit them. This was more than a fireworks display on Sinai or a glory cloud in the Temple. This was a redefinition of the Temple itself and a re-creation of those made in God's own image. It was the implementation of a new kind of Being.

This Spirit was the fulfillment of a promise Jesus gave before He ascended. His followers were to wait in Jerusalem for power. He had sent them on a mission, but they were not to begin it until the gift had come. He had earlier warned them that they could do nothing apart from Him. He had promised He would come to them, that His Spirit would fill them with His Presence. Now the moment had come.

This wasn't the first manifestation of God's Spirit in Scripture, and it certainly wouldn't be the last. But it was a defining one, marking the beginning of a new age. And simply by its inclusion in Scripture, it's an invitation to all who follow Jesus to be empowered in perceptible, life-altering ways. Many people were changed that day; you can be too. And it isn't a onetime event. The Spirit comes again and again. Ask Him to fill you more powerfully, more perceptibly than you've ever been filled before. He has waited long for such moments.

Spirit, fill me and empower me in such concrete ways that I know I'll never be the same again. Have Your way in me.

"In the last days," God says, "I will pour out my Spirit upon all people. Your sons and daughters will prophesy. Your young men will see visions, and your old men will dream dreams. In those days I will pour out my Spirit even on my servants—men and women alike—and they will prophesy."

ACTS 2:17-18

Peter stood up to preach, and one of the first things he said was a quote from Joel. The prophet had foretold a time when God's Spirit would be poured out. Clearly this event fit that description, but the prophetic language described an even greater scale. All people qualified—men, women, sons, daughters, Jews, Gentiles. And the prophecy described an even greater scope. In spite of only a few manifestations of the Spirit's Presence that day, God's people would be able to prophesy, see visions, and dream dreams. In other words, Peter interpreted a landmark event at one place and with limited manifestations as the beginning of the fulfillment of a prophecy with much greater ramifications. Pentecost wasn't seen as the exception; it was seen as the foreshadowing of more to come.

That isn't how many of us view this event—or other events in Scripture. We tend to see the astounding, miraculous incidents in the Bible as exceptions rather than examples. Or if we do see them as examples, they are grand examples that we can emulate only in lesser ways. But Jesus made it clear that His people would go on to do greater things than He did, and He promised to empower us not with a lesser spirit but with Himself. The Spirit who descended on the day of Pentecost is the exact same Spirit who comes to us today. And the prophecy of Joel is as true for us now as it was in Jerusalem then.

Spirit, fill me with prophecies, visions, and dreams. Whatever You offer, I want it—in abundance.

May 4

Each of you must repent of your sins and turn to
God, and be baptized in the name of Jesus Christ
for the forgiveness of your sins. Then you will
receive the gift of the Holy Spirit.

ACTS 2:38

The words have been spoken so often that they are almost institutionalized. No freshness, no relevance, no sense of insight. Just a script we've memorized already. But think of what you would have heard if you had been in the first audience: a promise that if you align your life with God, you'll be inhabited by an explosive power from above—a power being manifested right before your eyes. True, some people mistook the power for some other kind of influence, but clearly something remarkable was happening. And it could all be yours for . . . what, exactly?

That's the problem with words like "repent" or "turn from your sins" or "turn to God." The same could be said of "be baptized." They are religious-sounding words and phrases that hardly carry any impact anymore. What was required of this audience in order for them to become inhabited by the Spirit of the only true God? Simply this: they would have to acknowledge that they weren't like Him, express a desire to become like Him, let go of anything in the way, and identify with Him. It's as if God were saying, "I want to connect with hearts like Mine and change the world. If you can handle having a heart like Mine, come with Me." And three thousand people accepted the invitation.

Why don't we have more of God's power today? Perhaps it's because we haven't aligned our hearts with His in every area. We're stuck in old ways of thinking and old patterns of living. All it takes is an actual shift—not just the desire, but a real turn toward Him—and the gift of the Spirit is ours in increasing measure.

Spirit, is there any obstacle between us?
Any change of heart or mind I need to make?
Show me—and let me see more of You.

May 5

A deep sense of awe came over them all, and the apostles performed many miraculous signs and wonders.

ACTS 2:43

The Presence of God has consequences. In this case, there were many: a deep sense of awe, miracles, sacrificial generosity, worship and praise, unity, joy, favor, and growth. When divine power is obvious—when the weight of glory fills a room, a building, or a city—the attributes of that power begin to manifest themselves. Hearts fall in line with the character of the God they experience.

That's one reason it's so important to experience God rather than just know about Him or intellectually understand His truth. We can read His Word and try to develop habits from what we've learned, but that's an arduous process filled with fits and starts and many failures, and it works from the outside inward—eventually. But an encounter with God—or even just an increased awareness of His Presence—tends to impart His qualities to us. We begin to become like Him.

This happens when we're around people we admire too. We subconsciously begin to develop their attitudes, emulate their gestures and expressions, and see from their perspectives. We grow into the models of thought and behavior set before us. At a much more intense level, we grow into the character of God when we spend time with Him—not by effort but by impartation. We become what we behold.

Be intentional about what you behold—or rather *whom* you behold. Seek such a profound awareness of God's Presence that it provokes awe in you. Learn how to look at His works with wonder. Believe what Scripture says about Him, and notice the ways He graces your life. You will begin to incorporate His attributes into your own personality. And marvelous things may begin to happen.

Spirit, I want to experience the real You—not a false image or perception, but the reality of Your Presence. May Your character and Your ways "rub off" on me so that my heart can become like Yours.

Then God looked over all he had made, and
he saw that it was very good!

GENESIS 1:31

We look for God in the unusual and the miraculous, so we seek the supernatural as a point of contact with His Presence. If it's beyond explanation, then we can know we've encountered Him. We crave clear-cut evidence of the divine.

God certainly does supernatural things, and He loves inspiring awe and wonder with His works. But if our encounters with Him are dependent entirely on miraculous signs, we'll have a hit-and-miss relationship with Him that never quite satisfies. That's because His wonders aren't everyday occurrences; otherwise, they would become "normal" and cease to be wonders. They are encouraging when they happen, but they aren't the substance of a true relationship. We have to know Him more constantly than that.

Look for God in the "ordinary," realizing, of course, that nothing is really ordinary. All of His works are good, miracles of a voice that spoke creation into existence. If you can notice God's power and artistry in a sunrise, a smile, a blade of grass, a spider's web, or a conversation with a friend, you can encounter Him at any given moment of any given day. Any experience, no matter how unnoticed by others, can turn into a prayer of thanks, a hopeful impulse, a treasured moment, an awareness of the transcendent God. He stands by His creation and all its intricacies and relationships, observing with pleasure all that is good. When you do the same, your heart is in sync with His. And when you sense His heartbeat and His Presence, nothing is ordinary anymore.

Lord, I take so much for granted. Every moment
is a gift, and every observation can turn into
appreciation for the Giver. Help me appreciate You
in everything I see and experience today.

We fix our eyes not on what is seen, but on what is unseen, since what is seen is temporary, but what is unseen is eternal.

2 CORINTHIANS 4:18, NIV

"Fix your eyes on the unseen." That's like telling someone to listen to the silence or taste the air. It sounds like a joke. And it begs an obvious question: how? What eyes do we use to observe the unseen? How do we gaze at what isn't even visible? If anyone expected an experience of God's Presence to be simple, verses like this prove that it isn't. We have to tap into another realm.

Paul isn't teasing, of course. We *can* fix our eyes on the unseen. We don't use the eyes of the flesh, obviously; they're only good at perceiving visible light reflecting off of concrete objects. But we do have eyes of the heart, the very ones that Paul prayed would be enlightened to perceive God's wisdom and revelation (Ephesians 1:18). Those eyes can gaze into the eternal realm of spirits, where God and His angels are more real than the world our five senses perceive. When we view life through the eyes of the heart, we are able to recognize God and understand the limits of temporary experiences. We are not overcome by temptation, we endure hardship, we value souls over material things, we seek purpose over passing pleasures, and we draw close to God Himself. We can do all of that because we're focused on a higher reality than most people see.

The Presence is a palpable reality for those who have cultivated their eyes to see the unseen, and it's frustratingly elusive for those who haven't. Improve your vision by choosing God's truth over human wisdom, by refusing to bow to immediate impulses and demands, by noticing the flow of God's voice, and by asking Him to help. He loves to give sight to the blind.

Lord, give me eyes to see eternal realities. Change my focus. Divorce me from the tyranny of the tangible—what my physical senses perceive—and give me Kingdom eyes.

May 8

*Oh, magnify the LORD with me, and let us
exalt His name together.*

PSALM 34:3, NKJV

Some translators don't like to use the word *magnify* in verses like this, perhaps for concern of implying that the infinite God has the potential to become larger. And while we can certainly agree that God is already infinitely large, we know He isn't as big as He needs to be in our own hearts and minds. Our perspective is distorted. We need to magnify Him in our own vision.

In fact, we need to do that a lot. That's because we have a tendency to magnify our issues to be greater than God. And even if we don't underestimate His power, we easily underestimate His willingness to show it. We know He *can* overcome any obstacle we face or any problem we have, of course, but we don't expect that He *will*. We believe in His Presence without practically knowing it. And it's usually because we don't magnify Him and "exalt His name."

Fill your thoughts with God's greatness, and your experience of His greatness will increase. Focus on the depths of His love, and your experience of His love will grow deeper. When you face a crisis, be excited about the opportunity to magnify Him in the midst of the lesser issue, knowing that He already has a solution for whatever it is. Praise Him for His zeal to fight your battles and come to your defense. Your victories often depend on your acknowledgment of the Victor; your strength on your praise of the mighty Warrior; your healing on your trust in the Healer. Magnify Him in every way—thoughts, words, and deeds—and the infinite God will become larger to you.

*Lord, You are the great and mighty God, exalted
above every person, every passion, every problem. Fill
my heart with Your praise—and with You. Let me
experience the wonder of who You are.*

I prayed to the LORD, and he answered me.
He freed me from all my fears.

PSALM 34:4

This is the kind of prayer life we want. A request, an answer, and a heart at rest. No shot-in-the-dark prayer, no long wait, no more stress about whether God will or won't. That's the kind of interaction that lets us know He's with us and listening to our hearts. And that's the kind of relationship we long for.

Verses like this are implicit promises that we can have such a relationship, but they are condensed versions that may mislead us if we aren't careful. What David hasn't explained in this psalm is that he is still on the run from a king who wants to kill him, that he has had to hide out among Israel's enemies and feign insanity in order to stay alive, and that he has felt afraid, desperate, victimized, confused, and stressed at various times in the process. The psalm is a CliffsNotes version of a victory—the kind of summary that gets told on a day of celebration—but other psalms give us glimpses into the whole story: God's Presence and triumph in David's life have come at an often painful cost.

Be encouraged by psalms like this one when you're in a battle or struggling through a season of pain. They point to the same kind of celebration you'll have. You too will be able to say, "I prayed to the LORD, and he answered me. He freed me from all my fears." Just understand that for David, the process took longer than the succinct words imply, and it was considerably more complicated, too. The path to victory is often steep and twisting, but that's how God draws us close on the way. Even so, trust in Him for the outcome. He really does answer.

Lord, I really do want the kind of relationship
in which I make a request, You answer, and I
experience freedom and rest. Help me hang on to
that promise throughout the process of getting there.

May 10

Those who look to him for help will be
radiant with joy; no shadow of shame
will darken their faces.

PSALM 34:5

Underlying many of our prayers are two dueling attitudes: hope and a fear of disappointment. On some days, hope seems to reign; on others, fear of disappointment gets the upper hand. When we bathe in God's Presence, fill our minds with His promises, and take Him at His word, hope rises up within us. When we look around at circumstances, measure improbabilities, and expect the usual or "normal" course of events, fear of disappointment quenches the hope we thought we had. Eventually, one of these attitudes has to dominate the other.

God wants our hope to be pure. Hope fuels faith, and faith is almost always a necessary condition for answered prayer. Fear that somehow God will let us down, that His promises don't really mean what we thought they meant, corrupts our faith. Even if it doesn't quench faith completely, the mixture is toxic. It's what James called being "double-minded" (James 1:8, NIV), or literally, "double-souled," and it results in receiving nothing from the Lord (James 1:7). But if we look to Him for help—if our gaze is filled with hope and faith—we will be "radiant with joy." We will not be disappointed. Having gone out on a limb in faith, we will not end up ashamed.

Don't be afraid of going out on a limb in faith. Look to God for help. Even if you stumble and fall, He will honor the heart behind your faith and bring you to a place of joy. His Presence will radiate from your life because you chose to trust Him. He comes to those who let hope defeat fear and who invest their hopes in Him.

Lord, I easily look to human sources and earthly
wisdom for help—and easily end up disappointed.
Help me turn my gaze to You, to find my hope
only in You, and I will never be ashamed.

In my desperation I prayed, and the Lord
listened; he saved me from all my troubles.

PSALM 34:6

Many people think of fear as the opposite of faith. Perhaps that's true, but in many ways, it's simply another form of faith. It's faith in a negative possibility—in the power of Satan or the ways of the world. It's a statement that God might not protect or provide, that perhaps He isn't guiding our steps or looking out for the best interests of all involved. Fear isn't the absence of belief; it's the absence of a belief in something God has said or an attribute that He has. But it's a belief in its own right, or even a bundle of contrary beliefs that confuse and paralyze us. Fear reflects a real perspective.

David's remedy for fear, found in this psalm, is simple. He cried to the Lord in his suffering, and God heard him. That's it. There's no secret formula here, no probing into deep-rooted psychological issues, no victim mentality. Just a plea and the knowledge that God heard. Clearly God answered—the psalm is a celebration of victory—and the situation changed. This, apparently, was enough to set David free from his fears.

Don't let fear paralyze you. Let it serve as a symptom that faith is not yet fully developed in a certain area of your life. Recognize it as a sign that you are listening to a lie at some level in your heart. Expose the lie, replace it with truth, and believe. And God will set you free from all your fears.

Lord, I know You hear my pleas. You say so again and
again. Help me recognize the lies I'm hearing, give me
the resolve to stop agreeing with them, and fill my heart
with Your truth about Your will for me.

May 12

*Taste and see that the LORD is good. Oh, the joys
of those who take refuge in him!*

PSALM 34:8

A restaurant owner at the food court in the local mall is aggressive in his tactics. He offers a sample not only to those who walk by his counter; he waves and shouts loudly at those passing by on the other side of the dining area. He takes eye contact, even from a hundred feet away, as a commitment to try his food. He wants everyone to taste it because he believes it's the best around.

David urges his readers to taste and see that the Lord is good. In other words, "try Him out." That may seem a little too transactional for our spiritual sensibilities, but it's nonetheless biblical. God Himself, through the prophet Malachi, issued a similar invitation centuries later: "Test me in this," He said about tithing, "and see if I will not throw open the floodgates of heaven and pour out so much blessing that there will not be room enough to store it" (Malachi 3:10, NIV). He wants His promises to be tried and tested. He wants His Presence to be tasted. He wants to be sampled because He knows He's the best around.

There are times in our relationship with Him when we wonder if He's ever going to come through for us, when our current circumstances contradict our hopes for the future, when the tension between our desires and our experience is almost too much to bear. In those times, we can hear Him say, "Do you trust Me?" And if we can take a deep breath, let go of our intensity, and say yes, we will find Him to be trustworthy. That's the promise. If we can take a heartfelt step and cast ourselves completely on Him, we will find joy. Those who taste will experience the best there is.

*Lord, I cast myself on You—completely. I let go of my
anxieties and agendas and say yes to trusting You.
Let me taste and see the depth of Your goodness.*

*Even strong young lions sometimes go
hungry, but those who trust in the LORD
will lack no good thing.*

PSALM 34:10

Our God is a God of abundance. He experiences no shortages. There are instances in Scripture when He lacked something for a time, like in Isaiah when He looked for someone to intercede and saw no one, or when Jesus did only a few miracles in Nazareth because He found little faith among the people. But even when human responses are lacking, He still finds a way to accomplish His purposes. He can multiply bread to feed thousands, turn water into wine when normal supplies run out, and raise up laborers to go into the harvest. His only limits are the boundaries of His own character. Within His nature, all things are possible.

Why, then, do His people experience lack? If He is the God of abundance, why do we sometimes have trouble paying the bills? One reason may be that we can know Him as Provider only if we have needs that require His provision. We have to experience lack and depend on Him in order to see Him come through for us. Even so, there are delays in His provision that we sometimes don't understand and limits on what we can do because our supplies are short. Most of us don't have unlimited income; our resources are a factor in determining our options. We see lack every day.

But that's from our perspective, where we measure lack in terms of all our biggest desires. Whatever dream isn't being fulfilled at the moment causes us to feel like we're lacking in that moment. But God is always satisfying our needs and more. At any given moment, He is either providing or planning a provision. He may allow uncomfortable seasons, but He envisions no crisis of need in the lives of those who trust Him. We are promised His provision always.

*Father, I'm trusting You for all I need, and I
know You often provide much more. Please let me
experience Your abundance in every area of my life.*

*The LORD is close to the brokenhearted; he
rescues those whose spirits are crushed.*

PSALM 34:18

Sometimes when we look at God through the lens of our circumstances, He doesn't look very good. That's because our circumstances lie to us. They portray a careless God or an indifferent God or even a brutally painful God. If He is sovereign, we tell ourselves, He could have prevented the crisis or chaos we're going through. And yet He hasn't. Therefore . . . and we fill out the rest of the sentence with an indictment against His good intentions.

Never in Scripture does God define Himself by the hardships of His people. In fact, the hardships often set up a demonstration of His goodness. It takes a sickness to reveal a Healer, a captivity to reveal a Deliverer, or a war to reveal a Warrior. Our need creates an occasion for Him to show who He is. So when we are hurting, it isn't a sign of His disfavor. It may actually be a sign of His desire to meet us at a point of need.

Whatever is going on in your heart or in your life right now, it isn't a sign of God's displeasure or unconcern. It isn't hidden from Him, and it doesn't drive Him away. In fact, He is drawn to you in your times of need. Brokenheartedness and desperation are magnets for His attention. The key is lifting heartbreak and desperation up to Him as an offering, a gift of opportunity for Him to use. His love and compassion cannot refuse a heart that needs Him and knows it.

Tell God that you need His comfort. Acknowledge your discouragement and despair. Invite Him into your painful places. Know that He wants to meet you there.

*Your Word calls You the "God of all comfort," and
that's who I need. Lord, I'm broken. Please, in Your
mercy, fill my brokenness with Your wholeness.*

May 15

The righteous person faces many troubles, but the LORD comes to the rescue each time.

PSALM 34:19

Some Christians emphasize the first half of this verse: "the righteous person faces many troubles." And there are plenty of Scripture passages to back it up. In this world, we will have trials and experience pain. We live in a broken world, and suffering is a part of it. God doesn't keep His people from difficulties. In fact, our faith often subjects us to more intense battles and temptations. Trials are a part of our lives.

Other Christians emphasize the second half of this verse: "the LORD comes to the rescue each time." And there are plenty of Scripture passages to back this up too. God is our rescuer, our refuge, and our strength. He promises great successes and enables us to overcome great obstacles. Story after story in the Bible tells us of His power on our behalf. Victory is a part of our lives.

The problem is that those who emphasize the trials and troubles often live in defeat and never can really believe God for victory. And those who emphasize the victories often live in a state of denial about real human struggles and insist that faith always achieves predictable results. Neither emphasis is biblical, but a balance between them certainly is. The verse as a whole is the right perspective: we do face many trials, and God does deliver us from all of them in one way or another.

Whatever issue you face today—and we all face something at any given time—avoid a false emphasis. Don't ask "why me?" as though something is wrong when God allows you to go through a difficulty; but don't dwell in the difficulty as though God has no practical solution for it. He does—and He promises to rescue us every time.

Lord, I need Your rescue. You know I've been honest about my struggles, but You're honest about Your promises. In the process I'm going through, I trust Your deliverance.

Have faith in God.

MARK 11:22

Faith is a necessary way of life in the Kingdom of God. We have to have it in order to function the way God wants us to. And we always feel like we need more. But does that mean we try to muster it up by convincing ourselves of what we want to believe?

We can certainly do things to persuade our hearts of truth: dwell on God's promises, remember His past works, cultivate hope, and so on. But ultimately, faith is a gift of God (Ephesians 2:8). We get it from the work of His Spirit within us. When we cultivate His Presence, we develop faith. It comes from Him.

Greek scholars from a variety of theological perspectives suggest that this verse is better translated "have the faith *of* God." There are plenty of places in Scripture that speak of believing in God—clearly He's the object of our faith. But it only makes sense that if the Spirit of Jesus dwells within us, and Jesus lived with the kind of faith we're supposed to have, then He imparts faith to us. The more His Presence is allowed to move us, the more faith we'll have.

That's the way it is with all fruits of the Spirit and godly attributes. We don't muster them up. He has them, and He dwells in us. We get them by focusing on Him, communing with Him, and yielding to Him. The more we let Him have His way in us, the more we have the character and attributes we need to have. In your quest for greater, deeper, purer faith, ask for God's. He will give you the spiritual tenacity to hold on to His promises regardless of what you see. That's the kind of faith that can move mountains.

Lord, I need faith. Mine is weak and wavering, but I do believe. Help my unbelief. Please give me the faith that comes from Your Spirit.

*I will bless the LORD who guides me; even at
night my heart instructs me.*

PSALM 16:7

God's Presence doesn't leave us when we sleep. He doesn't guide us only when we're consciously focusing on Him and intellectually processing His Word. According to Proverbs 16:9, He determines our steps in spite of all our plans; and in Psalm 16:7, He moves in our hearts even while we sleep. When His Spirit is allowed to dwell freely within us, we are always being shaped.

That ought to put us at ease about getting direction for our lives. Yes, our path looks very uncertain from our perspective as we try to discern God's will and sort out the open and closed doors He has put in front of us. But He isn't worried at all about whether we "get it right." He has ways of moving us into the right spot at the right time. And He has ways of turning our hearts even during the night.

We need to seek God's will and zealously desire to walk in it. But we don't have to feel pressure to perfectly know which steps He wants us to take. If we're doing our best to follow Him and make a misstep, He'll get us back on the right path. Unless we're walking in rebellion, our Guide doesn't lead us on a pass-fail basis. He knows how to get us from point A to point B.

Trust God's Presence within you to guide you. Pay attention to the things He is doing in your heart. Ask Him every night before you go to sleep to fill you with His will—to "program" your mind with divine downloads that set your course from within. Then be sensitive to the ways He leads. You can let your heart instruct you because He instructs your heart.

*Father, I bless You as the Lord who guides me. Instruct
my heart at night, then teach me to hear the instructions
You have given. Help me always step into Your will.*

May 18

My God, my God, why have you abandoned me?
Why are you so far away when I groan for help?

PSALM 22:1

Anyone who has walked with God for a significant length of time has had such moments of despair. Joseph must have had one when his God-given dreams caused his brothers to send him far away into captivity. David must have had one when he was driven into exile by murderous King Saul. And Jesus certainly had one when He quoted this psalm on the cross. Those who are most acquainted with God's Presence are most sensitive to His absence.

God allows these crisis moments—times when we're completely disoriented about what He's doing and where He is. We can walk closely with Him for years, certain of His direction and Presence, and then suddenly experience a seemingly catastrophic turn of events and a sense that He's nowhere around. Like Isaac on the altar looking up at Abraham's knife and wondering what happened to love, we can look at our Father's actions toward us and feel like His victims. How we respond in these moments is crucial. Do we accuse Him of mishandling our affairs, of withholding something good, or perhaps even of betraying our trust? Or do we insist on trust even when we don't understand? We know the correct answer, but in a forsaken moment that answer isn't easy.

When you cry out to God because it seems that He has forsaken you, know that the contradiction to His Presence isn't unusual. In fact, if you have a heart for Him, you will feel His absence acutely at times. It's inevitable. It's one of the ways He prepares you for the next level in a high calling. Respond in trust, and His Presence and His purposes will soon become clear again.

Lord, I have felt forsaken at times. I don't always know what You're doing, and there are times when that hurts. Please help me move through those seasons with trust, and please restore the closeness we've had.

God looks down from heaven on all mankind to see if there are any who understand, any who seek God.

PSALM 53:2, NIV

A good parent notices the hungers of a child's heart and tries to cultivate the right ones. Is the child hungry only for more possessions, status, and achievements? Or is he or she also hungry for good relationships, wisdom, and love? Good parents want to see desires for truth, fairness, and understanding mixed in with the normal, less noble desires of childhood. When a kid's priorities are right, parenting is a lot easier and a parent is freed up to focus on benefits rather than discipline.

God looks into our souls to see if we long for understanding and seek Him. He notices the hungers of our hearts and helps us cultivate the right ones. If we're preoccupied with things that will eventually clutter our hearts or misdirect our steps, He will either frustrate those desires to protect us or satisfy them enough for us to realize how futile they are. Either way, His purpose is to turn us toward all that truly satisfies.

Your hunger is important to God. He understands all the directions your desires take, but when your hunger for His Presence exceeds all others, He satisfies it and is much more willing to satisfy the others, too. The context of Psalm 53 is God's disappointment that no one seeks Him or understands who He is—or even *that* He is. But this lament also reveals the positive attitudes He's looking for. When your longings are first and foremost for Him, He is pleased. And He rewards those longings by fulfilling them.

Lord, all my longings are in You. I know You are the root of every desire I have. I turn my heart toward You and pray for Your fulfillment. May You be pleased with my search for You and fully reward it.

I live in the high and holy place with those
whose spirits are contrite and humble.

ISAIAH 57:15

"I come down. Your religious instincts will always tell you that you have to come up to Me, but you can't unless I enable you by first coming down. Haven't you seen My ways throughout history? I sent Moses to 'go down' into Egypt in order to rescue My people. I sent My prophets into battles and captivities in order to bring My people out. I clothed Myself in flesh, coming down to bring salvation to all who believe. My Son went down into the grave in order to raise people up into life. I sent My apostles—and many servants since—into the depths of the world to bring people up into My Kingdom. The world's expectations are for a high and holy deity to insist that you reach higher. My way is to come down and lift you up to where I am.

"I am high and exalted, but that never keeps Me from entering into your condition. In your difficulties today, I come to empower you and guide you. In your limitations, I come down to defy them. Whatever depths you find yourself in tomorrow, I will be there to lift you up. I am the exalted One who exalts those who trust in Me.

"If you want to come up with Me, stop striving to go up yourself. Defy your instincts that drive you to 'achieve' spiritually. Those who strive for exaltation will never find it. I lift up the humble and contrite, the ones who rest in Me. Depend on My ability. Let My Spirit meet you where you are and bring you where I want you to be. Stop striving and know that I am God— and that the high and holy place is for *everyone* who is with Me."

Father, I want to live in the "high and holy place"
too. I want to rise above my circumstances and
live in Your power. Lift me up as I lay down my
efforts and humbly rest in You.

*I restore the crushed spirit of the humble and
revive the courage of those with repentant hearts.*

ISAIAH 57:15

"I know when it's hard for you to face the day. I've seen you wake up in the morning with a heavy heart. I've sensed the dread within you when you feel defeated by obstacles before you've even encountered them. When you have those days, you need to know: I want to refresh you, give you strength, and fill you with courage.

"Your issues are too big for you. They are never too big for the Spirit I've put within you. You feel intimidated by them for two reasons. First, you rightly understand your own limitations, and second, you make false assumptions about My readiness to come to your aid in the midst of them. When you walk boldly forward, depending on Me rather than on yourself, I am with you.

"The very thing that makes you humble—an awareness of your own weakness and flaws—is the very thing that qualifies you to overcome. Your humility draws Me into you and increases My desire to fill you with faith and courage. Your repentance brings Me close. But you often have more faith in your potential failures than in My potential successes. You envision how your life will turn out if I'm absent or don't come through. But I have promised My Presence—in *everything*. And in My Presence, you can have courage and strength to face any challenge in life without fear. Go into this day in the boldness of My Spirit, and nothing will overcome you."

*Lord, I need grace and strength to face this day—and
all days. May I always place my complete confidence
in You. Help me be as low as I need to be in order to
be lifted up in boldness and courage. Let me live as
one who is constantly refreshed by You.*

I will not fight against you forever.

ISAIAH 57:16

"Yes, I fight against you—sometimes. Are you surprised? It isn't because I'm opposed to you. I fight against you because I am on your side. If you want Me to support you in love, you also have to accept My truth. And My truth is sometimes opposed to your current direction, your current attitude, or your current perceptions. When that's the case, I have to oppose you in order to bring you in line with Me.

"This may seem like a contradiction, but there's no contradiction in My love for you and My desire to align you with My plans or to shape your heart in ways that might be uncomfortable. I want you to understand that in asking for My Presence, you are asking to conform. My Presence meets you where you are, but it doesn't adapt to you; you adapt to the Presence. If you want more experiences with Me, expect to make adjustments. I want us to work together in perfect harmony. I'm teaching you to harmonize with Me.

"If you saw the big picture, you would agree with what I'm doing and actually choose it for yourself. You would plead with Me to fight against you because you would know that My redirection will result in far greater blessings for you in the end. So I'm not really opposing you; I'm opposing something in your life that is less than best for you. And only temporarily. My purpose is to bless you beyond your wildest imagination—greater than you can ask or think.

"When you feel resistance, don't worry that I've abandoned you or am working against you. I'm not working against *you*; I'm working against an obstacle to My purposes for you. Rest in Me, trust Me, and follow My lead. I'll take you to places you truly want to go."

Lord, sometimes it seems You aren't on my side. But I want to be in perfect sync with You. Draw me into Your purposes completely.

Keep the Sabbath day holy. Don't pursue your own interests on that day, but enjoy the Sabbath and speak of it with delight as the LORD's holy day.

ISAIAH 58:13

"You can experience My Presence at any moment of any day. But you won't unless you quiet your physical senses and turn your spiritual senses toward Me. I love for you to do that at various times throughout each day. But I created a world that often keeps you occupied in earning a living, and most days are filled with activities that require your focus. And though you can learn to keep Me in mind as you focus on other things, I've designed you to need times of rest and refreshing in My Presence—times when you let Me fill your thoughts and feelings more than usual. I've set aside one day a week for you to joyfully experience Me.

"You need that day. I would never have commanded it if you didn't. It isn't a helpful suggestion; it's a vital necessity. And many of My people neglect it.

"Why do so many people lament that they can't experience My Presence when they don't even set aside a day to do so? My people fret about not hearing My voice, not sensing My Spirit, not having clear direction, not feeling refreshed, and not understanding My Word. Yet most who miss out on such blessings are ignoring one of the primary means to get them. That's like never seeking a job and then complaining about having no money. Do you really want to know Me? Then set aside a day to know Me. It isn't complicated.

"I take no pleasure in strict demands; that's not what My Sabbath is. I take pleasure in relationships, and you can't deepen the relationship without spending time with Me. I want to bless you with rest and My Presence. Please let Me."

Lord, so many things fill up my days of rest. It seems like I don't have time. Please multiply my efforts on other days, and help Me protect the day of rest and Presence.

Honor the Sabbath in everything you do on that day, and don't follow your own desires or talk idly. Then the LORD will be your delight.

ISAIAH 58:13-14

"I spoke these words long ago to a people living in rebellion. They set aside no time to honor me. Even though I am a God of justice, they treated people unjustly. Even though I am truth, they were careless with their lies. Even though I am welcoming, they showed no regard for strangers. They went to the Temple, prayed, and fasted—their religious impulses were active—but they didn't know My heart. They tried to serve Me and serve themselves at the same time.

"That never works—not then, not today. I told them I prefer a different kind of 'fast'—not a forsaking of food but a forsaking of selfishness and apathy toward others. If they would treat people fairly, seek justice, and share with those in need, I would come to them like the dawn and bring healing to them and their nation. And nothing has changed. I still love defending the defenseless, welcoming strangers, and sharing with those in need. My people see these as options; I see them as My attributes. And My attributes are anything but optional.

"I'll give you the same promise I gave My people long ago: if you align yourself with My heart, you will find that you really treasure and enjoy your experiences with Me. Honor Me in all you do, desire what I desire, and you will find yourself powerfully supported by infinite glory. Your experience of Me depends on Your aligning with Me. When a human soul willfully contradicts Me, I withhold My Presence. I don't fellowship with sin. But know My character and live accordingly, and I will inhabit your life."

Lord, I know it's foolish to seek Your Presence without seeking Your honor, integrity, and compassion, but it's easy to miss the mark. Help me have Your character. Fill my life with every aspect of Yourself.

*I will give you great honor and satisfy you with
the inheritance I promised to your ancestor
Jacob. I, the LORD, have spoken!*

ISAIAH 58:14

"No one knows the riches I bestow on those who love Me. You experience some of them in some measure, but no eye on earth has yet seen the height and depth and width of My favor. But you can see more than you have. Your vision can grow. The promises I gave long ago still apply. The blessings I spoke to Israel belong to all who have been grafted into My people. The more you honor Me, the more I show you My honor. And I have placed no upper limits on My blessings.

"Few accept My invitations because few understand how extravagant they are. I gave Israel a promised land as their inheritance, but that was only the beginning. I gave My Son an eternal, incorruptible inheritance, and all who are in Him can share in that inheritance. Everything has been created for Him. And He shares everything with those who love Him.

"Just as I promised honor to My people in the presence of nations around them, so do I offer honor to you in the society in which you live. Honor Me, and My favor will lift you up and raise you to places of influence. Love Me, and you will taste the fruits of My 'promised land.' Delight in Me, and I will give you the desires of your heart. As you give to Me, I will give back to you in greater measure. This is how My inheritance works. And you have all of eternity to fully explore it."

*Lord, Your promises are great, but they seem to exceed
my experience. How can I experience more? Turn my
heart to honor You and delight in You. Show me how to
access Your extravagant blessings more fully.*

*"This is my covenant with them," says the L*ORD*.
"My Spirit will not leave them, and neither will
these words I have given you."*

ISAIAH 59:21

"Most of what is visible in your life is temporary. Few things last forever. My words last forever, and those made and redeemed in My image have eternal life. But the ways of the world, its passing pleasures, its fleeting glories—these are not forever.

"I have given you 'forever' promises. My Spirit is with you forever, and My words will never fade away. You need to know this because I have foretold times of shaking (Hebrews 12:26-27). Even before the final shaking, when the entire earth will see My Kingdom, the earth around your feet will shake from time to time and reveal what's eternal in you. The things that can be shaken will fall away; the things that are eternal will continue to stand. The more you stand in Me—knowing My Spirit and being anchored in My Word—the better you weather these times. In a constantly shifting world, you need to stand firm in My words.

"Know the covenant I have made with you. My Spirit will never leave. This is a promise not only for those with good intentions and strong desires; it's a covenant for those who actually believe My words, turn to Me, and depend on Me. The connection between My Spirit and My words is not coincidental. In order to experience Me, you need to grab hold of My promises in faith. My Presence is always a reality, but in your experience it often seems more like a theory. To experience Me, let the truth of My Presence sink down into the depths of your beliefs—an unshakable confidence in the core of your heart that I am with you. The more you believe My words, the more you experience My Spirit."

*Lord, let Your words sink deep into my heart and
never be affected by the shaking around me.*

No longer will you need the sun to shine by day,
nor the moon to give its light by night, for the
LORD your God will be your everlasting light,
and your God will be your glory.

ISAIAH 60:19

"I want you to notice a trend. Everything I offer you in My Word eventually is fulfilled in Me. Long ago, I gave your forefathers bread. Centuries later, My Son became the Bread of Life. I gave your ancestors water, and He became the living water. I spoke truth in My Word, but He *is* the truth. In creation and in the Word, I gave you light, but in the end I become your light. Whatever your soul has longed for has been given in a transient form and will be fulfilled in a personal, eternal form. All you long for is ultimately in this relationship.

"Does that disappoint you? It's easier to receive gifts than the Giver; I realize that. You don't have to maintain your relationship with the gifts. You can enjoy them in your own way and your own time. But the joy and newness of gifts wear off, and they don't fulfill you forever. I do. I may require a deeper investment from your heart, but My benefits are far greater than anything you receive. I have the power to fill you with life, peace, and joy. I don't just *give* you these things; I *am* these things. I am the adventure you seek, the treasures you value, the excitement you crave. I am the light you live by and the glory you desire.

"Don't try to understand or analyze it. Just accept it. You'll see. You are living in days when this prophecy is more truly realized than when Isaiah uttered it. And it will be increasingly realized in days to come. Step into the glory of My Presence and experience Me."

Lord, this is a mystery. What does it mean for You to be
my glory? I'm not looking for an explanation—just a
demonstration. Show me Your glory in my life.

May 28

I want to know Christ—yes, to know the power of his resurrection and participation in his sufferings.

PHILIPPIANS 3:10, NIV

We tend to interpret adversity in terms of what God is teaching us—patience, submission, forgiveness, etc.—but could our trials serve a much greater purpose than training us in the right attitudes? I believe Jesus often speaks deep words to us:

"I'm allowing this pain to teach you some things, but not for the reasons you think. When you have to yield to difficult circumstances, show humility in the face of evil, feel the sting of rejection, suffer long delays, patiently endure insults and injustice and being misunderstood, or withstand obstacles and intense trials, I'm not just building your character. I'm giving you glimpses of Me. Every time you think of My story now, you will better understand what I went through. You will have tasted My adversity. I've longed for you to be able to put your arms around Me and say, 'Jesus, I know how it feels.' I'm sharing My heart with you. This is the fellowship of My suffering. I don't enjoy your pain, but I really enjoy your fellowship. And I want you to know My heart. But remember that the joy of My resurrection is more real than the pain of My rejection. And I am eager to share that with you too."

Our hardships are about much more than teaching us lessons in character. In nearly everything we go through, we can find some connecting point with Jesus' heart. We've been rejected? We can relate to His rejection. We're jealous for someone's love? We can bond with Him in His jealousy for ours. And on and on. If we let Him, He imparts His heart to us in everything we endure.

Jesus, I want to know Your heart, and the only way for that to happen is to experience some of what You went through. Please help me never squander those opportunities and learn to feel what You have felt.

*I will win her back once again. . . . I will be
faithful to you and make you mine.*

HOSEA 2:14, 20

God gave the prophet Hosea an unusual assignment. He was to marry someone who would be unfaithful to him again and again—but he was to remain faithful to her anyway. Why would God tell His prophet to do something so painful and strange? Because He wanted to paint a picture of His relationship with His people. Even though the Israelites had repeatedly been unfaithful to God, He still loved them. He wanted them back. He hated their sin, but He stood with open arms, waiting for them to return to His love—not because he was desperate but because it's His nature to love relentlessly.

One of the greatest hindrances to our sense of God's Presence in our lives is our awareness of our own sin. And though God hates sin, He loves us. So even when we disobey Him and grieve Him, He is single-minded in pursuing us. Why? Because He wants to be *with* us. He wants closeness. He may withdraw His Presence briefly sometimes, but it's only so we will see what we're missing and return to Him. His ultimate goal in creating human beings was for them to relate to Him. Why, after abolishing the record of our sins, would He withhold Himself? He wouldn't. He has always pursued relationship, and He always will.

Let nothing, not even your own flaws and mistakes, convince you that God prefers distance. When you most feel like hiding from Him, pursue Him even more zealously. Know that your instinct to withdraw is never a reflection of His attitude toward you. When your desire to be with Him outweighs your sense of guilt and shame, He is honored. And He welcomes you with open arms.

*Lord, even when I feel unworthy, I want You.
I choose You—to pursue You, to be with You—
knowing that my insecurity in our relationship is
unfounded. I accept the gift of Your open arms.*

May 30

I listen carefully to what God the LORD is saying,
for he speaks peace to his faithful people.

PSALM 85:8

Absence may make the heart grow fonder, but it certainly doesn't do much to deepen a relationship. For us to grow closer to God, we have to have some sense of His Presence. One of the best ways to do that is to actively listen for His voice. When we can hear Him speak, our hearts are drawn close to Him. When we can't—or don't *think* we can—He seems to be a distant God.

That's why listening carefully to Him is vital. But some Christians believe He doesn't speak anymore, even though Psalm 85:8 and many other verses insist that He has plenty to say to His people. And many who do believe He speaks are convinced they can't hear Him—or that if they are hearing Him, they can't distinguish His voice from all the others. In the absence of an audible voice, they assume all impressions and promptings are created equal—that all originate within the self. Meanwhile, God's Spirit is moving, inspiring, highlighting verses, setting up circumstances, sending signals, pouring forth knowledge, portraying parables, and prompting conversations that point to His truth for whatever season we're in. He floods our hearts with light (Ephesians 1:18), gives wisdom and understanding (Ephesians 1:17), reminds us of truth we've already been told (John 14:26), and tells us what's to come (John 16:13). And as today's verse makes clear, "he speaks peace to his faithful people." All we have to do is learn to recognize Him.

How do we do that? Ask. Ask again, and listen attentively. In fact, any area in which we're listening for His voice becomes an area in which He speaks. He isn't overly demanding or obscure. If we pursue the ability to hear, He will help us develop it.

Lord, teach me to hear. Speak in ways I can
understand. Tune my heart to the subtleties of Your
voice. And draw me close through what You say.

They raised their voices and praised the LORD
with these words: "He is good! His faithful
love endures forever!" At that moment a thick
cloud filled the Temple of the LORD.

2 CHRONICLES 5:13

Solomon had spent years—and quite a bit of Israel's human and material resources—to build the Temple. Now the day of dedication had come. The priests brought the Ark into the Holy Place, but God's Presence didn't manifest itself. The musicians began to play, but the Presence didn't manifest itself. The people raised their voices in praise, proclaiming God's goodness and faithfulness and love. *Then* the Presence filled the Temple. A visible, tangible cloud of glory became so thick that the priests couldn't even perform their duties. God responded to the worship of people hungry to encounter Him in His dwelling place.

That's always the way it is. God doesn't show up simply because of our rituals or behaviors, even when those rituals and behaviors are good. He shows up in response to heart attitudes, especially those that are expressed. Just as we're drawn to love, so is God. He comes close to those who love Him, hunger for Him, and say so.

We, the living temple of God in this age, are also inhabited by the cloud of glory when we worship Him from the heart, especially when we worship Him for His goodness and love. We may try to provoke His Presence through disciplines and postures and procedures, but even when those efforts are good, they alone do not draw Him. He is always present with us, but His Presence manifests itself most often when our hearts are turned toward Him in praise—and even more when we express that praise outwardly. When we create an environment appropriate to who He is, He fills it.

Lord, You are so good! Your faithful love endures forever!
And I don't tell you nearly enough. May my mouth
continually be filled with words that fit who You are, and
may my life be filled with Your cloud of glory.

June 1

The priests could not continue their service because of the cloud, for the glorious presence of the LORD filled the Temple of God.

2 CHRONICLES 5:14

Holy moments with God are often more than just a "quiet time" that passes when the allotted time is up. If there's a real encounter or an ongoing conversation, agendas have to be reset. A relationship with God can't fit into a schedule. He's more than an appointment on the calendar. When He shows up in a holy moment, the moment has to last as long as He wants it to.

We wouldn't want it otherwise, of course. No one truly engaged in a God-moment would prefer to get on with the daily routine or the to-do list. When we meet with God and something powerful happens, there can be no desire to disengage and say, "Okay, time's up." We can't walk casually away from holy ground. We live for such moments.

When you meet with God and expect His Presence, hold all agendas loosely. There's no need for that if you expect a routine relationship, but if you hope to encounter an unpredictable God however He chooses, you have to consider the possibilities. And those possibilities include getting lost in conversation with Him and losing track of time, services lasting longer than expected, or new guidance that radically redirects your day. Or you may just get overwhelmed and be ruined for anything else you had planned. When God shows up, all eyes are on Him. And when His glory fills a temple—like your heart—that's how it should be.

Lord, if You want to rearrange my day, You have my full cooperation. In fact, I invite You to do that however You choose. An encounter with You is worth changing plans or even getting behind. Fill me with Yourself and lead me wherever and whenever You will.

June 2

Then Solomon prayed, "O LORD, you have said
that you would live in a thick cloud of darkness.
Now I have built a glorious Temple for you, a
place where you can live forever!"

2 CHRONICLES 6:1-2

It's true. "Dark clouds surround him" (Psalm 97:2). Ever since Eden, God has been obscure to those who speculate, or even to those of us who diligently seek Him. Though He promises to reward seekers with the ability to find Him, He can seem elusive and hidden for years. He is not accessible to casual observers.

That's a deal-breaker for all but the truly hungry—which, perhaps, is why God waits in obscurity until a seeker persists. But when those who hunger for Him position themselves to receive Him—when a temple is prepared for Him to inhabit—He makes His Presence known. The thick cloud of darkness that hides Him is pierced by the desire of those who aren't swayed by it.

This is the progression of God's revelation since Eden—from hiddenness to revelation. That's just the way He chooses to show Himself. Some people are put off by His obscurity, as though if He isn't visible in the sky, then He must not be real. That isn't the way of faith.

Don't be swayed by the thick clouds that surround your God. If He seems distant, keep seeking. If He is slow to show Himself, keep pressing in. If you don't feel His touch, continue to position yourself for it anyway. Prepare the temple of your heart for a visitation, and don't give up hope that He will make His Presence known. If you believe, He already dwells in you by faith. Faith will hang on until you experience His indwelling.

Lord, I'm not giving up. In my driest time, even
when You seem far away, I'm seeking You with all
my heart and not giving up. I know You'll show
Yourself more clearly in Your own good time.

June 3

Will God really live on earth among people? Why,
even the highest heavens cannot contain you.

2 CHRONICLES 6:18

This question is deep in the heart of every human being. Many people look around them, experience a little bit of life, and answer, "I guess not." Or maybe their response is a little more nuanced: "I'm sure He's here—watching from a distance, perhaps, or only subtly and invisibly. But not in any noticeable way." That's because we've cultivated our natural vision but neglected our spiritual eyes. And we've trained ourselves to be disappointed.

When the Holy Spirit gives us new life from within, He gives us ample reason to hope that we can experience God in meaningful, practical ways. The world often quenches our hope, but we can rekindle it any time we want to by receiving and believing God's promises. We are told that the hope of a believer does not disappoint (Romans 5:5). So when we ask the rhetorical question Solomon asked—"Will God really live on earth among people?"—we have an emphatic answer. Yes, this God really has chosen to dwell with us. In fact, He is zealous about it.

That's why it's so important to cultivate our spiritual vision. We have to deliberately and consistently choose to see God in our lives. We need to learn to interpret the "coincidences" and "serendipity" and strange developments of our days as potential evidence of His voice. We must ask for discernment and avoid being tossed around by every hint of a whisper, but we must also stop dismissing the genuine whispers as "chance." God speaks and reveals Himself incessantly. We must watch with spiritual vision and listen with spiritual ears.

Lord, I know Your majesty and that You are
infinite. Heaven can't contain You, yet You choose
to dwell with us, in us, and all around us. Thank
You so much for choosing to live with us. I invite
You again to increase Your Presence in me.

June 4

O my God, may your eyes be open and your ears attentive to all the prayers made to you in this place.

2 CHRONICLES 6:40

I've prayed prayers that never got answered in any discernible way. So have you. Every Christian has experienced the frustration of a silent heaven. But we've also experienced the opposite—divine intervention that clearly answers our prayers. This diversity of experience has led to an abundance of sermons, books, and courses on how to pray effectively. The principles and techniques for what should be a relational conversation are almost endless.

Scripture gives us some simple answers to our questions about prayer. It's a genuine, two-way conversation, and it flourishes in intimate closeness with God. If we can remember the relational nature of prayer—that it isn't a formula or religious practice—we understand enough. We can deepen the relationship, draw closer to God, and let our hearts beat with His. Conversations grow richer and more fruitful with familiarity and affection. That's how prayer works.

So Solomon's request that God be attentive to the prayers made in His dwelling place is a great picture of prayer's true meaning. When we talk with God, it must be where He dwells—in the place where we cultivate familiarity and affection, where we worship and adore Him, where the bonds of friendship and intimacy are strengthened. It must be in that place of Presence we have established.

That place is no longer a temple of stone and curtains and holy furnishings. It's in the human heart that believes in Him, loves Him, and treasures His Presence. In other words, we can't have a rich prayer life if we don't have a rich sense of His Presence within us. If we want the conversation to flourish, we have to intentionally and relentlessly develop it. He is very attentive to the prayers made in that "place."

God, I'm setting apart places within me where we can talk, where I can sit in Your Presence and soak You in. Talk with me there; hear the desires of my heart; deepen our bond in those places.

June 5

And now arise, O LORD God, and enter
your resting place, along with the Ark,
the symbol of your power.

2 CHRONICLES 6:41

The progression of God's dwelling places took a landmark step in this Temple dedication. God had long before designated a Tabernacle and a Holy Place within it where His Presence would manifest. That Presence was most focused over the Ark and its mercy seat. This symbol of Presence had long represented God's favor to Israel. When the Ark went out with the army, God was "there." When the Ark was lost to the Philistines, the glory of Israel had "departed." When the Ark was recovered and then eventually brought to Jerusalem for David's Tabernacle, the Presence was celebrated. Now the Ark was placed in a magnificent permanent structure. Surely God would inhabit this place.

When Solomon finished praying, fire bolted from heaven and consumed Israel's offerings, and the glory of the Lord filled the Temple even more intensely than before. Solomon's prayer was answered. The designated "resting place" of the Lord was honored by the Lord Himself. He came.

A lot of preparation went into this request: a history of desire (Israel's love for the Ark and David's dream of a temple), a process of building (it was a seven-year project), an assembly of the people, and an elaborate celebration. This was no casual request. It took effort and was filled with expectation. It required faith and confidence that God actually *wanted* to be with His people. And according to His response, He did.

What kind of preparation and expectation goes into your request to encounter Him? What steps do you take to make your dwelling place ready? No amount of forethought, no level of preparation, no degree of hope is too much. He loves our readiness, and He responds with glory.

Now Lord, arise and enter this resting place
of yours—me—which You have chosen to
cleanse and set apart as holy. I welcome You
not only to be here, but to have free rein and
to make Yourself completely at home.

June 6

When Solomon finished praying, fire flashed down from heaven and burned up the burnt offerings and sacrifices, and the glorious presence of the LORD filled the Temple.

2 CHRONICLES 7:1

God is drawn to those who are humble, hungry for Him, brokenhearted, single-minded, pure-hearted, and willing to believe what He says. As Scripture consistently points out, He is also drawn to sacrifice. When we dedicate something to Him, especially at a cost to ourselves, He shows up on that issue or in that place. His fire of acceptance falls on our sacrifice.

This principle is written into the human heart, which explains why even idolaters expect the power of their gods in response to their sacrifices. An offering is not only an act of gratitude or adoration; it's often an invitation for a divine being to inhabit human devotion. True dedication cultivates a bond between the worshiper and the one being worshiped. And it very often prompts a response.

We don't always see God's responses to our offerings and sacrifices, but just because we don't see doesn't mean He is unresponsive. If an act of devotion is made in a true spirit of worship, He is drawn to it. His "fire" will fall on it in one way or another. He rewards those who draw near to Him by drawing near to them. No true devotion toward Him is ever ignored.

Understand the value of the sacrifices you make. They are important to God. They are tokens of your devotion, and He always responds to them—even when you don't see the response. A heart turned toward Him is always rewarded with more of Him.

Lord, I offer You everything I have. I offer You myself. I lay myself on Your altar, and I trust that Your fire will fall on this sacrifice—that You will fill me with Your Presence in deeper and deeper measure.

June 7

When all the people of Israel saw the fire coming down and the glorious presence of the LORD filling the Temple, they fell face down on the ground and worshiped and praised the LORD, saying, "He is good! His faithful love endures forever!"

2 CHRONICLES 7:3

We've read these words of praise before: "He is good! His faithful love endures forever!" The first time was right before God filled the Temple with His Presence (2 Chronicles 5:13). The cloud of His glory came in response to the Israelites' praises. Now their praises for His goodness, faithfulness, and love are a response to His Presence. In their encounter with Him, the natural reaction to His glory was falling facedown and worshiping. Their sense of His goodness and love was tangible. They had to cry out.

This is why we can legitimately say our faith is a relationship rather than simply a belief system. Our worship is not a monologue. God's acts are not a unilateral intervention in human affairs. We speak to God, He answers, we respond back to Him, He responds back to us. And on and on. His covenants with us are two-way interactions. Our praises are a response to His invitation to love Him and an invitation back to Him to grace us with His Presence. Anything less is not much of a relationship.

That's what we see in this Temple dedication—a dramatic conversation between human beings and a God who zealously seeks to live among His people. The implication for each of us is that when we express our worship to Him, we are setting the room at a temperature in which He is most at home, and He comes in. When He does, our response to Him is the same one we started with: worship. And an amazing conversation has begun.

Lord, let me never see my words to You, or Yours to me, as a one-way street. I know Your Spirit fills our conversations, even when I can't feel it. May those conversations become more and more saturated with Your Presence.

June 8

Though the LORD is great, he cares for the humble, but he keeps his distance from the proud.

PSALM 138:6

The Lord keeps His distance from the proud. We can relate; no one likes to be around those who are full of themselves. Arrogance has a way of alienating people. It alienates God, too.

In human relationships, we are repulsed by extreme cases of arrogance and annoyed by mild ones. We tolerate degrees of it in people with other redeeming qualities but are impatient toward those in whom it is conspicuous. We let it slide with those who can benefit us but quickly reject those who can do us no favors. And while we spot pride easily in others, we hardly notice it in ourselves. We have sliding scales of judgment based on our personal preferences and experiences. In other words, our perception of pride is skewed.

God's isn't. He detects pride immediately and precisely wherever it exists, and it always pushes Him away. It doesn't cause His love to fail—nothing can do that —but it certainly takes the pleasure out of the relationship. He can't honor those who elevate themselves; if He showered His favor on them, they would receive it as affirmation of their inflated self-esteem. He's too good for that. That's why He lets the proud fall and keeps His distance.

If you crave God's Presence, ruthlessly eliminate pride. We'd prefer that God give us the right attitude, but Scripture tells us to humble ourselves (James 4:10; 1 Peter 5:6). When He can trust you to remain humble—truly unassuming, not falsely modest—He is freed to enjoy and bless the relationship without fueling annoying attitudes. Good things come to those who aren't ruined by them.

Lord, I know where I stand before You. I'm not worthy of Your favor, but You give it anyway. I accept it as a gift—a free gift based entirely on Your goodness and not my merit. I know You don't have to bless me, but I'm so glad You do. And I'll remain forever grateful.

June 9

Because of our faith, Christ has brought us into this place of undeserved privilege where we now stand.

ROMANS 5:2

As much as we may talk of God's grace, few of us are thoroughly rooted in it. We're strong on the theology of grace and weak on its application—especially toward ourselves. In fact, most Christians relate to God in some level of "performance mode" almost constantly. We base our relationship on doing the right things. The result is the wrong kind of relationship.

God obviously has standards for our behavior, but His love and desire for us don't depend on them. Like the father of the Prodigal Son, He looks longingly toward His children even when they are squandering their privileged position—not because He's desperate but because that's what relentless love does. He designed behavior always to be a result of relationship, not vice versa. The relationship is primary.

Maybe you're one of the many who live in constant insecurity. You think you haven't done quite enough or done it right. But a sense of insufficiency in a relationship undermines its closeness. It's hard to feel affectionate toward someone you've let down. That attitude almost always alienates—the exact opposite of God's intentions for you. Remember that every moment of your life was laid out before you'd lived a single day (Psalm 139:16), so God knew about all your shortcomings ahead of time. And He still chose to make you and be with you.

God has based our relationship with Him on grace—a place of highest privilege—for a reason. The performance trap keeps us running on a spiritual treadmill. We're always striving and never arriving—and certainly never enjoying God. Determine to relate to Him on the basis of His extravagant love and nothing else. That's the only way to encounter Him as He truly is.

Father, I accept Your grace fully. I choose to believe that my behavior has nothing to do with Your love for me. Help me always relate to You from the privileged position You have freely given.

June 10

I pray that from his glorious, unlimited resources he will empower you with inner strength through his Spirit.

EPHESIANS 3:16

A lot of people live for the weekend. Or the next vacation. Or even the next good night's sleep. Why? Because we need to recharge. Life has a way of beating us down, draining our energy, and sapping our strength. And the only way many people know to recharge is to withdraw from stressful situations and relax.

There's nothing wrong with relaxing; God designed us to rest and refresh. But that isn't the only way for us to regain strength. In fact, we have a supernatural power supply. In the depths of our spirit, where the Holy Spirit dwells, God offers us "unlimited resources"—or as other translations put it, riches from His glory. So even when we can't get away from our stresses, we can tap into an unlimited source of divine strength.

Many of us forget our power supply. We rely on our own strength, and when it runs out, we default to natural means of coping. The Presence of the Spirit doesn't guarantee strength for us; we have to consciously depend on Him—to "plug in" to the supply. And in order to do that, we have to remember that He is readily available with the vast resources of God.

When you're feeling exhausted—spiritually, mentally, emotionally, physically, or any other way—look with eyes of faith to the Spirit that dwells within you. You'll have to consciously decide to do that, and you'll need to ask for His strength to sustain you. But you will find Him more than willing to show His strength in your weakness. He lives within you to show Himself in times of need.

Spirit, I'm out of strength. I've got nothing left. Even when I'm strong, I need to depend on You. That's even more true when I'm weak. Please show Yourself strong in me. Fill me with the riches and resources of God.

Christ will make his home in your hearts as you trust in him. Your roots will grow down into God's love and keep you strong.

EPHESIANS 3:17

Familiarity breeds contempt, it's often said. That's a reliable statement in many relationships, perhaps, but it's not true of our relationship with Jesus. True familiarity—real knowledge of Him rather than assumptions about Him—breeds depth. The more we get to know Him, the deeper He takes us.

The key mechanism by which that happens is faith. Jesus becomes more at home in our hearts as we trust Him. His Presence is always there—He assured us of that in the new birth—but His Presence doesn't have much practical benefit for us unless we learn to rely on Him, trust His work, and experience Him. And the only way to have that kind of faith is to know its roots. We believe not because we can muster up faith but because we're rooted in love. We can trust someone we love.

That's why Paul prays not only that his readers would know the Presence of Jesus through faith, but that their hearts would be deeply rooted in God's love. We aren't just after the practical benefits of His Presence; that would be utilitarian spirituality. No, this is personal. It's relational. We experience His Presence through faith in Him, and our faith is based in His love.

Know God's love. Then you can trust Jesus, and your trust will cultivate your awareness of His Presence. And He will be more and more at home in your heart.

Jesus, make Yourself at home in my heart. Let my roots grow deep into Your love, and let my trust in You grow stronger and fuller every day.

June 12

And may you have the power to understand,
as all God's people should, how wide, how
long, how high, and how deep his love is.

EPHESIANS 3:18

Imagine the most intense feelings of love you've ever felt—that time you felt your heart was about to explode because of your overwhelming affection for someone. Now imagine those feelings doubling. And doubling again. And again. Your heart would have a hard time handling such intensity, wouldn't it?

Yet that intensity is only a tiny fraction of God's love for each of His children. The dimensions of His love are incomprehensible, but we're encouraged to try to understand it anyway. Paul prays for God to reveal it to us—the only way we can really even begin to grasp it. And even though we'll never truly understand the magnitude of that love, it's encouraging enough just to be told that it's beyond our wildest imagination. Though we can't measure it, we can experience it.

That's important. It's one thing to know *of* God's love—even the youngest children in Sunday school have been told about it—but knowledge isn't enough. A marriage certificate or an old love letter may testify to love, but a spouse still needs to be reminded of it and feel it often. A child may "know" a parent's love, but knowing, without personal and affectionate embraces and conversations, doesn't satisfy. Those who love want the objects of their love to experience it fully. Anything less is disappointing, to both the lover and the loved.

Accept the truth of God's love, but do more than that. Ask to understand it, grasp it, feel it, experience it, and dive into its depths. God isn't satisfied with our head knowledge, and neither are we. His love is meant to be fully encountered.

Lord, I know you don't offer Your love to be experienced
halfway. You want us to experience it as fully as we can.
I believe that and ask for it. Help me understand—
and feel—the enormity of Your love.

June 13

*May you experience the love of Christ, though
it is too great to understand fully. Then you
will be made complete with all the fullness of
life and power that comes from God.*

EPHESIANS 3:19

"It is too great to understand fully." Paul has grasped the irony of what he's
asking. He has prayed that his readers will understand and experience the
love of Christ—and its width, length, height, and depth—but knows they
will never understand it fully. Even so, the promise behind the prayer is stag-
gering: "that you may be filled with all the fullness of God" (v. 19, NKJV).

Some translations rearrange Paul's words because the literal translation
is incomprehensible. We can "be filled with all the fullness of God"? Really?
We're finite and He's infinite; "all" His fullness is too much for us. But the
extravagant words of the original text are meant to stretch us, to drive us to
our knees at the shocking suggestion that we are vessels not just of a small
taste of God but of God in abundance. Though the promise seems too great,
it accurately expresses God's heart. He *wants* to fill us with all His fullness.
Like a smitten lover or beaming parent, He longs to pour all of Himself into
us. His heart overflows.

Soak in the depths of His love. It's perhaps the most widely known yet
least-experienced aspect of His character. Most Christian minds are amply
aware of it, but few Christian hearts have let it really sink in. Spend some time
letting it sink in—deeply and thoroughly. Yes, the promise is unimaginable,
but imagine it anyway. The fullness of God's life and power is in it.

*Jesus, thank You for pouring Yourself out into me.
Let Your love sink into my heart. I want to soak
in it, savor it, and overflow with love back to You.
Please increase my capacity to experience You.*

June 14

Now to him who is able to do immeasurably
more than all we ask or imagine, according to
his power that is at work within us.

EPHESIANS 3:20, NIV

We wait for God to open doors, to move mountains, to part waters. We pray for deliverance and healing and provision. We look upward and outward for His intervention. He hears our prayers and often moves on our behalf. Yet more often, as alarming as it seems, God points us back to the power that works "within us."

It's true that God works *for* His people, but His preferred modus operandi is to work *through* us. That's why He didn't tell His disciples just to pray for people to be healed, raised, cured, and delivered. He told them to "heal the sick, raise the dead, cure those with leprosy, and cast out demons" (Matthew 10:8)—to do these things themselves. Sure, they would need faith and supernatural power to do that, but He still put the action on them. Why? Because God was setting a pattern and a mind-set for the new creation. We are more than poor creatures of dust appealing to an awesome deity to intervene. We are inhabited by that deity Himself. We have become one with Him.

That seems too remarkable to be true, as well as a little arrogant. But it's thoroughly biblical. In our natural selves, we have no power to do anything lasting or ultimately worthwhile. But inhabited by the Spirit of Jesus, we have the power of the Resurrection within us—the same power that healed the sick, raised the dead, cleansed lepers, and cast out demons. Any mind-set that convinces us otherwise will keep us living within natural limits, but when we become deeply, thoroughly convinced of the Presence and power at work within us, we begin to experience more of that Presence and power. He does immeasurably more than asked or imagined—in and through us.

Holy Spirit, this truth is beyond my experience.
Please bring my experience up to the level of Your
truth. Teach me to operate in the power of the
Resurrection that works within me.

*Do not rebel against the LORD, and don't be
afraid of the people of the land. They are only
helpless prey to us! They have no protection, but
the LORD is with us! Don't be afraid of them!*

NUMBERS 14:9

It's not exactly comforting that Scripture sometimes portrays fear as a form of rebellion against God, but it does. In light of God's overwhelming promise and clear favor on Israel, Caleb and Joshua saw the people's terror as defiance against His plans. When God speaks victory and our fears speak defeat, we have a choice of which to believe. One of those choices is the kind of faith that pleases Him; the other is mutiny.

Fear quenches our sense of God's Presence in our lives. Why? Because it doesn't reflect the attitude of heaven. It's out of sync with who He is and what He has said. It turns our hearts into alien territory for Him. When we know the favor He has given us, hear the promises He has spoken, and see the calling He has put within us, our worries and anxieties form a contradiction to the divine agenda. Our hearts become a hostile environment for faith.

From ample scriptural assurances, we can hear what He says to us about our worries: "Do not fear. I see your future, and I know how present circumstances will turn out. In every possibility you worry about, I'm already there. I'm not incapable of bringing you into your destiny, and I'm not unwilling either. In fact, it's My delight to direct and guard your every step. I love the statement you make about Me and My goodness when you believe. So let go of fear and embrace faith. You can trust Me."

*Lord, I believe. I struggle with trust, but I know who
You are—that You are good and trustworthy. I place
all my confidence in You and not in any negative
possibility that might happen. I choose to trust You.*

June 16

And the LORD said to Moses, "How long will these people treat me with contempt? Will they never believe me, even after all the miraculous signs I have done among them?"

NUMBERS 14:11

Just as fear is treated as rebellion against God, unbelief is treated as rejection of Him and even contempt for Him. It, too, makes our hearts hostile territory for His truth and blocks our sense of His Presence. God speaks good plans and purposes over us; He sees our destiny in full. And when we entertain unbelief and let it sink in and affect us, we become rocky soil for His seeds. We unintentionally go to battle against His calling.

Belief cooperates with God. It agrees with who He says He is and what He has said He will do. Unbelief, on the other hand, contradicts who He says He is and what He has said He will do. Belief draws us close to Him while unbelief separates us from Him. One causes us to beat with His heartbeat; the other weakens our pulse completely.

One negative thought of unbelief can be the catalyst for a downward spiral of discouragement and depression. Just as faith feeds faith, unbelief feeds unbelief. When we allow our minds to begin going down a hopeless path, we find ourselves on a very slippery slope, and it's hard to climb back up. We have to learn to cut off unbelief when it first appears.

Hear God's encouragement: "In a fallen world separated from My visible Presence, faith is the only way to connect with Me. And My heart *longs* for you to connect with Me. So believe—every word I speak, every direction I lead, every promise I give. Entertain no contradicting voices. My voice is absolute. I *will* accomplish the things I have spoken. If you believe them, I will honor your faith by showing Myself to you."

Lord, I confess that I tend to live by sight, not by faith. Please help me reverse that tendency. I choose to hang on to Your truth, even when it contradicts my visible world. I want to be a believer—in every way.

Because you complained against me, every one of you who is twenty years old or older and was included in the registration will die. You will not enter and occupy the land I swore to give you.

NUMBERS 14:29-30

The Israelites faced an enormous obstacle on their way to the Promised Land. It wasn't the Red Sea; God parted that with ease. It wasn't the vast stretch of wilderness between Egypt and the Jordan; God provided bread from heaven and water from a rock to sustain them. It wasn't the giants in the land; God had promised victory. No, the biggest obstacle the Israelites faced was their own attitude. Their complaints kept them from experiencing God's best.

Complaints—or "grumbling," as some translations express it—give voice to the fear and unbelief of our hearts. They are an audible expression of contradictions to God. Though God often invites wrestling and entertains our questions, He doesn't respond favorably to accusations that He isn't treating us well or is perhaps holding out on us. When we're dissatisfied or confused, He has no problem with our honestly expressing questions and doubts (not in a spirit of unbelief but in a spirit of seeking). But if our true heart is making judgments against His ways, we are walking in the opposite direction of our promised land or, at the very least, prolonging our time in the wilderness. Grumbling and complaining don't get us anywhere with God.

The Israelites who complained—and whose attitude was contagious to others, as attitudes always are—had to defer their promise to the next generation. Complaining doesn't fit the culture of His Kingdom. Caleb and Joshua had a different spirit, so God preserved their lives until they entered the land. That's a common dynamic among God's followers. Those who submit to His processes experience fulfillment of promises; those who complain about the processes don't. As those who seek the promise of His Presence and His abundance, we have a clear choice.

Lord, forgive any complaints I've uttered. I don't always understand Your processes, but I submit to them. I know they will lead me into the fullness of Your promises.

Jesus responded, "Didn't I tell you that you would see God's glory if you believe?"

JOHN 11:40

God has been pretty indiscriminate in publishing His stories. His dealings with human beings have been recorded in the bestselling book of all time, as have His extravagant promises. He has not kept secrets or established a highly exclusive club. Whoever chooses to follow Him may do so. Membership in His family is still wide open.

If that's true, why do some people experience His blessings and His Presence while others don't? What distinguishes those who only know of His promises from those who see them fulfilled? Belief. God has chosen faith to be the currency of His Kingdom. If we believe what He promises, we can experience it. If we remain in unbelief, His promises remain nothing more than words to us. God divides people into two categories: those who believe and those who don't.

That sounds awfully conditional for a God who doesn't show partiality (Acts 10:34), but it's true. Though God's love is unconditional, His responses to us aren't. Scripture contains a repeated and emphatic "if" when it comes to faith. *If* we believe, we can experience what He promises. *If* we believe, we can see His glory. *If* we believe, we can be saved. And if not? Then we have refused to use the currency of His Kingdom. And we can't receive very much without it.

Unbelief will block the Presence, not because God is weak and can't overcome our faithlessness, but because He chooses to encounter us on His terms. When we have faith that has been tried and tested and has endured, we will eventually see His promises, including His manifest Presence, come to pass in our lives. If we believe, we will see His glory.

Jesus, I accept Your words—and Your conditions— as true. I know my faith is necessary to experience You the way I was meant to. When You say I will see Your glory if I believe, You're implying that I won't if I don't. So I choose to believe You—in everything—and ask You to show me Your glory.

*Your favor, O LORD, made me as secure
as a mountain. Then you turned away
from me, and I was shattered.*

PSALM 30:7

God turned away. He hid His face, and David was dismayed. This psalm of dedication for a temple that hasn't even been built yet is full of joy and gratitude for God's goodness, but one line interrupts the joy with an absentee God and shattered hopes. Why?

It could be for one of the many moments when David's life was in danger or when his family was in turmoil as a result of David's sin. That would give us a tidy explanation of God's seeming absence—He only *appeared* absent because of the crisis, or He righteously punished His servant's misdeeds—but David doesn't point out any particular circumstances. In fact, he almost seems to fit the absence of God into the natural flow of life. Sometimes God seems very present, sometimes He doesn't. It just happens, and there's no explanation.

We've all experienced that. We sometimes feel very close to God, and then for no discernible reason, we don't. Sometimes He leads us through green pastures, and other times through dry deserts. We don't understand why—and the psalms do an honest job of mentioning life's disappointments—but God values our trust in those times more than our understanding. Perhaps He allows our isolation to see how we respond in the absence of outward evidence of Him. Will we believe and hope or doubt and despair? Whatever the reason, God can hide His face, and we're dismayed.

The good news is that dry times don't end that way. Mourning is turned to dancing (v. 11). But when life includes seasons of longing for a God who seems strangely silent, sandwich your lament in the middle of your life's psalm of praise. Don't get stuck in the middle of the story. God turns disappointments into joy.

*Lord, I don't understand my disappointments, but
I know they aren't how my story ends. I know
Your face even when I don't see it. In the midst of
dismay, I choose hope and faith.*

June 20

In him we live and move and exist.

ACTS 17:28

We don't really notice air. It's the environment we live in. It's always all around us, and we can feel it when it moves as a swift breeze. If we were suddenly deprived of it, we would certainly notice its absence. But other than that, we give it little attention. If we want to be conscious of it, we have to intentionally choose to think about it.

God is like that. He's always around us, and we can often detect Him when He moves. And if we were suddenly deprived of Him . . . well, we would certainly notice His absence. But we often have to choose to be aware of Him.

Many passages of Scripture suggest that God is nearer to us at some times than at others—that He's near to the brokenhearted or the humble, for example, or that He will draw near to us if we draw near to Him. But verses like Acts 17:28 remind us that He is always near, as pervasive as the air we breathe. Though much of our experience of His Presence depends on His drawing near, much of it depends on our increasing our awareness of Him. We need to become noticers who, like Brother Lawrence long ago, "practice the Presence of God."

In our quest for a deeper sense of God's Presence, we need to remember that much of what we seek is already all around us. We live and move and exist in God. He is present in every atom of creation, and if we're observant, we can see not only His past handiwork as Creator but His current activity as Lord, Guide, Shield, Provider, Comforter, and Healer. Even when it seems like He is far away, He never is. Whether we sense His Presence or not, He is near.

Lord, I know You're sitting next to me right now. You're watching me, protecting me, even sharing Your heart with me. Help me become a noticer of Your Presence and acknowledge You in every situation.

June 21

Then he breathed on them and said,
"Receive the Holy Spirit."

JOHN 20:22

The resurrected Jesus surprised a gathering of disciples with His Presence, and they gathered around Him in joy. He declared their mission: "As the Father has sent me, so I am sending you" (John 20:21). Then He breathed on them and made a startling statement: "Receive the Holy Spirit."

That isn't a startling statement to us because we have a couple of millennia of church history behind us to contemplate the gift of the Spirit. But to disciples who knew that God's Spirit was with Moses, Elijah, and Daniel—and not many people of lower profile—they had to marvel at the idea. More than that, they must have marveled at how they got such a Spirit. They didn't have to go grab Him or jump through all the right hoops to appease Him. They simply had to receive Him. Like breath being drawn into lungs, the Spirit was available to anyone who had the urge to inhale. There was nothing to earn, but everything to gain.

We experience the Spirit the way He was first imparted—by simply receiving. Soaking in God's Presence can often be far more effective for our growth and intimacy with God than acts of service or desperate prayers. Though pursuing Him is certainly appropriate at times, an attitude of quiet receiving is essential. God doesn't always call us to come and get; He calls us to be still and know.

Spend some time soaking in God today. Be a passive recipient of the Spirit He offers. Don't feel guilty about not making an effort; sometimes effort is counterproductive. Fulfill Jesus' command: "receive."

Spirit, I open myself to You. Flow into me. Let me
inhale You fully. I receive You into my spirit so we can
experience greater and greater oneness.

June 22

The Lord is near.
PHILIPPIANS 4:5, NIV

The toddler was perfectly content playing with his toys until he looked around and couldn't see his mother. He panicked. His eyes widened, his mouth contorted, and his soft whimper transitioned into a louder cry. Then, suddenly, he spotted Mom in the far corner. The fearful face relaxed, the wailing ceased, and he turned back to his toys as though nothing had happened.

Why does a child, without any other circumstances changing, feel comfortable with a parent in the room and afraid when no one seems near? Because nearness matters—especially in an uncertain mind that isn't fully developed. And we, spiritual children who certainly aren't fully developed, are exactly the same way. When we sense that God is with us, we can be perfectly content going about our business and handling life "on our own." But when uncertainty strikes, we look around for reassurance, and if God seems to be absent, we panic. We need to remember that He's still "in the room."

Remind yourself that the Lord is near. (Though many interpreters apply this verse to His second coming, it just as easily refers to His current Presence.) Declare, even out loud if it helps, what you know to be true: that God is all around you, that He hasn't left you or forsaken you. Then look around for the many evidences of His nearness—the provision He gave last month, or the blessing He bestowed last week, or the word He whispered last night. The more you notice His many personal touches, the more you realize how fully surrounded you are with His Presence. Then you can relax and be content in whatever you are doing.

> *Father, I need to know You are in the room. Help me notice all Your personal touches. May Your Spirit remind me how close You are. Let me be content knowing that I'm completely safe with You.*

June 23

*I said to myself, "I will get up and roam the
city, searching in all its streets and squares.
I will search for the one I love."*

SONG OF SONGS 3:2

"Close your eyes and count to one hundred," says one child to the other,
and the game begins. The hider finds the most obscure, unexpected spot
within the designated boundaries, and the seeker finishes counting and sets
out looking and listening for evidence of a friend who doesn't (but really
does) want to be found. It could be frustrating if it went on too long, but
it doesn't. All hiding places are eventually discovered. The revelation of the
hider is only a matter of time.

God plays games of divine hide-and-seek, and they are meant to be fun.
He makes Himself obscure—frustratingly so for those who don't understand
there's a game on—and waits for us to find Him. There's something about
our quest that warms His heart; He enjoys our searching. And He rewards it
too. He doesn't hold His position so long that those with true faith will lose
heart and give up. He shows Himself to those who keep seeking (Jeremiah
29:13). He wants to be found.

If God seems obscure, don't give up your search. Let Him enjoy your
seeking—an endeavor He fully intends to reward. Like the beloved in the
Song of Songs, go into all the streets and squares of your life in pursuit of the
One who loves you. Know that "it is the glory of God to conceal a matter"
(Proverbs 25:2, NIV), and He does it simply to see who is serious enough
about Him to search it out. If you really desire His Presence, you won't quit
until you've found Him. And He will make your quest worthwhile.

*Lord, I know You're there. I'm certain, even when You
make Yourself scarce, that You enjoy our companionship.
Please lead me in my search for You as I journey deeper
and deeper into Your will and Your ways.*

June 24

Ever since the world was created, people have
seen the earth and sky. Through everything
God made, they can clearly see his invisible
qualities—his eternal power and divine nature.
So they have no excuse for not knowing God.

ROMANS 1:20

Philosopher Bertrand Russell, an atheist and critic of Christianity, once declared that if God confronted him in the afterlife and asked why he didn't
believe, he would claim there was "not enough evidence." In fact, many agnostics and atheists claim not only that there isn't enough evidence to believe
in God, but that there is ample evidence to prove that the God of the Bible
doesn't exist. They reject the idea that this world exists because of a creator—
especially the one described in Scripture.

Paul asserts that creation itself demands belief in a creator and that God's
"invisible qualities" can be seen by those who look for them. His conclusion?
There's no excuse for not knowing God. With some visible evidence to go
on and a heart inclined to seek, He can be found.

That argument applies not only to discovering the existence of God;
it applies also to knowing Him more deeply. Every Christian who wields
this verse against agnostics and atheists and then spends his or her days in
complacency toward God is being somewhat hypocritical. Anytime we get
a taste of God and choose not to explore Him more fully, we are rejecting
His invitation. The glimpses we see and whispers we hear are the opening
lines of a conversation. We can choose to engage or not. When we don't, we
are settling for our spiritual status quo. But when we do, God shows more of
Himself. Our acceptance of His invitation stirs His heart, and He in turn stirs
ours. Wherever you see Him today, let it lead you further in that direction.

Lord, just as there's no excuse for not knowing You,
there's no excuse for not knowing You more. Any
whisper I hear from You, I'll follow. Any glimpse I
get, I'll look closer. Show me more of You.

June 25

I will never leave you nor forsake you.

JOSHUA 1:5, NIV

Joshua was about to lead a vast number of wilderness wanderers into the Land of Promise. The parents of these wanderers had once noted how intimidating the land's inhabitants were, but Joshua had defended God's promise. Now he would see God's promise fulfilled. But he would have to be strong and courageous. And he would have to remember that God would never leave him or forsake him.

We have to remember that too. We know in our heads that God will never leave us or forsake us, but when a crisis hits, we often feel like He already has. In moments of confusion or pain, we can get really disoriented. The God who seemed like He was on our side yesterday suddenly seems like He doesn't even know our names. In those times of confusion, we need to insist to ourselves what we know to be true: that He hasn't left and He isn't going to. He is still on our side.

Like Joshua, we face big moments of decision, times when we have to put our faith on the line and be strong and courageous. We may fear the outcome, but we don't have to. Even if the outcome isn't what we expected, God will be with us in the surprise or disappointment. But He will also be with us in many victories. Whatever we have to walk through, He is there.

Stake everything on that, no matter how present or absent He seems to be. Trust Him even when you can't sense Him. He made a binding promise to be with you. And He *never* breaks a promise.

Father, thank You for being with me. No matter what happens, I know you place victory—in one way or another—in my path. You will lead me into many lands of promise. And on the way there, Your being with me means everything.

*I remember the days of old. I ponder
all your great works and think
about what you have done.*

PSALM 143:5

One day God gave me some profound encouragement in a much-needed answer to prayer, and I thanked Him all that day. The next day, a situation came up that caused me quite a bit of stress, and I began to worry that God was going to let me down. When I recalled how encouraged I had been just a day earlier—and that the recent turn of events in no way nullified what had been true then—I realized I had a choice. I could choose to see God through the lens of disappointment, or I could choose to see Him through the lens of gratitude. I chose to embrace the attitude of the first day as a true reflection of God's goodness and the mood of the second day as a false one.

God often allows us to be in a position to make that choice. The praises we declare one day are often challenged by circumstances the next, and that's when we find out if we really believed what our mouths said. If our opinion of God changes with every shifting circumstance or mood, our faith is still immature. We need to let the blessings and victories of one season speak just as loudly as the appearances of the next season. If we once were convinced of God's goodness, then we ought to remain convinced through difficult times.

The best way to do that is to remember. We easily forget past graces and focus on current stresses, but we end up with distorted perceptions when we do. Choosing to remember what God did in the past—whether it was long ago or just days or hours earlier—will give our hearts and minds the right perspective on what God is doing.

*Lord, Your past works in my life remind me who
You are. Remembering keeps me grounded in
truth. Please help me bring them to mind often
and continue to thank You for them.*

*Let us run with endurance the race God
has set before us. We do this by keeping
our eyes on Jesus, the champion who
initiates and perfects our faith.*

HEBREWS 12:1-2

If a marathoner focused on each painful, jarring step—and the burning thirst
and mounting fatigue—the race would be lost long before it was ever finished. Some racers focus on the glory of the prize, others on some pleasant
memory or future hope, and some simply on the finish line. But on the needs
of each moment and the pain of getting there? That would quench the motivation to continue. It would intimidate any expectation of going all the way.
Marathons can only be accomplished when the mind of the runner sees the
big picture. The details kill faith.

That's certainly true of the spiritual marathon we run. When we focus on
the details—the overwhelming needs of this day or the what-ifs of how certain situations might turn out—faith drains out of us, motivation disappears,
and discouragement sets in. Our obsession with details takes our minds off
the big picture, and we lose hope. Our perspective becomes skewed. The race
then becomes a painful chore that we may or may not even finish.

In order to run well—and specifically to run with endurance *this day*—
we have to gaze at someone who has finished the race successfully. We have
to look at Jesus, who not only finished well but makes Himself available to
fill us with His strength and endurance. He endured every temptation, over-
came every obstacle, and won every victory. Now He lives in us. If we gaze at
ourselves, our pain and needs and our moment-by-moment details, we lose
heart. If we gaze at Him, we overcome. It's as simple as that. The only way to
finish the race is to keep our eyes on the One who won it.

*Jesus, I turn my eyes toward You. In every step of
this day, I run with my focus on You. Fill me with
Your strength, Your faith, Your victory.*

June 28

God showed his great love for us by sending
Christ to die for us while we were still sinners.

ROMANS 5:8

The more we sacrifice for something, the more valuable it is to us. The same goes with relationships: the more we invest in a person, the more treasured that person becomes. Jesus made it clear that our heart will follow our treasure, and the heart-treasure connection seems to flow the other way too. Our treasures follow our affections. We give ourselves to whatever and whomever we love.

This is God's heart too. His most priceless offering flowed in the direction of His love. He gave Jesus because His love compelled Him to rescue us. We know we are valuable simply from the fact that God created us—He only creates things of value—and from the fact that He created us in His image, which makes us uniquely valuable among creation. But if we ever wonder just *how* valuable we are, all we have to do is look at the offering made on our behalf. The beloved Son was brutally slaughtered as the price of our rescue. That's a major statement on what God treasures.

If God values our relationship with Him that much, then neglecting that relationship or being casual about it is a shocking waste. If we aren't pursuing a deeper relationship with Him from the very core of our being, we are disappointing the heart of God. That statement is not meant to induce guilt and shame; it's an encouragement to boldly chase what has been offered. If God has poured so much into this relationship, we never need to fear making too much of it or overstepping our privileges in it. Our royal position and privileges as the King's children were bought at an enormous price. Underestimating them would be underestimating His desire for closeness. Seeking to experience them honors His heart.

Lord, I want our relationship to live up to Your
desires fully—to be worth the price You paid.
I don't want to miss anything You've planned
for us. Please draw me closer into You.

Even though the fig trees have no blossoms, and there are no grapes on the vines; even though the olive crop fails, and the fields lie empty and barren; even though the flocks die in the fields, and the cattle barns are empty, yet I will rejoice in the LORD! I will be joyful in the God of my salvation!

HABAKKUK 3:17-18

God is drawn to naked faith—the kind of faith that believes, hopes, and endures in spite of appearances. Anyone can trust God when life is smooth and pleasant, and He often gives us those seasons. But when everything seems to be falling apart—when the God of all grace and comfort seems to be hiding His grace and comfort—faith is tested. Those times are dividing lines; faith either endures or fails. When it endures, God draws near.

This sets up an odd situation of God withdrawing His Presence in order to eventually make His Presence even more felt. He steps back to stretch and strengthen our faith, then He steps in to reward our faith with His closeness. The result is a divine dance in which He and we experience choreographed spaces and then bridge them in an expressive rhythm. The cycle of yearning and satisfaction is repeated again and again—if we make it through the yearning phases without losing our trust. When circumstances make Him seem absent—when He's on one side of the stage and we're on the other—we hold on, knowing that the choreography will bring us back into an intimate, face-to-face encounter.

Many people drop out of the dance when the distance comes, assuming that God is unavailable or uninterested in closing the gap. Nothing could be further from the truth. Hard times and a seemingly distant God have a purpose, but that purpose is never to alienate us. It's to keep us seeking, to draw us closer, to elicit the cry of our hearts to be near. And when that cry persists, it's always answered.

Lord, please help me see every turn of events with You as a step in the choreography, not as a measure of Your desire to be with me. I know your ultimate purpose is for us to be united as one and to experience the closest intimacy possible, and everything works toward that goal. Please bring my heart into the rhythm of that process.

June 30

Always be joyful.
1 THESSALONIANS 5:16

We rely on laws and rules to govern behavior, but everyone knows they can't govern the human heart. External forces can't command internal responses. Still, God works into His Word several unexpected instructions: to love Him with all our hearts, to have no anxiety, and to be joyful. How is this possible? How can an outward command be imposed on inward attitudes? How can an untamable heart be tamed by words?

It takes more than words, of course. In a command to "be joyful," self-discipline isn't the goal. It isn't an effective response or even a realistic one. We can't change our hearts simply by telling them to change. We can, however, realize that our attitudes are off-kilter and ask Him to supernaturally change them. He holds hearts in His hand; He can certainly sway them with His thoughts and fill them with His Spirit. If we are going to be people who are always joyful, this is how it has to be. We can't follow this instruction in the midst of trying circumstances unless we have a radical change of perspective and supernatural help. Biblical commands to rejoice—especially in suffering, persecution, and the intense trials of life—can only be fulfilled when we depend on Him.

Hear His heart: "I designed you for joy. I sent My Son to you so your joy might be full, abundant, overflowing. I didn't create you for joy only on pleasant days but for deep, abiding joy in any circumstance. Yes, this seems unrealistic to you. And yes, you can't simply flip a switch and rejoice. But you can focus on Me, change your perspective, and ask for My heart to fill you. I will gladly give you joy if you ask."

*Father, I'm asking. I want joy—Your joy, the kind
I was designed to have and that Jesus promised.
Please let me experience it, even in my most trying
circumstances. I want the joy that overcomes all
obstacles and runs deeper than any pain.*

July 1

Never stop praying.
1 THESSALONIANS 5:17

God is persistent. His rescue plan for humanity took millennia to unfold, but even after repeated rejection by His people, He continued to redeem, restore, and prepare for the Messiah. He relentlessly pursues our love and does not abandon us, no matter how many times we fall. He has promised to complete the work He has begun in us, no matter how long it takes or how winding the road seems to be. God does not give up.

It only makes sense, then, that this God of persistence tells us to be persistent. He continues to make us in His image, and this is one of the ways we are to reflect Him. That's why Jesus told His disciples to pray and "never give up" (Luke 18:1), giving them parables about knocking on a neighbor's door repeatedly (Luke 11:5-8) and pestering a judge until he gives a favorable decision (Luke 18:1-8). In our pursuit of God, His Kingdom, and His will for our lives, we are to be relentless just as He is relentless—even if the one we petition is Him. He invites us to remind Him of His promises and take no rest in doing so (Isaiah 62:6-7). He urges us to "pester" Him.

Hear His heart: "I don't ask for your persistent prayers because I'm hard of hearing. I ask for them because in the process of asking, listening for My answers, waiting on Me to act, and continuing to seek out My will, you are being drawn close to Me. My delays are rarely a no; they are an invitation to come closer. If you learn this, you will find yourself growing deeper and stronger in Me."

Father, forgive me for giving up too quickly when I pray. There's no reason for me not to come to You for everything at all times. May Your Spirit remind me often to pray, and may You hear my requests and answer them according to Your power and purpose.

July 2

Be thankful in all circumstances, for this is God's
will for you who belong to Christ Jesus.
1 THESSALONIANS 5:18

Ingratitude drives a wedge into relationships. When one person has gone out of his or her way to benefit another and the gesture is taken for granted, the relationship cools. Gratitude, on the other hand, draws people close. Appreciation causes a person to feel valued, and when we feel valued, we increase our openness to those who value us. Everyone likes to be affirmed.

God doesn't really need our affirmation, but the dynamics of gratitude apply to our relationship with Him anyway, just as they do to our relationships with others. Ingratitude does nothing to draw Him deeper into a relationship with us, but gratitude certainly does. Giving thanks reflects an accurate perception of what He has done. It stirs up intimacy.

Gratitude for obvious blessings is good. Gratitude for less obvious blessings is better. But gratitude in spite of known adversity is the most mature form of all. The person who can thank God for His work even when His work seems to be painful or is completely hidden from view is a spiritually mature believer. When we thank God for an answer to prayer that isn't even slightly apparent yet, we are demonstrating true faith. God draws near to those who are thankful no matter what happens.

Hear His heart: "Your gratitude is My will in every circumstance. I don't expect you to enjoy adversity, but know that you don't see the whole picture, and trust the One who does: Me. No matter what happens, give thanks. Stubbornly insist on it, regardless of your reservations. It's always an appropriate attitude, and it makes Me want to come closer."

Father, thank You for everything You are doing on my
behalf—the things I see and the things I don't see.
Help me have radical gratitude, a stubborn insistence on
acknowledging that You are good—no matter what I see.

July 3

Do not stifle the Holy Spirit.
1 THESSALONIANS 5:19

The God of all power and strength has put His Spirit within us—a Spirit who can sway hearts, inspire heroic acts, raise the spiritually and physically dead into new life, perform supernatural miracles, and bear supernatural fruit. As a member of the sovereign Trinity, there is no limit to His power. Even so, according to the Word this Spirit breathed into His people, He can be stifled.

How? By resisting Him. By functioning out of our assumptions or principles instead of by His unpredictable leading. By refusing to go with His flow because we have an agenda or a program. By living in a way that's decidedly out of line with His character. There are so many ways. Whenever we wonder where He is and why He doesn't seem more powerful in our lives, one of those ways is probably the reason.

Do not stifle the Spirit. He is all-powerful, but He prefers to work with us and through us, not over us and around us. When His movement is flowing and we decide to assert our own agenda rather than His—even when ours is a good agenda that we believe is God's will—the flowing ceases. He works powerfully when we respond to Him, not when we attempt to manipulate His response to us. The only way not to stifle Him is to listen attentively to Him, heed every prompt He gives, and depend on Him for the outcomes. Anything else is human, fleshly effort.

Hear His heart: "When you depend on Me—in faith, without worry, and without assuming your own plans are the right ones—I am free to work. I love that dynamic between us. That's how our relationship flows as it should. Seek that alone, and you *will* experience Me."

Spirit, I want to experience You. Forgive me for living by principles and not by relationship with You, for assuming my best-laid plans are Yours, and for not depending on You. I invite You to flow through me and from me freely.

July 4

Do not scoff at prophecies, but test everything that is said.

1 THESSALONIANS 5:20-21

God speaks. Always has, always will. A lot of Christians don't believe that, assuming that once Scripture was complete, He had said all He would ever say. But that idea defies the content of Scripture itself, which portrays a God who loves to communicate with His people and gives no indication He will stop. He won't establish any new or contrary doctrines, but He certainly still guides, comforts, corrects, and encourages. He speaks to us individually because . . . well, we're individuals.

That was certainly true in the early church, which seemed to have a vibrant, member-to-member prophetic ministry. People listened to God's voice on behalf of each other and shared His words. And Paul told the Thessalonians not to scoff at such prophecies. We know he wasn't talking about the Old Testament prophets—an instruction not to scoff at Scripture would be ridiculously unnecessary. He was referring to the kind of interpersonal ministry he mentioned in 1 Corinthians 14:3: "One who prophesies strengthens others, encourages them, and comforts them." Christians need to be able to hear God—for themselves and for each other—not dictating intrusive guidance but strengthening, encouraging, and comforting. Having contempt for such words is forbidden by Scripture.

Hear God's heart: "You cannot sense My closeness without believing that I speak and minister to you personally. It's impossible to know My touch if you think I only speak generally or have confined My words to the past. Many of My people are starved for My voice today while simultaneously having contempt for anyone who claims to have heard it. Speak it to them anyway. And hear it for yourself. I am speaking to you if you will listen."

Lord, I believe You speak, and I'm listening. Let me hear Your heartbeat. Open my ears. Help me hear Your voice so I can encourage, strengthen, and comfort others, and let me hear it for my own needs.

July 5

God will make this happen, for he who
calls you is faithful.

1 THESSALONIANS 5:24

Paul urged the Thessalonians to live a "blameless" life and, anticipating their sense of futility over such a suggestion, gave them a key to much of the Christian life: "God will make this happen." In any faith endeavor, we need to know this. The God who called us to live in impossibilities will accomplish what He has designed us to do and be.

In our quest for a sense of God's Presence, for becoming a God-carrier in our world, or for any other over-our-head pursuit, we don't have to fear being in over our heads. We always want to know "how," but it's a faith-killing, self-focused question. We look for step-by-step instructions, the key to make it happen, but that's the wrong approach. We ask; He answers. How does He accomplish it? We don't know. We don't have to. The One who called us is faithful, and He will make it happen.

Don't overanalyze this pursuit of God's Presence or any other faith adventure. Just ask to experience Him more, to become sensitive to His voice and His touch, to be an effective vessel filled with Him. When you do that, it becomes His responsibility to get you from point A to point B. The request may seem monumental to you, but you are essentially taking this monumental impossibility from your hands and putting it in His. He will accomplish it. You may not even notice it happening; one day you'll look back and realize how much progress has been made, but you still may have no idea how. The goal is not for you to learn principles for spiritual success; it's for you to trust Him to do what only He can do. And, according to His Word, He will.

Father, I'm trusting You for the process. I'm
believing that You will get me where I need to go,
to do the impossible in my life. All you ask me to
do is dream big, pray big, and watch You work.

July 6

*If you remain in me and my words
remain in you, you may ask for anything
you want, and it will be granted!*

JOHN 15:7

Two single people make decisions and go in directions independently of each other. They may cooperate on certain endeavors or for specific seasons, but they don't need to synchronize their lives permanently. They are unconnected entities. They act individually. Married couples, however, have to be on the same page to function well. They need to make decisions together—to have the same vision, work toward the same goals, dream the same dreams. The more that happens, the more satisfying the relationship is.

Jesus binds us to Himself in a permanent relationship, and for it to function well, we have to have the same agenda He has. When we're operating on our own agendas or focusing on the microscopic details of our lives, our prayer lives can become pretty frustrating. But when we work toward the same goals and dream His dreams, we see Him respond. It isn't that He doesn't care about what's on our hearts; He absolutely does and very often answers our personal prayers. But He does that much more often when His agenda becomes our priority. When we lift up our eyes to see the big picture in His heart, He looks much more favorably at the pictures in our hearts. When we take up His desires, He takes up ours.

This is why fellowship with Him matters. Soaking in His Presence shapes your heart with His desires and brings you in line with His purposes. When that happens, you can "ask for anything you want," and it will be answered. A spirit synchronized with Jesus—joined to Him and saturated in His words—finds Him rising up on its behalf.

*Jesus, the closer I get to You, the more our desires
blend. So bring me close. Surround me with Your
Presence and impart Your heart to me. Then hear
me when I pray my heart out.*

July 7

How long, LORD? Will you forget me forever?
How long will you hide your face from me?

PSALM 13:1, NIV

"Behind a frowning providence He hides a smiling face." Those words from a hymn by William Cowper describe how many of us feel on any given day. There are times when God gives a vision or a promise, attends to it with His Presence and witness and confirmations, and then flees the scene. Or so it seems. He did it with Joseph's dreams and with David's anointing. Either could have questioned the revelation in those long years when circumstances seemed to mock and God seemed painfully absent. Joseph sat in prison while holding a vision of his brothers bowing before him, and David hid from Saul in caves while holding a vision of the throne. All the while, God's "frowning providence" was hiding His pleasure in them both.

Faith is the evidence of "things we cannot see," according to Hebrews 11:1. If we could see them, we wouldn't be employing faith. So why are we surprised when God leads us down roads on which the fulfillment of His promise is invisible? If He is pleased with faith, and if faith is required to receive a promise, then the evidence of the promise has to hide for a season. Circumstances must contradict it. And we must hold on in assurance that what God has spoken is true.

We seek the Presence of God in every situation, but don't be surprised when He hides His face for a time. We may go through trials that mock our faith, but God is smiling behind those situations. He is pleased with our endurance and our insistence on His trustworthiness. The answer to the psalmist's question—"How long will you hide your face from me?"—is "not forever." His absence is for a moment, but His Presence is eternal.

Lord, I don't want to be presumptuous, but unless
You clearly direct otherwise, I choose to hang on to
what I believe You have said. No matter what my
circumstances say, I know You smile at me.

July 8

As the waters fill the sea, the earth will be filled
with an awareness of the glory of the LORD.

HABAKKUK 2:14

Scripture is filled with majestic, sweeping verses like this one. Some of them envision nations streaming to Jerusalem for worship or every knee bowing before Jesus. Many portray a level of victory for God's Kingdom that, in light of the headlines we read, seems hopelessly far-fetched. So what do we do? We take the really good promises and defer them to that "one day" after Jesus comes back—the millennial kingdom or the heavenly city. We modify an old adage with a spiritual twist: "If something seems too good to be true, it probably is—this side of heaven."

We've been conditioned not to believe extravagantly. We've been disappointed too often, even by other Christians and our own perceptions of God. So if an extravagant declaration from Scripture doesn't seem realistic to us, we assume it belongs in another age. The problem is that in doing so with something God plans for this age, we forfeit any meaningful participation in it. To be specific, we don't pursue greater manifestations of His glory because we don't believe He will give them now. In our beliefs, we default to the status quo.

Do you really want to experience God? Then have a big vision—a vision that honors what He has said prophetically and that fits His heart for the world. Small visions don't capture His heart and don't reflect who He is. He doesn't fill nearsighted hearts with faith because they don't really need it. But those who lift up their eyes and envision God's victories in this world will find His strong support within and around them. His Presence accompanies His agenda.

Father, I not only want to see Your glory fill me, I want
to see it fill the earth. Increase my vision to believe such
things and to pursue them. In my lifetime, let me see
Your Kingdom advance in ways I never imagined.

July 9

As they flew, their wings sounded to me like waves crashing against the shore or like the voice of the Almighty or like the shouting of a mighty army. When they stopped, they let down their wings. As they stood with wings lowered, a voice spoke from beyond the crystal surface above them.

EZEKIEL 1:24-25

Ezekiel saw a vision of wheels, majestic angelic creatures, and the glory of the Lord. The wings of the living beings sounded like crashing waves or a vast army in this awe-inspiring scene. The sights and sounds of cosmic activity must have been terrifying for a lone human prophet. But when the Lord was ready to speak, there was a holy hush. The creatures lowered their wings and stood in silence. All was still and quiet.

That immense picture is played out in various ways in human life too. The cacophony of our lives can turn any scene into a seeming chaos—sights and sounds begging for our attention and demanding our energy. The difference (other than the enormous scale of the heavenly vision) is that when God is ready to speak, few people "let down their wings" and stand in silent stillness waiting for the voice that matters. As much as people look, few really see.

Think about it: the scene Ezekiel saw is still going on. The mysterious living creatures still exist. Their wings still make deafening noises. Wheels still turn. The Lord still sits enthroned on clouds and speaks. Be like the prophet and know those scenes. Sense the sacred moments that call for stillness. In the Spirit, you live in spectacles like this. Why? Because you have been born of this Spirit who can overwhelm the hearts of mortals. You are invited to envision divine glimpses like this. Accept the invitation and see what He reveals.

God, when I envision what the prophet saw, I'm overwhelmed with the mystery of it all. Yet this is You—Your throne, Your lightning and thunder, Your environment. I choose to enter in. Open my spirit to be in awe of You.

July 10

Don't be afraid, for I am with you. Don't be discouraged, for I am your God. I will strengthen you and help you. I will hold you up with my victorious right hand.

ISAIAH 41:10

As our relationship with God deepens, we hear His voice more and more clearly. That's an amazing privilege, but it's also a weighty responsibility. Why? Because when we believe we've heard direction from Him, we have to choose whether to follow it or not, even when it seems risky or potentially embarrassing. Once we hear, we can't remain neutral. And when we follow in faith, faith gets tested. Delays and adverse circumstances seem to mock our beliefs and our resolve. The tests can be fierce.

God is with us in these tests. When He has spoken, we need encouragement to believe. In adversity and delays, we will face doubts, obstacles, wise-sounding but uninformed counsel, temptations to give up, and much discouragement. That's when He tells us, "Don't be afraid . . . don't be discouraged . . . I will strengthen you." God promises victory to those who endure, so He gives us enough strength—usually just enough so faith is still required—to keep us going. He wants us to succeed and not give up.

In the walk of faith, we can't afford to doubt, worry, fear, or complain—the very symptoms that kept a generation of Israelites out of their Promised Land. All of these attitudes severely undermine God's work on our behalf, not because He can't do whatever He wants but because He has chosen to relate to us on the basis of our faith. Negative attitudes and words undermine faith. They devalue the very currency we have to use in God's Kingdom. Wherever God's voice and your faith are leading you, do not be afraid or dismayed.

Lord, if I've misheard You, I'll trust You to correct me. But until You do, I'm hanging on in faith. I reject doubt, fear, worry, and complaining. I won't give up.

July 11

The LORD must wait for you to come to him so he can show you his love and compassion. For the LORD is a faithful God. Blessed are those who wait for his help.

ISAIAH 30:18

Imagine the heart of a father whose runaway daughter is wandering the city. The girl is making reckless decisions, bowing to addictions, squandering the love of those who truly care for her, and offering herself to those who don't. The father knows the horrors of the street, and he grieves constantly. But his love isn't diminished at all. He stands ready to throw his arms around her the second she returns.

God portrays Himself in Scripture as just such a Father—one who isn't alienated by even the worst decisions we've made. Like any good father, He grieves for our self-inflicted wounds and the pain they cause, but He doesn't turn His back on us. He waits for us to return. Why? Not so He can rebuke us but so He can show His deep love.

God wants to show His love. A lot of people aren't convinced of that, but Isaiah's words are clear. Having made a move toward us, He waits for us to make a move in response toward Him so He can pour out His heart on us. And not only does He *wait* to do so, the sense of the original language is that He *longs* to do so. It's His passion. He is standing by in anticipation of our response.

Don't assume you're the only one waiting in your relationship with God. He might be waiting on you, too—not to measure up but to turn your heart more fully in His direction. Many of us "live on the streets" spiritually, catering to our habits and giving ourselves to unworthy loves. But He longs for us to engage fully with Him. When we do, He shows us the depths of His love.

Father, I want to respond to You fully and give You no cause to wait on me. Let me feel Your passion and experience Your love.

July 12

*Why was no one there when I came? Why
didn't anyone answer when I called? Is it
because I have no power to rescue?*

ISAIAH 50:2

Think of how you would feel if, in spite of your long history of faithful devotion, a loved one refused to trust you. How would you interpret his or her
suspicious suggestions that perhaps you aren't reliable or fears that you might
have harmful intentions? What if you had always demonstrated great skill and
power yet were treated as incapable of handling difficult situations? The slan-
der of your character, however unintentional, would hurt. When someone
mistrusts you for no reason, you take it personally.

This is how we often treat God. Despite repeated assurances that He
loves us, is taking care of us, will keep His promises, and is mighty to save, it
can take a long time for those truths to sink into our hearts. That's because
we come from a background of being alienated from Him, and it takes time
to adjust to the Kingdom culture. We can somewhat attribute our difficulty
in trusting God to the fact that He's invisible, but that isn't the whole story.
We have epic battles with trust in part because of our old nature and in part
because of our current spiritual enemy. Meanwhile, the most reliable Person
in the universe waits for us to have confidence in Him.

God responds to trust. His Presence seems to accompany a heart that has
chosen to have confidence in Him regardless of contrary appearances. He is
not too weak to save, even when a desperate situation lingers and tempts you
to believe otherwise. Whatever obstacles stand in the way of your trust today,
choose trust anyway. God takes that attitude personally too, and He loves it.

*Lord, I trust You. Forgive me if my lack of
trust has hurt Your heart. No matter what, I
choose to place my confidence in You.*

I will give them hearts that recognize me as the LORD. They will be my people, and I will be their God, for they will return to me wholeheartedly.

JEREMIAH 24:7

Imagine a man whose true love doesn't yet know or care that he longs for her. He's certain they will be married one day, but in the meantime, he feels the pain of her indifference. She seeks other loves, ignores his signs of affection, and lives as though he is largely irrelevant. In the depths of his love, he watches and waits. And his heart aches.

God portrays Himself that way in Scripture. This God who is entirely self-sufficient describes Himself in terms of a man who loves and waits. He longs to share Himself with those who can appreciate Him, but they often don't recognize Him or realize how perfectly He fits their desires and needs. Though they look elsewhere for fulfillment, one day they will see Him as "the One." But for now, He observes their futile search and longs to enjoy their affections.

God will impart His heart to us if we ask Him to. He will stoke the flames of love within us and cause us to recognize Him for who He is. Even as He waits for us to catch on to the fact that we are deeply loved, He will begin to win us over. Our love may develop slowly, but His doesn't. He knows our hearts will eventually find their true home in Him.

Don't underestimate God's emotional investment in your relationship with Him. He isn't casual about you. The more you realize that and return His affections, the quicker and deeper your spiritual life will progress. Your heart will be fulfilled in the relationship—and so will His.

Lord, give me a heart that recognizes who You are, not just on the surface but in deeply personal ways. I want You to be fully satisfied with my love for You and for me to be fully satisfied in Your love for me.

July 14

What I always feared has happened to me.
What I dreaded has come true.

JOB 3:25

It's a strange statement that could be taken a couple of ways. Does Job mean that he feared disaster and, coincidentally, it happened just as he feared? Or is he saying that his fears had cause-and-effect implications? If the latter, all those warnings in Scripture about fear, worry, doubt, and grumbling suddenly become much more profound. That would mean the Bible isn't just encouraging us to cheer up; it's telling us that our attitude is a statement of faith that has consequences. If we are thinking negatively even when God has spoken positively, we are agreeing in faith to an unholy agenda. And that faith is unfortunately rewarded.

We could put this in psychological terms and say that those fears, worries, doubts, and complaints tend to pick up steam and send us on a downward spiral into more of the same. But this dynamic seems so much more powerful than psychology alone. There's a spiritual dynamic. Our attitudes actually seem to open doors into our lives for a spiritual presence. When we agree with God's words and ways, we invite Him further into our lives. When we agree with an unholy perspective, we invite something altogether different.

Refuse to give any ground to fears and doubts and all related contradictions to God's heart. We can't afford to express faith in the enemy's plans, which is often what these attitudes amount to. God attends to attitudes, words, and actions that line up with His revealed truth. His Presence is strong when we think like Him. So when Scripture says, "Do not fear," take the warning seriously. And the same for doubts, worries, discontentment, and self-pity. Agreeing with God in all things opens the door for His Presence and power.

Lord, I don't want to agree with any unholy
agendas, even if unintentionally through my fears
and doubts. I want to agree with You. Please accept
my faith as an invitation to enter my life more
fully and accomplish Your plans with power.

July 15

Because of your faith, it will happen.
MATTHEW 9:29

The things that Job feared came upon him. The things believed by the blind men (mentioned in Matthew 9:27-30) came upon them. Though the correlation is never exact and there may be lots of variables involved, there seems to be a general trend: God honors what we believe. If we feed our minds with fears, those fears can torment us and open the door to influences we don't want. If we feed our hearts with faith, our faith is fulfilled.

That means that if we ask God for a deeper relationship with Him, a heightened sense of His Presence, supernatural experiences with His power, and answers to the prayers He has put within our hearts and we still think and act as if those things will never happen, they may very well not. But if we ask those things believing that God will accomplish them, He responds to our faith. To put it another way, God's Presence seems to attend to those attitudes and actions that place full confidence in Him. He doesn't seem to respond to those attitudes and actions that don't.

Cast your faith unreservedly on God—on the promises He has made, on the calling He has put in your heart, on the Spirit who is working within you to shape your desires and guide your actions for His good pleasure. When you believe, you are inviting Him into your circumstances. When you don't, you are shutting the door to Him. As someone who trusts Him to inhabit you, you can't afford to vacillate between fear and faith, having a divided heart that doesn't know what to expect from Him. Expect Him to do what He said. Trust His promise to be with you and work on your behalf. He responds "because of your faith."

Jesus, You love faith because it honors You for who You are. I want my attitudes to reflect You well. Help me. Impart Your faith to me. Let me be a believer who actually believes.

The jailer woke up to see the prison doors wide open. He assumed the prisoners had escaped, so he drew his sword to kill himself. But Paul shouted to him, "Stop! Don't kill yourself! We are all here!"

ACTS 16:27-28

Paul and Silas had been beaten and held overnight in prison, but God shook the earth, the doors opened, and the prisoners' chains fell off. This was their moment of escape—a "get out of jail free" card, divinely delivered. But even though God was manifestly present and working in the situation, obviously arranging the release of His servants, Paul stayed. Why? Because he saw the bigger picture of God's work. God was not only present to save Paul, He was present to save a Philippian jailer and perhaps many more people. Paul considered himself free to go with the flow, not to run.

That's what happens when the Presence becomes our highest priority. All other priorities play a smaller part in our lives. Crisis situations become opportunities for God to manifest Himself in the crisis. We see them as catalyst events for encounters with those who need to see Him. It's true that the Presence benefits us in amazing ways, but there's almost always a bigger picture at play. Whatever God is doing *in* us, He is also setting the stage to do something *through* us. When we really believe that, we are free to go with the flow of His Spirit.

Is there a crisis blowing up around you today? Are you being pressed in a hard place? You may be tempted to flee, especially if God provides a legitimate way of escape. But before you do, look around and see what He is doing in the situation. Has He strategically positioned you for a big-picture purpose? Is He present within you for the sake of those around you? Ask Him, and keep your eyes open. And be free to go with the flow.

Lord, what are You doing in this situation? What do You want to do through me? I'm open to whatever You want to accomplish.

July 17

God loved the world so much that he
gave his one and only Son.
JOHN 3:16

Imagine loving someone with heart-bursting intensity—from afar. All you want to do is pour out your love, but you aren't even able to be close to that person. You want to express deep affection and experience the joys of passion, but there's a gap making such intimacy impossible. Your heart, longing to give, is frustrated.

That's a picture of God's love. What other kind of love would say, "Yes, this is worth the brutal death of My beloved Son"? No one makes such a sacrifice for a casual, take-it-or-leave-it companionship. God would not have done what He did for the sake of moderate affections. The intensity of His sacrifice reflects the intensity of His passion. When Jesus said in John 3:16 that God was offering His Son for love, He was making a powerful claim. The divine agenda was to bridge the gap between the Lover and the beloved at all costs. God's heart beats for closeness.

Lost in the familiarity of this verse and its promise of eternal life for those who believe is God's motivation. He loved the world so much that He made an enormous sacrifice. And while that truth applies globally, it also applies personally. God loves *you* with such passion that He paid an incomprehensible price to get close to you.

That God's heart beats for closeness—specifically with you—implies an invitation. Offer love back to Him, not as an obligation but as a delight, and expect Him to reveal more of His heart to you. Take full advantage of the price He paid to share His love.

Father, thank You for pouring out Your love on me.
I want to pour my heart out to You too. I want all
the closeness made possible by Your sacrifice.

July 18

The eyes of the LORD search the whole earth
in order to strengthen those whose hearts
are fully committed to him.

2 CHRONICLES 16:9

The words were spoken to someone who didn't fit God's criteria, but they still invite a response from those who will. God isn't looking for those who have behaved perfectly, or for those who have discovered His principles for life, or for those who impress Him with their achievements. He looks for those whose hearts are devoted—those who seek Him, trust Him, and love Him. He searches for those like David, who, in spite of their flaws, are continually running in His direction. And when He finds them, He rises up to support them.

The image of God's eyes looking back and forth throughout the earth is a startling one. Why is He searching? Why does this God seem to care so much? Does He just need servants who will do what He says? No, He wants those who will recognize Him for who He is—His strength and love and wisdom—and who will relate to Him on that basis. He searches for those who see dire circumstances, hear of His faithfulness, and choose to trust the truth of the latter over the power of the former. He longs for those who will believe Him and love Him. He is always trying to cultivate relationship.

When people ask, "Why doesn't God do something?" this is sometimes the reason. We can be reluctant to trust, slow to fully commit, hesitant to invest ourselves with reckless abandon. But that's exactly what God is looking for—those who will abandon themselves to Him. He strongly supports those who do.

Lord, I don't want Your eyes to look past me. I
want to have one of those hearts You stop to gaze
at. I devote myself completely to You and trust that
You will show me Your strong support.

July 19

Take delight in the LORD . . .

PSALM 37:4

We love the last half of this verse. The first half isn't bad either; we just don't fully understand what it means. How exactly do we "delight" in the Lord? We serve Him, believe in Him, even love Him. But delight? Most of us don't get chill bumps and rapid heartbeats about God for more than a few moments at a time. It isn't always pure pleasure.

If our relationship with God isn't full of delight, then we have some misperceptions about Him. Perhaps we assume He's down on us for not measuring up to His high standards, or maybe we resent that He didn't seem to answer that desperate prayer we prayed. We might have interpreted His apparent distance as a lack of love, or His words as a system of sterile doctrine. But if we really saw Him for who He is—the beauty of His face or the majesty and mystery of His throne room—we would be completely captivated. If we truly understood His purposes and the love behind His ways, we would be profoundly grateful.

The rewards for delighting in the Lord are appealing, but in many ways the delight is a reward in itself. If you push past the false assumptions and ask to see Him as He is, He will completely capture your imagination. The intrigue of a relationship with Him, with all His passion and zeal, makes for a fascinating adventure. No one can be bored in His Presence. He urges us to delight in Him because He is worthy of our delight.

Lord, break through my false assumptions about You. I want to see You as You are. Capture my imagination. Fill my heart with delight. Thrill me with the joy of knowing You.

July 20

We are drawn to those who love us, and we enjoy doing things for them. In fact, we go out of our way to please those who express affection for us. So does God. He responds to our affection for Him with signs of His affection for us.

Those who delight in God—who turn their hearts toward Him and enjoy His Presence, regardless of the trials and contradictions in their lives—notice an unusual phenomenon. Their desires begin to be fulfilled. Part of the reason for that is that when we are saturated in love for God, His Spirit can shape our desires. He plants His desires within us. But another reason is that when our hearts are drawn to Him, He is drawn to us. He rises up to defend and provide for those who have enjoyed His intimacy.

This is why Jesus tells His disciples that if they remain united to Him and His words thrive in them, they can ask any request they want and He will do it for them (John 15:7). God doesn't just impose His sovereign will on those who love Him. Our desires affect Him. He interacts with us at the level of our longings. He shapes who we are and then trusts us to desire worthwhile things. Then He supports those desires and fulfills them.

However this extravagant promise functions, the result is that our desires and His answers line up. We no longer live in futility and frustration with our longings remaining perpetually unfulfilled. Somehow our pleasure in God results in His pleasure in fulfilling the matters on our hearts.

Father, in spite of all my questions, and in spite of whatever contradictions my faith experiences, I delight in who You are. My relationship with You is my highest priority. Shape my heart, fill me with Your desires, and let me experience satisfaction and fulfillment.

July 21

While the harp was being played, the power
of the LORD came upon Elisha.

2 KINGS 3:15

The kings of Israel, Judah, and Edom went out with their armies together to quell a rebellion by Moab, but when they got into the wilderness, they realized there was no water for their troops. The king of Israel panicked and assumed God had abandoned them, but Jehoshaphat, the king of Judah, wanted to inquire of the Lord. So the kings went to consult with the prophet Elisha. And when Elisha finally agreed to listen to God's voice for them, he began with an unusual request: he called for a harpist.

Why did Elisha need a harpist in order to hear from God? Because the Lord's Presence can often be experienced in music—or any other creative expression—far more easily than in an analytical, deductive approach. The Lord speaks to the heart, or to our right-brained, intuitive side, more often than to our logical, skeptical side. As mathematician Blaise Pascal once said, "The heart has its reasons that reason cannot know." God's Spirit seems to connect with us at a creative, imaginative level. His power comes upon those who can perceive Him without having to analyze Him.

So Elisha heard the Lord better when a harpist was playing—when music was activating his spiritual perceptions. And we can hear Him better that way too. Experiencing God requires some level of creative aptitude, or at least a willingness to know Him beyond our own understanding or explanations. He stretches us to the point that we must embrace Him intuitively, subjectively, and instinctively. When we're open to that, He opens up to us.

Lord, sensitize me to Your Presence—in me and around
me. Awaken my heart to know when You are speaking
creatively and subjectively to me. Free me to experience
You any way You want to be experienced.

*I will climb up to my watchtower and
stand at my guardpost. There I will wait
to see what the LORD says.*

HABAKKUK 2:1

Habakkuk wanted to "see" what God would say. John also "turned to see the voice that spoke" (Revelation 1:12, NKJV). Both knew that God's language is often visual, and they kept their eyes open for messages from Him. They heard by watching.

Habakkuk also heard by positioning himself. He climbed up in his watchtower and waited. He understood that God's voice rarely comes to those who aren't vigilant enough to hear it or to those who aren't patient enough to wait for it. God allows us to experience Him, but not if we're casual about the prospect. In preparing people to encounter Him, He filters out those who are halfhearted—the spiritual dilettantes among us who are more interested in the things of God than in God Himself. Some people seem to have the attitude that if God wants to speak, He knows their address and will find a way to get their attention. And while God has in some situations manifested His Presence to people who weren't looking for Him, that isn't His preference. He honors our level of hunger. When we climb up into our watchtower and wait, He eventually speaks.

Don't make the mistake of thinking Habakkuk is an exception among God's people. It's true that Old Testament prophets were somewhat rare, but God wants to speak to everyone. Scripture implies that God and His chosen servants call all people to some degree of prophetic insight (Numbers 11:29; 1 Corinthians 14:5). The living Word wants to be heard by those who have ears to hear Him. And those who set themselves apart for Him, wait, and listen are apt to recognize His voice. Those who seek will find.

*Lord, I seek Your face. I'm desperate to hear Your
voice. I'm watching to see what You will say, and
I will wait as long as necessary to hear You. Help
me position myself favorably—in vigilance and
patience—and let me encounter You.*

July 23

*If the LORD is with us, why has all this
happened to us? And where are all the
miracles our ancestors told us about?*

JUDGES 6:13

Gideon was focused on what God hadn't done—at least what He hadn't done recently. He hadn't kept Israel from being oppressed by Midian, He hadn't performed any dramatic miracles, He hadn't delivered His people. Yet. So when God came to his cowering servant, Gideon did as any skeptic does. He asked if/then questions and assumed God hadn't been with Israel.

That's a common train of thought, but it isn't a good one. And God's answer to Gideon is the same one he gives us in our skepticism: "Go with the strength you have" (v. 14). He turns our focus away from what's lacking and puts it on what we have. Just as the disciples saw a hungry crowd and Jesus saw two loaves and five fish, we tend to emphasize the evidence that God isn't at work—or perhaps that He doesn't even exist—while God emphasizes what He has done. In matters of faith, we have to have a glass-half-full perspective, not a focus on the emptiness that remains.

This is an essential truth to grasp if we want to experience God's Presence. As long as we're asking why He wasn't there when that crisis happened or that mistake was made, we won't see Him. But if we focus on all the reminders He gives us that He's there, we'll notice Him more and more. His Presence—along with His provision, miracles, and comfort—will become a regular experience. Faith chooses what to see and then sees it.

Refuse to look at all the ways you think God hasn't been there for you. Instead, look at all the ways He has. Then you can go into your day in the strength you have, knowing He's there to empower, deliver, and defend.

*Lord, my perceptions haven't judged You well. Thank
You for all You have done, and help me now focus
only on what You have said You will do.*

July 24

Be still, and know that I am God.

PSALM 46:10, NIV

Sometimes in Scripture, God wants us to stand still and see His salvation—to simply receive. Other times, He tells His people to move forward, to take a step in faith. Both are legitimate scriptural approaches. But He never tells us to allow our insecurities, doubts, and anxieties to drive us obsessively into the future. We can't seize our destiny on our own, and we can't receive the fulfillment of God's promises restlessly or by striving. Yes, we may wrestle with Him, endure, and persist in faith, but in the end we have to depend entirely on His strength. We experience Him and His provision by resting in who He is.

The place of God's Presence is a place of stillness. When we know who God is—not just intellectually, but in our core—we have the peace that passes understanding. We know His will is good and His power is able to carry it out, and we're fine with however He works it all out. We're able to calm down, stop striving, and rest in Him. It may be an active, intentional rest, but it's still rest.

How do we get to that place? By choice, for one thing. We simply decide to believe in His wisdom, power, and love. But it also helps to focus on the words that follow this verse. God *will* be exalted in the nations, on the earth, and even in our own lives and circumstances. It's guaranteed. And in whatever we go through, "the LORD Almighty is with us" (v. 11, NIV). As always, His Presence is the key. If we really believe that, if it really sinks down into our hearts, if we live in that place of knowing and sensing the Presence, the peace comes. We can take a deep breath, be still, and know that He is God.

Lord, my heart is restless. I worry. I know You're on Your throne, but I don't know what You're going to do. Help me trust—and give me rest—in who You are.

*Just as our bodies have many parts and
each part has a special function, so it is with
Christ's body. We are many parts of one body,
and we all belong to each other.*

ROMANS 12:4-5

We often experience God's Presence in privacy with Him—those moments of solitude when we're able to pull away from other people and focus on Him alone. But there are sides of Him we can't experience unless we encounter them through others. He shows His compassion through one and His joy through someone else; His patience in the ministry of one fellow believer and His zeal in the face of another. In the same way we need others to experience all the spiritual gifts, so we need others to see each face of God. He never fully expresses Himself through one person, other than Jesus. He spreads Himself abroad so we'll have to encounter Him in fellowship.

The reason for this is clear: God wants us together, not in isolation. If there are aspects of His character we can only get from someone else, we are compelled to seek unity and remain in fellowship. The body functions as a coordinated body. We get a clear picture of His unconditional love when a human being loves us unconditionally, or a glimpse of His power when an average person is supernaturally empowered. Our desire for Him keeps us seeking the treasures in each other.

Even though the body of Christ doesn't always live up to that ideal, learn the importance of fellowship. You'll never be able to fully experience God in isolation. Recognize that you and other believers are carriers of His Presence. In coming together, you offer each other a taste of His character and personality. Understanding that truth will make fellowship a sacred experience and will unveil God's Presence in surprising ways.

*Lord, I love our private times, but I know You
show Yourself through others—that there are
some things I can't get from You unless I get them
through other people. Let me see Your Presence in
each believer I meet, and help me be a careful and
intentional bearer of Your Presence for others.*

July 26

*I saw a throne in heaven and
someone sitting on it.*
REVELATION 4:2

A college professor once told me, "Who knows? Maybe heaven is boring."
His misperception was illogical—why would an amazingly creative God surround Himself with tedium?—but it's also common. Many people think of
white clouds, angels singing in predictable four-four time, and King James
English as the only acceptable tongue. No passion, no adventure, no exciting
pleasures. Just an eternal state of uneventful peace.

Any perception that God's Presence is boring or in any way less than
exhilarating is misguided. That kind of deception comes from only one place,
and it keeps people from seeking the one Person who can fully satisfy and
excite them. Though God's Presence can calm a troubled heart, it can really
stir up a complacent one.

Revelation 4 tells us what's going on in God's environment, and it's
thrilling to think that this scene is playing out *right now*. At this moment in an
unseen realm, lightning flashes and thunder booms around God's throne. Intense colors dance around Him, elders and angels cry out loudly, and bizarre,
intriguing creatures stand beside Him. It's a sensory overload for mortals like
us who are accustomed to an earthly environment, even for those of us who
have enjoyed Hollywood's most impressive special effects. What's normal for
God would be an overwhelming, heart-pounding experience for us.

If you're stagnating, ask God for more excitement in your relationship
with Him. There's nothing wrong with wanting more enjoyment in that
relationship. Life can be hard, and God's ways can be confusing, but He still
wants you to experience His joy. Glimpses of His electrifying surroundings
are available for those who seek them.

*Lord, I want more excitement with You. I want
to experience the thrill of Your Presence—for my
spiritual senses to perceive the glorious commotion
around Your throne. Let my heart beat faster when
You draw near and let me feel the heartbeat of the
creatures who worship in Your Presence.*

July 27

Let all that I am praise the Lord; with my
whole heart, I will praise his holy name.

PSALM 103:1

If you were God—and granted, the suggestion takes some imagination and a sense of reverence—to whom would you reveal yourself most clearly? To those with a scattered focus? To those with an I'll-believe-it-when-I-see-it attitude? To those with a halfhearted interest? No, it's much easier to imagine offering deeper intimacy to those who come with a whole heart—who bring every crack and corner of their soul into the relationship. That's who will treasure a deep relationship most.

In human relationships, we give ourselves more fully to those who have given themselves more fully to us. God, an intensely relational God, is the same. Fragmented hearts receive a fragmented experience, but a whole heart receives a whole experience of God. If we scatter our affections abroad—a little of this or that treasure with God added on—we'll know God at some level, but not as fully as we could. Though He loves all of us, He opens His heart to us in direct proportion to our desire for Him.

That's why David determined to praise God with a whole heart. Saul before him had come to God without much heart at all, and Solomon, his son, would display a highly fragmented heart later. But David knew that God was worthy of a complete investment of his soul, and he knew he would experience God accordingly. Throwing everything into the relationship, he received everything in return. He enjoyed the benefits of knowing God deeply.

If your relationship with God seems to be falling short of your expectations or desire, ask yourself how divided your heart is. That isn't always the reason for disappointment, but it often is. Then resolve to invest everything—every impulse of your heart—into seeking Him.

Lord, my heart is easily divided and scattered among
other interests. And You even support our interests, but
not when they overshadow You. Help me seek You
above all else—and enjoy You above all else.

July 28

*May I never forget the good things
he does for me.*

PSALM 103:2

Surrounded by self-serving Christianity, many believers have determined to
worship God for who He is, not for what He does. The desire is admirable,
but the practice isn't really possible. Nor is it biblical. For one thing, we only
know God by the works He has done. We call Him Deliverer because He has
actually delivered people, for example, or Provider because He has actually
provided—not because of abstract theology. But in addition to knowing Him
in the context of His actions, it's entirely biblical to praise Him for what He
has done. David's statement in verse 2 clearly expresses a desire to praise God
for His benefits.

And those benefits are many. He promises to forgive sins, heal diseases,
ransom us from death, surround us with mercy and good things, renew our
youth, and defend us with righteousness and justice (vv. 3-6). God never tells
us to ignore the blessings of His Presence in order to focus on His Person. It's
true that we can become preoccupied *only* with His blessings and treat Him as
our heavenly Santa Claus, but an equally troubling error is to become so "spiritual" that we neglect what He has offered. His Presence is meant to benefit
us in a multitude of ways. He knows we're needy and meets us in our need.

What needs do you have today? Seek God's Presence for His ability to
meet those needs. Certainly seek Him for more than that, but know that He
enjoys opportunities to provide, deliver, comfort, heal, redeem, restore, empower, and more. He wants to help you, not just in your spiritual growth but
also in your practical circumstances. Know Him for who He is—but never
forget the good things He does for you.

*Father, I enjoy Your blessings, and I know it's okay to
seek them. I want You for more than those, of course; I
need You, not just Your gifts. But I do need Your gifts and
Your help. Please let me fully experience Your benefits.*

July 29

His unfailing love toward those who fear him is as great as the height of the heavens above the earth.

PSALM 103:11

Few people have experienced relentless love in human relationships. Even those who have experienced it realize that human love often springs from mixed motives or unhealthy emotional needs. But pure, selfless, extravagant, passionate, unbending love is hard to comprehend. We've seen few, if any, examples of it.

So when we're told about God's unfailing love—and how high and deep and wide it is—we often nod our heads in agreement while our hearts remain untouched. It isn't that we don't believe it. We just don't *feel* it. It becomes an intellectual solution for us rather than a warm embrace. Meanwhile, the God whose love is bigger than we can imagine looks for hearts that can receive Him.

How can the power of God's love make the journey from our heads to our hearts? Not by better reasoning and analysis, nor by repetition of the verses that describe it, nor by more explanations and understanding. Mental processes do little for the heart; they further establish things in our minds. The only way we can know this kind of love is through spiritual and emotional processes, through experience, through the kind of faith that can accept truths the mind can't understand. And the only way for any of these things to happen is not by self-effort but by receiving them from God.

Step one in almost everything in the Christian life is to ask for it. Religion gives us step-by-step instructions, but in a relationship, we experience life and all its blessings by simply receiving. Don't strive to understand God's love; accept it. Ask for a greater revelation of it. Embrace it as true even if your mind objects. According to God's Word, His love will always be greater than we can understand.

Lord, I don't understand Your love, but I know it's true. I know I'm deeply loved beyond my comprehension. I choose to soak in it. As I do, please let it become more and more real to me.

July 30

*He has removed our sins as far from us
as the east is from the west.*

PSALM 103:12

We are sinners saved by grace. We know that. It's the underlying truth we embraced when we came into the Kingdom. But many of us remain there, with that descriptor as our identity. It's always our current status. We forget to move on to "child of the King" or "co-inheritor with Jesus" or "ruling with Him from His throne." All of these descriptors are biblical too, but we can remain so conscious of our sinfulness that we never feel empowered to rise above it. We depend on the fact that we are saved without realizing we are saved for a great purpose.

We need to understand that salvation isn't the ultimate objective. Salvation is the entrance into the Kingdom, not the final result. When we're born physically, we enter a life full of promise and destiny. But many of us don't see the same dynamic in being born again. We're like babies constantly celebrating our birth rather than looking ahead to the great Kingdom exploits we're called to do. And one of the main reasons for that shortsightedness is an obsessive focus on the darkness and death from which we were redeemed rather than the light and life into which we have been brought.

God's Presence brings life. God doesn't hold our sins in front of our faces and constantly remind us where we came from. He removes them as far as the east is from the west, presumably too far for us to hang on to them. We can be grateful for God's grace and remember why we needed it, but God doesn't want us dwelling on our sin. He wants us to enjoy Him, adventures in His Kingdom, and victories over His enemies. And He sent our sins so far away that we can.

*Lord, thank You for the freedom of not having to think
about my sin anymore. Thank You for the invitation to
enjoy life in Your Kingdom, safe and secure in Your love.*

July 31

He knows how weak we are; he remembers we are only dust.

PSALM 103:14

A parent's heart is moved by the scrapes and bruises a toddler gets while learning to walk. Or by the tears that flow when a child is the only one not to get an invitation to the party. Or by the lasting hardship that may result from a young person's unwise decisions. Life can be unyielding in the way it imposes the law of reaping what we sow. In His mercy, God is not.

The psalmist David has just described God as a tender and compassionate Father, mostly in the context of how He deals with our sins and flaws. In that or any other hardship of life, God is on our side. He offers us mercy, waits for us patiently, and sent us a Savior who can sympathize with our weaknesses. He looks on us with understanding about our frailties. He condemns persistent rebellion but not consistent failures. He hates willful pride but meets us in our weakness. When we read of His wrath in Scripture, it's always directed at those who have arrogantly chosen to shun Him, not those who have made mistakes or who are trying but falling short. God is slow to anger and willing to help us overcome.

God's Presence gives us a sense of acceptance, comfort, and encouragement. His Spirit may also convict us of sin, but the purpose is constructive—to help us deal with it correctly, not to condemn us for it. Feeling beaten down and rejected are not signs of His Presence. Futility and frustration are not fruits of His Spirit. When His Presence is strong in us, we will be encouraged and strengthened.

Lord, I need the encouragement of Your Presence. I get discouraged easily, especially over my own shortcomings. But I trust in Your compassion. You know my weaknesses and are patient with me. You strengthen me. Help me reject any spirit that says otherwise and embrace Your compassion.

August 1

*Praise the LORD, you angels, you mighty
ones who carry out his plans, listening
for each of his commands.*

PSALM 103:20

A president's or prime minister's children may act as if they are going out in public on their own, but they have highly trained guardians watching them. These guardians not only specialize in observing and protecting, they also specialize in blending into the background. They do their job without being noticed, but they do it well. They have to; the stakes are very high.

Angels are like God's secret service agents. They are ministering spirits sent to serve those who will receive salvation (Hebrews 1:14). They are messengers and warriors for God's Kingdom agenda. They worship around His throne. They are not only present among us as created beings, they are also agents of the Presence of God. They minister at His command. Wherever He meets needs and encounters His people, they are present to help.

We see this often in biblical thought, where "an angel of the Lord" and "the Lord" were often used almost interchangeably. That's because in ancient Jewish understanding, an angel's task was so perfectly aligned with God's instruction that an encounter with an angel was an encounter with God Himself. God created angels as agents of His own expression. They speak His words, carry out His plans, and listen for His instructions. They are an integral part of His relationship with us.

Why is this important to know? Because God has surrounded us with ministering spirits who carry out His will. We have warriors who battle on our behalf. We aren't simply guarded and guided by an ethereal, amorphous Presence. We are guarded and guided by living beings who manifest the purposes and plans of God. Even when we feel alone, we aren't. God makes sure of it.

*Father, thank You for surrounding me with Your
agents. You haven't left me isolated and abandoned.
You minister to me with Your own hand and Your
own specially assigned creatures. Help me always
remember how well-watched I am.*

August 2

My sheep listen to my voice; I know
them, and they follow me.

JOHN 10:27

You've asked to hear God's voice. You've believed His promise that you can. Still, all you seem to hear are your own thoughts. Maybe some of those thoughts are planted there by God, but you can't be sure. They seem so subjective. So you wonder. And while you hope that's His voice, you can't say so with any confidence.

Does this sound familiar? It's a common battle in the mind. Jesus promised we would hear His voice, then we wonder if we ever have. Occasionally we get some guidance that seems clear, but only when circumstances and convictions converge to the point that we're reasonably sure of God's direction. But to hear an inner voice telling us something specific? We question such subjectivity relentlessly, and our questioning is helped by the fact that we've known people who used the "God told me" rationale a little too often. We usually convince ourselves that the internal voice isn't God's.

We need to remember that God's voice rarely sounds like a booming voice from heaven or even a voice outside of ourselves. Jesus said that the river of living water springs from our innermost being. The Presence is an internal flow of thoughts and ideas. He is constantly speaking to us. We just have to recognize which voice is His.

Don't listen to any thoughts trying to convince you that you don't hear God. Surrender yourself to Him and see what comes through your heart and mind. Be discerning, of course, but don't overanalyze. (True discernment is a function of the spirit; analysis is a function of the brain. The redeemed spirit is qualified to process the things of God's Spirit, but a mental process isn't.) Trust the Spirit within you. When you think it's God's voice, it probably is.

Jesus, I trust You to speak to me. I believe Your promise
of Your Spirit flowing within me. Help me recognize
which internal voice is Yours and follow it faithfully.

August 3

*Around midnight Paul and Silas were
praying and singing hymns to God.*

ACTS 16:25

Paul and Silas had been beaten brutally in a punishment that normally left its victims with broken bones and internal bleeding. But instead of trying to recover in a comfortable bed, they had to spend the night on a stone floor with their feet clamped in stocks designed to inflict further pain. Their response? They prayed and sang hymns loud enough for other prisoners to hear.

The result was an earthquake that shook the prison, broke chains, and opened doors—physically and spiritually. God showed up in power. He heard the worship of His servants and rose up to defend them. He used them to change lives and impact a city.

Would God have showed up as powerfully if Paul and Silas had had a negative attitude during their long, painful night? We don't know. But we do know that God responds in unusual ways to the praises of His people. He defeated a coalition of three armies when Jehoshaphat and Judah's people praised Him in battle, and He responded in such glory when the nation praised Him at Solomon's dedication of the Temple that the priests couldn't even stand up. Whether in peace or under stress, we are in sync with God when we worship Him. And His Presence comes.

Worship creates a pathway for God's Presence and power. Praising Him is like rolling out a red carpet for Him into the middle of your circumstances. Whatever situation you face today will have to bow in His Presence when you bow in His Presence. When you acknowledge the power of God, you acknowledge the impotence of your problems, and God responds to such faith. His Presence accompanies your praise.

*Lord, I choose to worship You in every
circumstance. I know You will respond to my praise,
sometimes visibly and sometimes invisibly. But
either way, Your Presence is real when my heart is
in sync with the truth of Your glory.*

August 4

*With a shriek, he screamed, "Why are
you interfering with me, Jesus, Son of the
Most High God? In the name of God, I
beg you, don't torture me!"*

MARK 5:7

If we really want to know the effects of God's Presence on us, all we need to do is look at Jesus. He, Immanuel, was and is the Presence of God among us. While He walked this earth in the flesh, He was a carrier of the Presence, the incarnation of God Himself. The responses He received tell us a lot about the effects of being in the company of God.

Demons had a common reaction to the Presence: terror. They couldn't stand His nearness. When Jesus commanded them to leave, they had to leave (though usually not without some resistance). But even before He said a word, they recognized Him, and they feared. They equated His Presence with torment. They felt compelled to cry out, to argue that the appointed time of judgment had not yet come, or even to loudly reveal Him as the Son of God before He wanted it known. Their darkness could not survive in His light.

That's one of the great benefits of inviting God's manifest Presence into our lives. Whatever darkness remains, whatever evil we encounter, whatever confusion and despair we struggle with, it has to go when He comes near. It can't stand in His Presence. The more we saturate ourselves in His Spirit, the less any evil influences can affect us. Ungodly spirits may harass us, and old thought patterns may try to recapture us, but a continuing insistence on being "in the Spirit" will give them no hold on us. What was true of Jesus' encounters is true in our lives today: darkness gives way to light.

*Jesus, I want no darkness in my life. I'm tired of
confusing and depressing thoughts, deceptive reasoning,
and all the fatigue and futility that come with them.
I know I don't have to figure it all out; I just need to
invite You to come near. So please, Jesus, come near.*

August 5

They picked up the pieces and filled twelve baskets with scraps left by the people who had eaten from the five barley loaves.

JOHN 6:13

On at least two occasions, Jesus fed hungry multitudes from a paltry stock. No one knows quite how it happened. Even the scriptural accounts simply report the before-and-after and skip over the how. Somehow between breaking a few loaves and blessing a few fish, the amounts grew. Men began handing out the supplies, and they never ran out. The phenomenon would drive an inventory manager crazy. The normal laws of physics and economics were suspended until everyone was fed.

In Jesus' Presence, resources multiply. He is the Lord of abundance, not of the never-quite-enough. It's true that His people sometimes go through lean seasons and that we learn to seek Him and depend on Him in those seasons. But insufficiency is never His end result for us. He is fully able to provide whatever we need whenever we need it.

Sometimes that provision comes at the last minute. From all appearances, the crowds following Jesus were going to have to leave hungry. Neither they nor the disciples knew ahead of time that an abundant supply was coming. Why? Because God strengthens faith by stretching it, and faith isn't stretched when everything is given far in advance. Even so, God does not intend to leave His children lacking. His Presence brings not only fullness of joy but fullness of life. He gives extravagant promises about taking care of us.

What does this mean when you're underemployed? How does it apply when you're hit with a sudden financial crisis? It means you can confidently continue to seek the Provider side of God and expect that, in His Presence, things like time and resources will seem to multiply to fit your needs. God is never in short supply.

*God of provision, let me see Your abundance. As I sit—
and live and work—in Your Presence, multiply my time
and resources. Maximize my efficiency. I'm trusting You
to make a lot out of the little I have to offer.*

August 6

*The blind see, the lame walk, the lepers
are cured, the deaf hear, the dead are
raised to life, and the Good News is being
preached to the poor.*

MATTHEW 11:5

In heaven, where God's Presence is most tangible and obvious, there's no pain. There's no sickness or deafness or blindness. No one is crippled, and certainly no one is dead. Everyone is healthy and whole.

Jesus, God incarnate and filled with the Holy Spirit, carried the environment of heaven with Him during His ministry. In His Presence, sickness and pain had to bow. Blind eyes and deaf ears were opened. Both the disease of leprosy and its stigma were undone. Cripples—and even a few dead people—got up and walked. Wherever He went, circumstances had to recognize His authority.

That ought to tell us something. We often pray for healing for our infirmities, knowing that Jesus has the power to make us healthy and whole. But is it really healing we seek? Or would we be wiser to pray for His Presence? When we pray for healing, He certainly may give it, and we'd be made well and have a wonderful testimony of His power. But if we pray for His Presence, we get more. He makes us well simply by His nearness, but we also get Him—a fuller, more satisfying outcome. A prayer for healing is a prayer for a wonderful gift from God, but a prayer for Presence is a prayer for the God who brings gifts with Him. It's a plea for relationship, which always hits closer to God's heart.

Whatever you need from God, ask for the whole package—His Presence, first and foremost, and then everything that comes with it. Wherever He is, so is the environment of heaven.

*Jesus, I want You and all that You bring. I
know my greatest need isn't the request I'm
asking; it's the Person I'm asking. Please
answer in every way, but mostly with Yourself.*

*The house where he was staying was so
packed with visitors that there was no more
room, even outside the door.*

MARK 2:2

Jesus has a magnetic personality. When He walked this earth, people flocked
to Him—partly because of the powerful things He could do, but also because of their fascination with Him personally. He was intriguing, surprising,
and friendly to many, even those who had few friends. People wanted to be
around Him.

People still do. Well, those who have an accurate perception of who He
is want to be with Him. Some try to stay far away from Him because they
misperceive Him, thinking Him to be cold or pious or a figure only of the
past. But when we see Him rightly, we are drawn. Considering that we were
made for Jesus (Colossians 1:16), it only makes sense that we would be attracted to Him. We have longings planted within us that can be filled only
in Him. The way our hearts ache for fulfillment is all about our need for the
ultimate relationship.

A taste of Jesus' Presence doesn't satisfy us; it only whets our appetite.
Those who think God is boring haven't actually spent much time with Him.
When we sit with Him and sense His nearness, we want more. And according
to His purpose in making us, so does He.

Choose to be one of the people drawn to Jesus simply because of a desire to be with Him. Say yes to every aspect of the relationship. Spend some
time today cultivating closeness. He will find a way to answer, and there is
always room in His Presence now.

*Jesus, if You were in a nearby house today, I would
be in the crowd trying to see You. I have needs
that only You can meet, and I also have desires
that only You can satisfy. Most of all, I want Your
personal touch. Please let me feel it today.*

*Don't imagine that I came to bring peace to the
earth! I came not to bring peace, but a sword.*

MATTHEW 10:34

Jesus, the Prince of Peace, came to reconcile people to God. But when people are reconciled to God, they are simultaneously estranged from their previous influences. That's because unity with Jesus puts us at odds with anything or anyone not aligned with Him. The Prince of Peace is inherently controversial.

Sometimes that controversy occurs within ourselves. At times, the Presence of Jesus makes us restless. Our imperfect thoughts and assumptions are challenged by surprising truth. Our false expectations are dashed by His winding paths or unpredictable plans. Our circumstances often function as persistent contradictions to His promises. And, when we need correction, He has the right and the ability to offend us. The Presence of Jesus can be disorienting.

How do you respond when you sense His correction? What do you think of Him when His actions toward you seem to contradict His words to you? How do you feel when your questions of "why" or "why not" remain unanswered? Jesus pronounced a blessing on those who are not offended by Him (Matthew 11:6), knowing that offenses are common among those who relate to Him. How you respond to those offenses has a lot to do with how consistently you experience Him.

Feel the love of God and be encouraged by His Presence, but also know that He doesn't come to endorse the status quo in our lives. He often comes to rearrange—circumstances, relationships, even our own hearts. Whenever you find yourself in a season of challenge or rearranging, let Him do His uncomfortable work. If we let Him, the restlessness He causes always leads to peace.

*Jesus, I love Your peace, but I accept the conflicts You
create in my life. I know You bring change, and change
can be uncomfortable. Even so, I want the discomfort if it
leads me closer to You and further into Your will.*

August 9

I am leaving you with a gift—peace of mind and heart. And the peace I give is a gift the world cannot give. So don't be troubled or afraid.

JOHN 14:27

One of Jesus' favorite classrooms was the storm-tossed Sea of Galilee. Once He was asleep in the back of the boat when a storm raged and His friends panicked, but He calmly woke up and told the storm to be quiet—and it obeyed. On another occasion, He sent the disciples across the lake ahead of Him, and when they were being tossed around in a dangerous storm, He came to them walking on the water. In both cases, His Presence changed the nature of the crisis. And in both cases, He taught foundational lessons about fear and faith.

This is not an unusual dynamic. Jesus still allows storms in our lives, He continues to teach lessons about fear and faith, and His Presence still changes the nature of the crisis. He comes to us in the midst of a storm—often after He has allowed us to reach a point of panic—and calms us, the storm, or both. He reminds us that faith is the key to overcoming, that fear undermines faith, and that keeping our focus on Him destroys fear and builds faith. He teaches and strengthens us best not when the weather is calm but when the waves are about to overwhelm us.

If you're going through a crisis, remember that this is normal for the Kingdom of God. Nothing is unusual about His children experiencing storms. What *would* be unusual is if He never showed up in them or let them go on longer than necessary. In your crisis, trust that He is aware, He has already timed His entrance, and He will calm it at the perfect time. Meanwhile, trust Him. The storm is designed to teach you how.

Jesus, I hate the storms, but I'm so grateful that You meet me in them. Please don't delay. Strengthen my faith and calm my fears.

August 10

Zacchaeus stood before the Lord and said, "I will give half my wealth to the poor, Lord, and if I have cheated people on their taxes, I will give them back four times as much!"

LUKE 19:8

Zacchaeus had a reputation for greed, corruption, and fraud. Some of that notoriety came with the title of "tax collector," but even he admitted that his reputation was deserved. When he met Jesus, he vowed to give his wealth to the poor and repay more than God's laws of restitution required to those whom he had overtaxed. He stands in stark contrast to the rich young ruler, who met Jesus and decided to hold on to his wealth. Zacchaeus encountered Jesus and wanted to let go of everything else.

The elders around the throne of God couldn't even hold on to their crowns in the glory of the Presence. How much more difficult it is to hold on to our sins—or even our less-offensive attachments—when we encounter God. If the rich young ruler had truly recognized who Jesus was, he would have gladly let go of his relatively worthless treasures. When we know we are truly in the Presence of God, everything else fades. As an old hymn says, "The things of earth will grow strangely dim in the light of His glory and grace."

We pray for purity and wholehearted passion, but as is often the case, that's a prayer for an outcome rather than a relational dynamic that produces the outcome. Why not pray for a deeper encounter with Him, a growing sense of His nearness? The purity and passion will take care of themselves when we see Him for who He is.

Jesus, help me see You more clearly and sense You more fully. I want pure and deep devotion to You, and I know Your Presence will provoke it in me. Please draw near, Lord.

August 11

Seeing their faith, Jesus said to the paralyzed
man, "My child, your sins are forgiven."

MARK 2:5

Many of us would be disappointed with the above statement. The paralytic's friends went to great lengths to get him into the Presence of Jesus, lowering him on a stretcher through a clay–and–thatch roof in order to break to the front of the line. Clearly they came for one thing: healing. They wanted their friend to walk. *He* wanted to walk. A miracle was all they had on their minds. So a declaration of forgiveness, while a nice spiritual touch, might have been a letdown.

There are times, of course, when we realize that our sin is the heaviest weight we carry. It's a burden that keeps us down. But usually when we come to God with a request, it's for something more practical than absolution. Just like the paralytic and his friends, we want a miracle.

We know the right perspective, of course—that knowing God is our greatest need. But a remarkable tendency of Jesus is to meet our practical needs in addition to our deep, spiritual needs. Often in Scripture He healed, fed, or brought deliverance to prepare people to receive His mercy and to know Him, but sometimes He simply met the need without a lot of spiritual explanation. Why? Because He cares. Because He wants us to know His heart more than His doctrine. Because as the God of compassion, that's what He does.

Still, His primary focus is to get our sin out of the way because He hates obstacles in our relationship. Like the father of the Prodigal Son, He bypasses lectures about wrongdoing and goes straight to the hugs and celebration of our return. And in the process, He deals with us as whole, integrated people, with practical, material, physical needs. We are free to accept every blessing He offers.

Jesus, I seek Your face for all my needs—spiritual,
physical, material, emotional, psychological,
relational, and everything else. Thank You for Your
comprehensive touch in every part of my being.

August 12

"Yes, Lord, I believe!" the man said.

JOHN 9:38

Jesus healed a blind man and a controversy erupted. To the religious leaders, Jesus had obviously sinned because He healed the man on a Sabbath. But how could a sinner heal? So these leaders attempted to discredit the miracle. They asked the man's parents, in hopes that it had all been staged, but the parents assured them that the healed beggar was their son who had been blind from birth. The contradiction—an "ordinary sinner" who could perform miraculous signs—created quite a theological predicament for the experts. They couldn't handle the truth.

The Presence of God creates such crisis moments when a decision must be made, when neutrality is no longer an option. Do we give Him credit for His works even when those works blow our theology away? Or do we stick to doctrine that confines Him to the boxes we think we've discerned from Scripture? It's a harder choice than it seems for those who are well established in a system of beliefs. Yet it's one of God's favorite tools for revealing whose hearts really belong to Him.

God's Presence and His works prompt faith in the openhearted but go unnoticed by closed minds. When we sense Him, we are faced with a choice: believe or don't believe. The choice we make may very well determine whether we continue to experience Him or not.

Jesus brought out the very best in some people and the very worst in others. Whatever was in them came to the surface. When we commune with Him, we experience the same dynamic. Whatever is truly in us—whether faith, unbelief, love, apathy, hope, despair, or any other relational attribute—will eventually be exposed. Some people avoid Him for this reason, but it's wiser to deal with the condition of the heart. As you sit with Him, notice what rises up in you. Whatever is of faith, hang on to it.

Jesus, whenever You shatter my assumptions,
I'll choose faith. Deal with any unbelief in
my heart and help me trust You fully.

August 13

"My Lord and my God!" Thomas exclaimed.

JOHN 20:28

Does Scripture really claim that Jesus is God incarnate? Many people say no because Jesus never explicitly said, "I am God." But the Bible affirms His deity in many other ways: calling the Messiah "Immanuel," which means God with us; reporting Jesus' statements that He and the Father are "one"; and describing the many instances in which someone worshiped Jesus directly. Someone who was simply a good teacher would never accept worship if He wasn't divine, but Jesus always did. Wise men, a Gentile woman, a blind man who had been healed, women at the tomb, and His own disciples bowed down and praised Him. Thomas even called Him "my Lord and my God."

In God's Presence, this is a normal reaction. Many people saw Jesus only as a self-styled prophet or a religious instigator—they argued with Him, tried to trap Him with trick questions, and insulted his birthplace or questionable heritage. But most who encountered Him were in awe of His teaching, His attitude, and His supernatural power. They got glimpses of the holy, the God empowering this messianic figure. As a result, their lives were changed.

We need glimpses of the holy—to walk with a sense of reverence for the One who is near. The more we immerse ourselves in our relationship with Him, the more we recognize each moment as sacred. When we do, all of life becomes a powerful experience and a divine offering. Nothing is mundane anymore.

Cultivate awe. Learn to recognize the power of the risen Jesus in your circumstances and in the other believers around you. Go through this day with an awareness that every moment can be a sacred intersection between your earthly life and the eternal realm. In God's Presence in your life, heaven touches earth, and earth becomes much more meaningful.

Jesus, at times I'm in awe of You. But I want it to be more than just "at times." Help me be aware of Your sacred Presence at every moment in every situation. Help me live in wonder and amazement.

August 14

*She had heard about Jesus, so she came up behind him
through the crowd and touched his robe.*

MARK 5:27

The woman who had been bleeding for twelve years risked a lot to touch
Jesus. She was considered unclean—not necessarily sinful, but ritually impure
enough to be excluded from Temple worship and prohibited from touching
priests. There was a stigma associated with her condition and an understanding that she would keep herself at an appropriate distance. Still, she pushed
through a crowd to touch the garment of a holy man of messianic stature.
And when He noticed—and publicly questioned her—she owned up to
what she did.

Some people try to keep their decorum around God. Others behave
appropriately. That is to say, some people inappropriately put on airs or remain dignified in His Presence, while a heart that is truly captivated by Him
will forget all propriety and risk everything to pursue Him. Whenever that
happened—with a synagogue leader whose child was dying, with a Roman
centurion, with a Gentile woman whose daughter was demon-possessed, and
with this hemorrhaging woman in Mark 5—Jesus responded with great affirmation. He applauded their faith. He commended their ability to breach
protocol in order to access the divine answer to their true needs. Jesus seemed
to honor boldness.

When we recognize how unworthy we are to approach Jesus, how utterly
holy and awesome His glory is, and are desperate enough to reach out and grab
Him anyway, we are honoring Him. We are recognizing the heart that designed
us for Himself and saying yes to it. We are taking God at His Word.

What do you need from Him? Pursue it boldly. Chase Him recklessly.
Forget decorum and cry out to God. He is pleased with such abandon and
responds to it. He calls it great faith.

*Jesus, I have needs, and only You can meet them. Some
people might be appalled at my boldness, but I'm
shamelessly asking You to give me what I need. I know
Your generous heart, and I'm risking everything on it.*

August 15

They left their nets at once and followed him.

MARK 1:18

When the disciples followed Jesus, they left their past behind. For some of them, "the past" was not only a family business but the family members still working at it. When the woman at the well encountered Jesus, she left her water jar behind. Zacchaeus left his fraudulent ways and his wealth. Lazarus left his grave clothes. It's a pattern that's repeated often in the Gospels. Jesus makes some aspects of our past irrelevant.

We come into the Presence of God with a lot of baggage that we don't take with us when we go. That's because He has a way of helping us rearrange our priorities, reorient our vision, and reassess our needs. What we see as necessary becomes a lot less so when we get a glimpse of Him. We begin to realize that He's all we need; everything else is peripheral.

Those moments of realization that nothing else matters are precious, but they can be few and far between. The details of life and all the responsibilities we bear have a way of screaming for attention. They squeeze our God-moments out of our schedules. We still pray—sometimes on the fly—but it takes time to let deep truths sink in, and the right perspective on God is a deep truth. Exalting Him above everything else in our hearts is a process.

Take time today to sit in His Presence and sift through your priorities, your vision, and your needs. Let Him grow larger in your eyes, and notice what becomes smaller. Realize that when He is first in your day, everything else falls into its proper place. Whatever you bring into His Presence, be prepared to leave it behind.

Jesus, I carry a lot of things around with me—
responsibilities, attachments, to-do lists . . . You
know the issues. But I hold them loosely as I come
to You, and I'm prepared to let anything go. As
You increase in importance to me, let other things
decrease. And let me walk away lighter.

August 16

You desire honesty from the womb,
teaching me wisdom even there.

PSALM 51:6

Human beings take a face-saving, image-casting, best-foot-forward approach to relationships. We wear masks, some of them quite subtle and unintentional. Sometimes our persona is a hypocritical display, but more often it springs from an appropriate awareness that some aspects of life are personal and private. Still, in our relationships with others, we exhibit varying degrees of openness. We are rarely completely transparent.

The social patterns we have with others don't apply to our relationship with God, but we don't really know how to function any other way. So we continue to wear masks, albeit thinner ones; and we still clean up our image in order to express the "right" thoughts and words to Him. We forget that God knows every impulse of our brains before we even have them. He knows our suspicions and doubts, our frustrations and complaints. He sees right through us.

That's why it's essential to be completely honest with God. Just as we never draw close to another person when we aren't being real—we're aware they are relating to a false image, after all—we never draw close to God if we "dress up" spiritually in order to interact with Him. He can move us from point A to point B if we acknowledge point A. But when we feign faith, joy, maturity, a "spiritual" focus, or any other attitude, He has to undo the false self before working with the true one. He loves it when we approach Him in blunt honesty.

If you want to cultivate closeness with God, be completely transparent. Acknowledge every ugly attitude and ask Him to deal with it. Avoid rationalizing misguided behavior and own up to your actions and their true motives. God will meet you at raw and real places in your soul much more readily than in places of pretense.

Father, You know every corner of my being, so why
should I hide anything? I'll share every unappealing
part of me if You'll help me change it.

August 17

*I am trusting you, O Lord, saying, "You are
my God!" My future is in your hands.*

PSALM 31:14-15

Many of us have a pretty strong sense of agenda. Some items on our personal agenda have been placed in us by God's Spirit; some are the products of our own dreams and goals. And God cares for both kinds, though He may need to refine or redirect some things on our list. But when our sense of agenda becomes a stronger pull than our sense of need for God Himself, we find ourselves mentally on the other side of the fence from Him, as though we aren't working together. We're trying to convince Him of our agenda, or maybe just struggling with His. When that happens, the Presence is hard to detect.

God doesn't forbid us from wrestling with Him. In fact, He invites us to do so from time to time. But there are times when our hearts are in turmoil until we're able to simply let go and rest in His will, not knowing what it is. This is often called "surrender," and it opens a door to His Presence.

Surrendering our will to God's is a vital part of experiencing Him; His Spirit rushes into a heart that is fully yielded to Him. Why? Not because He wants automatons or completely empty vessels with no personality. No, it's because a surrendered heart is a heart that's in the process of aligning with His deepest desires and purposes. When we yield to Him, He begins to give us His very own heartbeat. That's a relationship that warmly invites closeness.

In order to align with His heart, you may have to unalign with something currently in yours—or at least be willing to. Don't fear that decision or the process. The result is a beautiful sense of closeness.

*Father, I'm Yours, along with everything in me.
I yield my will to Yours and trust my future
completely to You. I'm at peace and rest in Your
care. Please work out Your will in me.*

August 18

Why am I discouraged? Why is my heart so sad? I will put my hope in God! I will praise him again—my Savior and my God!

PSALM 43:5

The psalmist talked to himself as an exercise in Presence. He spoke to his own soul about truth. That happened a lot in the Psalms, in fact. David told his soul to bless the Lord (Psalm 103:1-2, NKJV) and resolved to constantly praise and boast in the Lord (Psalm 34:1-2), for two examples among many. Here, an unnamed psalmist asks some probing questions about his own discouragement and then declares an intent to praise. There are times, it seems, when self-talk is entirely appropriate.

It's easy to see why. God wants us not only to know truth intellectually but to believe it deep in our hearts. When we mentally agree with Scripture but let circumstances or feelings dictate an opposite view—for example, when we believe God can do the impossible but then despair in an impossible situation—we are not in sync with Him. We have to assert truth against circumstances and feelings, just like Abraham, who "against all hope" continued to hope and believe (Romans 4:18, NIV). The hearts of those who tell themselves to do that will beat with God's heartbeat.

Hear His desire: "My truth is real and unchanging, regardless of how you feel in any given moment or what you see with your eyes. Much of life is a decision about how and what to see—the reality I tell you about or the 'reality' you perceive. My people, those with My heart, learn to insist on seeing from My perspective rather than theirs. That pleases Me more than you know. I show My favor to those who look past apparent contradictions to see Me. When you choose to tell yourself the truth, I choose to fill your decision with My Presence."

Father, I choose Your truth and adamantly tell my own soul to embrace it. I know my perceptions aren't always accurate and my feelings aren't always reliable. But You are. What You have said is trustworthy, and I can depend on it.

August 19

Do not worship any other god, for the LORD,
whose name is Jealous, is a jealous God.

EXODUS 34:14, NIV

Jealousy is considered a negative emotion, even a harmful one. But it's a natural response when one's true love turns toward other affections. In an exclusive relationship, the nonexclusive love of a wandering heart hurts. In fact, a love that isn't jealous in the face of betrayal isn't a very strong love at all. Jealousy is a sign of deep caring.

Try meditating on God's jealousy today. This holy God apparently burns with passion for His people (Zechariah 8:2). Think of the implications: what His jealousy says about His love for each of us, the intensity with which an infinite heart must feel, and what kind of response such jealousy provokes in us. When the depth of His love begins to sink in, so does the sense of His nearness.

In fact, this is a great exercise in Presence that can be done with any of God's names. When we dwell on one of His names or attributes, the implications of His character begin to sink into our souls. We realize not only what God is like, we realize what He is like *for us*. His attributes become personal. We begin to notice how He has dealt with us and to feel His heartbeat in ways we've never felt it before. Every time you have a few moments to spare—waiting in line, in your drive time, in a waiting room—spend time dwelling on one of His characteristics. Closeness is established when we focus on who He is.

Lord, there are so many sides of You to experience.
I want to know You as fully as I can—every aspect
of Your character, every emotion of Your heart,
every thought You have toward me. As I think
about Your attributes, open my eyes to what they
mean and what they reveal about You.

My heart says of you, "Seek his face!"
Your face, LORD, I will seek.

PSALM 27:8, NIV

You have a need. You know God can meet that need. You've asked Him to do so and believe He will. But while you wait—and you will almost always have to wait for at least some period of time—what do you do? What attitude do you hold in your heart?

You know the obvious answers to that question: patience, trust, and faith, for example. But one of the best ways to interact with God in the meantime is to worship Him. And one of the best ways to do that is to worship Him specifically for the "face" you need to see. If you need provision, worship Him as Provider. If you need healing, worship Him as Healer. If you need victory, worship Him as Victor. Every need you have—comfort, strength, mercy, etc.—corresponds to one of His attributes. While you wait for Him to step into a situation to resolve it, praise Him for the way He can step into it.

What does that accomplish? For one thing, it cultivates faith in God in the area in which you most need it. It acknowledges that God can meet your need for that issue, and the more you do that, the stronger your confidence in Him grows. But more than that, worship of God becomes a testimony of His goodness and power. Daniel's friends declared God's ability to save them from the furnace before they entered it, and their praise glorified Him before and after the crisis (Daniel 3:16-18). Jesus praised the God who hears prayer before He raised Lazarus, and His declaration became a testimony for those who believed (John 11:41-42). God honors those who go out on a limb because of what they believe about Him.

Father, You are able and willing to meet any need I have.
While I'm waiting for Your intervention, I acknowledge
who You are, what You can do, and how faithful You are.
You are exactly what I need in every way.

August 21

Guard your heart above all else, for it
determines the course of your life.

PROVERBS 4:23

First and foremost, the Presence of God is a heart issue. That's where we experience Him most profoundly. Jesus told His disciples that the Spirit would be like a river flowing outward from within them, not flowing inward from outside of them. If we want to experience the tangible touch of God, the living Presence, we will have to become attuned to His movements within us.

That's why meditating on verses of Scripture is an effective exercise in Presence. True meditation goes well beyond memorizing a verse or exploring knowledge about a truth from different angles. It's a spiritual practice of chewing and swallowing the truth, digesting it to the point that it becomes a part of who you are. When you embrace a scriptural truth and then turn it over and around within your soul, letting it sink into every corner and crevice, it changes you. It becomes part of your nature. When that happens, you don't have to obey it against your inclinations; you simply fulfill it by being who you are. That's how transformation happens.

Scripture says to guard our hearts. Most people interpret that as, "Keep the bad stuff from getting in"—a good practice, but only part of the full meaning of this verse. We are to be diligent about our internal state—to keep the bad stuff out, to keep the good stuff in, to dwell on truth and peace and the Presence, and to anchor ourselves in Kingdom reality. Filling our hearts with scriptural truth is a vital part of that process. It's one of the most important and foundational ways we experience God.

Father, I'll do what I can to guard my heart—to
fill it with all the right things. But You are the true
Master of my heart, and I'm trusting it into Your
hands. Shape it, fill it, and meet me there. Let it be
a place where Your Presence always reigns.

August 22

Do not be afraid or discouraged, for the LORD will personally go ahead of you. He will be with you; he will neither fail you nor abandon you.

DEUTERONOMY 31:8

Numerous passages of Scripture remind us that God is always with us. The fact of His Presence isn't in question. The issue is whether we remain aware of His Presence or not. And surprisingly, the degree to which we are aware of Him seems to correlate to the level at which we experience Him. In other words, though His Presence is always with us, He seems more available to us when we notice.

Perhaps that's because when we're aware of Him, we tend to talk to Him more. We ask for His help, therefore we receive it. When we don't ask for His help—well, He helps in some ways anyway because His mercy is great. But He doesn't step into our circumstances as often. As James said, "You don't have what you want because you don't ask God for it" (James 4:2). Apparently, asking is important. And awareness is the first step in asking.

But even before our increased asking, simply noticing His Presence seems to motivate Him to speak to us and to move on our behalf. He knows when He has our attention and when He doesn't. And when He does, He seems to intervene much more often than He otherwise would.

One of the most important exercises in Presence is one of the simplest: remind yourself that He is there. Whatever it takes, call Him to mind frequently. There's nothing superspiritual about that; it's a mental practice like remembering the items on your to-do list or keeping track of the time. Reminding yourself of the truth of His Presence as often as you can—every day, every hour, every minute—will increase the power of His Presence in your life.

Lord, help me remember. I give you complete permission to jar my memory as often as You need to. I always want to be aware that You are here.

*I will ask the Father, and he will give you
another Advocate, who will never leave you.*

JOHN 14:16

Imagine yourself alone with Jesus in a place where your spirit and His freely commune. It can be anywhere: a beach, a hillside, a living room, wherever. Ask Him to inspire your thoughts and fill your heart with Himself. Picture His face—don't worry if you get all the details right or not—envision His gestures, and hear the tone of His voice. Ask Him questions. How does He respond? What do you hear?

This is an exercise in Presence that bothers some people for its subjectivity. But relationships are subjective by nature, and if we're going to have one with Jesus, it will need to be so. Granted, it takes practice; no one sees and hears completely in the Spirit. But all are invited to meet Him there. In fact, He promised that we would. He assured us we would have an Advocate or Counselor—a highly relational term—and implied that we would be able to communicate with this Counselor and He with us. Do we trust that He will speak to us when we ask Him to? That He can fill our thoughts with Himself? Or do we believe instead that when we ask this relational God for clear communication with Him, He will ignore our request and abandon us to deception? Clearly, Jesus meant for us to experience Him through His Spirit who lives within us, not just in some abstract theological sense but in real person-to-Person communication. We can trust Him to follow through.

Spend ample time communing with Jesus—picturing Him, listening for His voice, trusting His Presence. Measure what you see and hear against Scripture, but be open to His personal touch. He wants to give it. Meet Him in the secret place where His Spirit and yours can freely commune.

*Jesus, I envision Your Presence because You've
assured me it's true—that You speak, counsel, and
commune with me. Make our relationship rich and
full with Your nearness and love.*

August 24

The heavens proclaim the glory of God. . . . They speak without a sound or word; their voice is never heard. Yet their message has gone throughout the earth, and their words to all the world.

PSALM 19:1, 3-4

The heavens have a story to tell. If you go out at night and look up into the sky, you'll hear the testimony. An unimaginably awesome Being spoke universes into existence and continues to hold them in His hand. Even now, He is sustaining the fiery explosion of gases in stars hundreds of times larger than our sun and farther than our most powerful telescopes can see. He is moving in the midst of immense nebulae and galaxies. The enormity of creation is mind-blowing, the glory of the Creator even more so.

One might think that pondering such vastness would make God seem distant, but the opposite is true. Contemplating His relational nature in the context of such dominion is a powerful exercise in experiencing His Presence. To know that the God of distant galaxies is the God sitting next to us as we gaze at them makes His nearness all the more real. To think—this is the God to whom we pray. Is anything too difficult for Him? Is any problem beyond His reach? No, and our finite minds learn contentment when we realize an infinite mind is involved in our lives. We grasp that His ways are beyond our understanding, and we're okay with that. We trust this King when we perceive the enormity of His realm.

Are your days filled with His Presence? Do you take long walks with Him and talk with Him? Do you see Him in the things He has made? Realize that this vast God is not only *with* you, He is *in* you. Personally, deeply, intimately. Closer than you can imagine.

Father, I can't even begin to comprehend Your greatness and glory. But who can deal with my concerns more faithfully? Who can touch my spirit more meaningfully? I'm grateful that the God of an immense creation is mindful of me and every detail of my life.

August 25

A child is born to us, a son is given to us. The government will rest on his shoulders. And he will be called: Wonderful Counselor, Mighty God, Everlasting Father, Prince of Peace.

ISAIAH 9:6

Long ago in Eden, we had *shalom*. The familiar translation of this Hebrew word is "peace," but it means so much more than that: fullness, wholeness, abundance, a sense that things are right, a state of well-being in every area of life. It's that feeling of rest and satisfaction we expect to have when every item is crossed off a to-do list, or when we finally get away from it all on that perfect vacation, or when that big dream is fulfilled and life seems right again. This *shalom* is what we're all striving for, but the reason we have to strive is that we lost it long ago. In Eden, we had it all without any sense of lack. Now we don't. Our desire for *shalom* drives us relentlessly toward whatever we think we need for fulfillment.

Scripture tells us that Jesus is our Prince of *Shalom*. We can't get it apart from Him. We may strive for wholeness, fulfillment, abundance, and well-being in all sorts of ways, but we won't find it unless He's at the center of our search. Wherever He is, there's *shalom*. He's the one who gives it.

One of the great benefits of His Presence is that the *shalom* we lost in Eden is restored to us. That's why so many people who sense the Lord simultaneously have a sense of great peace. He stills restless hearts and fills empty ones. Whenever we have a restless or empty heart, the solution isn't to seek peace or fulfillment; it's to seek Him. His Presence provides what we're looking for. He Himself is the environment of Eden that we seek. He is where our hearts find rest.

Jesus, You are my peace, my completeness, my shalom. I realize I won't get what I'm looking for in anyone or anything else. Help me find my rest in You.

August 26

You will keep in perfect peace all who trust in you, all whose thoughts are fixed on you!

ISAIAH 26:3

We've seen that there are two ways for our sense of God's Presence to increase: for us to draw near to Him by "practicing" His Presence and for Him to draw near to us by manifesting His Presence. Brother Lawrence, the famous monk best known for practicing the Presence, became an intensely focused worshiper. He saw many around him trying to experience God's love by learning methods and principles, and it seemed unnecessarily complicated to him. He chose instead to intentionally worship as constantly as possible, to fix his thoughts on Jesus' Presence. This, he learned, made all the difference. Theological training wasn't the key to experiencing God; focusing on God was the key to experiencing God.

When we fix our thoughts on Him, He keeps us in perfect peace—or perfect *shalom*, actually. Not only does He put our hearts at rest, He gives us that sense of wholeness and fullness we seek. Isaiah 26:3 delivers a powerful truth that can affect our satisfaction in life for the rest of our days: when we are able to focus on God in trust, He is able to grant us *shalom*. The satisfaction every human heart hungers for, so elusive and frustrating to so many throughout history, can be ours. We don't get it by striving for it but by trusting in the One who offers it. All we are required to do is keep our thoughts on Him as He truly is.

This is why so many Christians who are born of God's Spirit are still discontented and somewhat empty. They have God's life in them but are too distracted from Him to benefit from His Presence. But it doesn't have to be that way. If you keep your trust fully focused on Him, you will live in perfect *shalom*.

Father, help me keep my focus. Turn my eyes toward You. I want to experience Your perfect peace in all its fullness.

August 27

May the LORD bless you and protect you.
May the LORD smile on you and be gracious
to you. May the LORD show you his favor
and give you his peace.

NUMBERS 6:24-26

We often think of blessings as nice words, a "best wishes" sentiment appropriate for greeting cards and special occasions. But from a biblical perspective, a blessing is much more than a happy thought, and spoken words are much more than just words. Words—and especially words spoken in a blessing, curse, or prophetic declaration—carry a lot of weight. They are tangible expressions that shape reality.

In light of that perspective, it makes sense that God would tell His people to pronounce blessings on each other. A blessing like Aaron's in Numbers 6 sets people up to encounter God. It invokes Him for His protection, His favor, and even His smile. It appeals to His grace. And it promises His *shalom*.

If you want to upgrade your sense of God's Presence, try blessing others. Ask God to bless them and, when appropriate, pronounce a blessing on them. God's favor and *shalom* will increase in their lives, and it will also increase in yours. A blessing can create a pathway into someone's life for fullness, completeness, abundance, and well-being. It benefits not only the one being blessed but also the one who blesses. Why? Because God enjoys watching His people align their words with His heart and His purposes. The God who desires to bless responds to words declaring that He will.

Many Christians have lost the art of blessing others verbally, but you can regain it. In fact, it's still God's desire for the encouragement and building up of His people. Words carry weight, even the power of life and death (Proverbs 18:21). And in a very real sense, they can carry His Presence.

Lord, may my tongue be an instrument of Your shalom.
May I impart Your goodness to others through my words,
and may Your Spirit inhabit those words in power.

August 28

*I love all who love me. Those who
search will surely find me.*

PROVERBS 8:17

The voice of Wisdom in Proverbs—and also the voice of God in many other verses—reveals a deep, divine truth. God loves to be sought. He is available in many ways to many people, even those who haven't looked for Him, and He certainly seeks and finds those who are lost. In fact, He is a pursuer at heart. But in any relationship of true love, pursuing goes both ways. And God loves not only to pursue but to be pursued.

God can get our attention, of course, even when we aren't looking for Him. He did that often in Scripture—in a burning bush that commanded Moses' response, in a vision on the Damascus road that jolted Paul into awareness, and so on. But which is better: for God to have to get our attention or for Him to already have it? Which does He prefer? Which has more value for the relationship and indicates more potential for knowing and loving Him? Clearly He responds to those who seek Him because their hearts are open and ready for Him. As the writer of Hebrews expressed, "He is a rewarder of those who diligently seek Him" (Hebrews 11:6, NKJV).

The greatest reward is Himself. If we seek to know Him better, we will know Him better. He will make sure of that. We don't have to figure out how; we only need to express a desire for greater intimacy with Him and ask for it earnestly. Our persistence will be rewarded, and in the gift of Himself, we will also receive the *shalom* He offers as well as all the other benefits of His Presence. When we seek, we will find. It's a promise.

*Father, I seek You for a lot of reasons, but I know all
of Your gifts come not as separate blessings but wrapped
up in Yourself. I continue to seek Your face, Lord. Please
reward my search beyond my greatest expectations.*

August 29

The creation was subjected to frustration,
not by its own choice, but by the will of
the one who subjected it, in hope that the
creation itself will be liberated from its
bondage to decay and brought into the
freedom and glory of the children of God.

ROMANS 8:20-21, NIV

If *shalom* is the fullness of life in God, its opposite is the frustration and futility we all feel from living in a broken world. Our longing for *shalom* shows up in that deep-down feeling that things aren't right—that life isn't working out the way we want it to, that we need to put our out-of-control existence into some kind of order. The angst we feel over our lack of fulfillment gnaws at us and prompts all kinds of why questions. We know this isn't the way things were meant to be.

God subjects this world to futility and frustration without Him so we will seek the *shalom* that can be experienced with Him. If brokenness were comfortable, we could be content with it. We wouldn't have the restlessness that sends us searching for more. We would never embark on a quest for meaning and purpose. Our emptiness becomes a blessing when it drives us toward the *shalom* of God's Presence.

Let every ache, every pang of hunger, every frustration in life push you in the right direction. Some people wander from the God who allows futility, assuming it's a sign of His lack of love—or even of His nonexistence. But hardships, obstacles, and frustrations are designed to draw you into His arms and His solutions. He offers His peace to those who seek it in Him. Every obstacle in life is designed to bring you close.

Lord, draw me. In my difficulties, let me not only
seek You but also find You. Please show Yourself as
the shalom *I've been searching for.*

August 30

In peace I will lie down and sleep, for you
alone, O LORD, will keep me safe.

PSALM 4:8

David was bombarded with accusations and concerned for his reputation. He was the subject of rumors and lies and was trying not to let anger get the best of him. We don't know the exact situation behind this psalm, but we know the relevant dynamics. The environment was tumultuous, and David felt besieged.

We can relate. We may not be plagued by the political intrigue David experienced, but we know what it's like to have difficult circumstances swirling around us. Life has a way of making us feel "under siege." And when it does, we lie awake wondering how things will play out. We envision various scenarios, plan how we might respond in each one, and speculate about what others are doing to make matters more complicated. Turbulent thoughts can keep us awake for hours.

David could lie down in peace—in *shalom*—and sleep. Why? Because he knew God was sovereign over his circumstances and present to help. Only God could ultimately vindicate him. Only God could defend him from his enemies. Only God could still the storm that raged around him. And David trusted that He would.

Where do you find peace in a storm? Certainly not in focusing on the storm. That never calms any situation. No, the way to lie down in *shalom* and sleep is to know beyond the shadow of a doubt that God is present, working on your behalf, and able to accomplish anything He wants to in the midst of it. Whatever storm you face in this season of life, trust in God's desire and ability to keep you safe. He promises to be your help, your vindication, and your peace.

Lord, things are beyond my control. I know they always
are, but they seem especially so now. I can't fix my
circumstances, but You can—and You can bring me peace
in the midst of them. Please calm my heart and speak
words of peace to me. And give me rest.

August 31

He himself is our peace.
EPHESIANS 2:14, NIV

Jesus doesn't just give us *shalom*. He *is* our *shalom*. In other words, peace isn't just a condition imparted to us. It's a state of being that comes about through a relationship. When we are born into God's Kingdom, we are *in* Christ—a Person of perfect wholeness and pure integrity. There's no conflict within Him, no division, no incongruity. The more we become aware of our true position in Him and experience it, the more like Him we become. Unity with Jesus gives us peace.

That doesn't mean we won't experience conflict with the world, our circumstances, the enemy of our faith, or even our own flesh. We will. This verse in Ephesians is written in the context of people who have long been separated by culture and religious conviction but have been made one in Christ. It implies a history of conflict. But we can experience rest in the midst of whatever conflict we face, and we can have the wholeness and fulfillment of Christ in our relationship with Him regardless of what's going on around us. Turmoil can't touch our true state if His Presence is strong in us.

Whatever turbulence is shaking your life right now, it's no match for the Presence. Whatever friction you feel with other people can be neutralized by His Spirit. Whatever personal battle you're fighting within yourself, Your identity in Christ can resolve it. Don't seek peace as a condition; seek Him, and let peace result. Take a deep breath, invite Him to fill you and show Himself strong within you, relinquish yourself to His good purposes for you, and relax. His closeness will create the conditions you seek, and the turbulence in your life will eventually have to submit to Him.

Jesus, You are my peace. You are my wholeness, my comfort, and my blessing. I can take a deep breath and fall into Your arms because I trust You to hold me well. And I trust You to bring peace and enforce it in my life.

September 1

Let the peace that comes from Christ rule in your hearts. For as members of one body you are called to live in peace.

COLOSSIANS 3:15

Studies show that if you put several people of normal emotional state into a room with an agitated person, they all become more agitated. Put them in a room with a depressed person, and they all become more depressed. And if you put them in a room with a person overflowing with joy, they become happier. That's because strong emotional states are contagious. In an otherwise neutral environment, stronger feelings affect people with milder ones.

We want the peace of Christ—the rest and comfort and unity He gives us—to rule in our hearts. But Paul, with his Hebrew-oriented mind, was surely thinking in terms of *shalom* in this verse, not just "peace" as we define it. In addition to rest, comfort, and unity, Jesus fills our hearts with contentment, abundance, and a sense that we are as whole as we were meant to be. The condition that rules our heart is the fullness of Jesus.

That's a huge personal blessing, but it's more. We become carriers of the *shalom*, vessels of God's Presence wherever we go. In God's design for His people, we are not to be shaped by our environment but shapers of it. When we carry the *shalom* of God into a room full of people, they should somehow be impacted by it. They may not know how or why, but their mood can be impacted by exposure to the Presence within us.

Determine to be a shaper of your environment rather than letting your environment shape you. The Presence in you is stronger than the internal state of those who aren't filled with Him. Let the *shalom* of Christ impact not only your heart but other hearts too.

Jesus, rule my heart. Let Your peace reign not just in me but also around me. It's an honor and privilege to carry Your Presence everywhere I go, and I trust that You'll accomplish great things through me.

September 2

*Love the LORD your God with all your heart, all
your soul, and all your strength.*

DEUTERONOMY 6:5

These are words from the mouth of Moses, but they come straight from the
heart of God. It's repeated several times in Deuteronomy, again in Joshua and
the Psalms, and then deemed the most important commandment by numerous rabbis and by Jesus Himself. And this "commandment" is also a plea—not
from a God desperate for love but from a God who created us for that purpose and wants it fulfilled. God wants an emotional closeness to and heartfelt
commitment from those made in His image.

It's easy to hear the divine heartbeat on this subject: "Why do you think
I made you to be like Me? There's no reason for your design other than relating to Me. Haven't you noticed? I have pursued you for centuries. I've waited
patiently and planned your restoration in detail. I haven't called your straying
'disobedience' only, I've also called it 'adultery.' Why? Because it's personal.
Because I want your heart and you've given it to others. I can be hurt and
grieved by your attitude toward Me. But I've continued to call you back to
Me. I've made enormous sacrifices for you. I've placed My affection on you.
I've made extravagant promises that include giving you an eternal inheritance and letting you rule the earth together with Me. And I've shown you
love that's higher and wider and deeper than a finite mind can comprehend.
Don't misread the cues. Don't underestimate My commitment to you—or
My desire for you. I want you for Myself."

*God, I want to love You with my whole heart. I know this is
Your greatest desire for me, that it's the reason I was made.
But You know how weak my love can be, and how easily I'm
distracted by lesser, more visible things. Please help my heart
respond to You and love You with passion.*

September 3

Those who sacrifice thank offerings honor me,
and to the blameless I will show my salvation.

PSALM 50:23, NIV

Before Jesus fed multitudes with a few loaves of bread and some fish, He gave thanks. Before He raised Lazarus from the dead, He gave thanks. Even in consuming the bread and wine that symbolized His body and blood, He gave thanks. He was able to be grateful in advance because He had confidence in what God would do. And His gratitude prepared the way for God to step in.

Like worship, gratitude creates a highway for God to ride into our circumstances. It's a relational attitude that prioritizes a focus on God over and above His benefits. It's also a statement of faith, an acknowledgment that God is able and willing to intervene according to His promises. When we are confident in Him, He rewards our confidence with His solutions.

But giving thanks when our dreams, desires, and plans hang in the balance is hard to do. That's because we aren't sure how or even if God wants to intervene. We wonder what God is doing—if He wants to prolong our discomfort to teach us patience or faith, or if He's working on some plan much bigger than our own situation that we don't know about, or if His mysterious ways are simply beyond us. In such cases, gratitude almost seems presumptuous. But that's only when our gratitude is contingent on one particular outcome rather than on God's goodness in general. When we anticipate His goodness in one way or another, even if we can't predict the outcome, gratitude is appropriate. When we give it, He responds with both His Presence and His solutions.

Thank You, Father. I don't know how You want to intervene
in my circumstances today, but I know I can expect goodness
from You. I'm grateful for the certainty of all Your promises
and for the assurance of Your Presence.

September 4

My power works best in weakness.

2 CORINTHIANS 12:9

He has been called "God of the gaps" by those who suggest humanity needs a deity only when we can't explain mysteries. The assumption is that as science increases our understanding, the need to believe in God decreases—and that one day we will have enough natural explanations not to need a deity at all. While that approach is superficial and that sort of "God of the gaps" is a completely unnecessary reduction of His role, we can certainly embrace another sense of the term. In the gaps of our lives, we need Him desperately.

We can believe in a God of our own gaps. In fact, that's where He shows up in power most often. Wherever we're needy, broken, and weak, that's where He rises up in strength to provide, repair, and defend. While we try to cover up our vulnerabilities and establish our strength, He waits for us to realize how incapable we are without Him. When we're finally at the end of our rope, that's when He is finally able to act without anyone mistaking His victories for our self-effort. He loves to fill feeble vessels with divine strength. His Presence attends our weakness.

Present your weakness to God. Do the same with your lack and your brokenness. Whatever gaps you have, let God fill them with His strength, His provision, and His healing. He is glorified far more in the deserts and valleys of our lives than in the gardens and peaks. That's good news for us because we have far more deserts and valleys to offer Him than gardens and peaks. He welcomes that—and promises to fill those places with Himself.

Lord, I have plenty of weakness to give You. You know the cracks and crevices of my life, the fault lines and frailties that keep me feeling insufficient. But You are my sufficiency and my strength. I depend on You. Please step into my gaps with Yourself and Your help.

September 5

*You open Your hand and satisfy the
desire of every living thing.*

PSALM 145:16, NKJV

I was going through some of the toys my son has outgrown, reminiscing about each one before putting it in the giveaway pile. Most of them had teeth marks and other signs of being fully enjoyed. All of them brought back images of playtime on the floor, and I realized that these cheap chunks of plastic were precious to me. Why? Because they had been precious to him.

God promises to satisfy the desires of those who love Him, fear Him, and delight in Him. We know that doesn't mean every whim, as some people seem to think, or on the other hand only every basic need, as other people assert. Somewhere in between, in the places of our heart where we have deep longings and lasting desires, God opens His hands and meets them. He doesn't often fulfill them immediately, nor does He always fulfill them exactly as we expect Him to. But He does care for the things we care about. The things that are on our hearts are on His. Certain things become precious to Him simply because they are precious to us.

Avoid the error of two extremes on this issue. We can't dictate our desires to God and expect Him to satisfy every one of them, just as kids can't demand every passing wish on their Christmas lists. But we can't be too dogmatic in our declarations that "God will give you what you need, not what you want." According to Scripture, He often gives us what we want. When we are filled with Him, our desires and His provision begin to line up. The treasures of our hearts and the treasures of His heart begin to overlap, and our desires begin to be fulfilled.

*Lord, You know the desires of my heart. My prayer
is that You will fulfill the ones You want to fulfill
and remove the ones You don't. Strengthen my
longings that fit Your purposes and let all others
fade away. Let my heart be satisfied.*

September 6

Many will say to me, "Lord! Lord! We prophesied
in your name and cast out demons in your name
and performed many miracles in your name."
But I will reply, "I never knew you. Get away
from me, you who break God's laws."

MATTHEW 7:22-23

It's one of the scariest passages in Scripture but also one of the most revealing. This Jesus will later tell His disciples—and us, by implication—to do supernatural works in His name. "Heal the sick, raise the dead, cure those with leprosy, and cast out demons. Give as freely as you have received!" (Matthew 10:8). But here He tells them that many will do exactly these things while calling Him "Lord" and find themselves outside His Kingdom. Why? Because He never *knew* them.

It makes little sense to us. It would make slightly more sense if He said, "*You* never knew *Me*," but the issue is actually His knowledge of them. Clearly He isn't talking about knowledge *of* them; He is in no way ignorant. No, He must be talking about relational knowledge—His communion and fellowship with them. If that's lacking, so apparently is salvation itself.

Jesus' words imply that it's possible to do supernatural miracles in His name without belonging to Him—to tap into His power outside of a genuine relationship with Him. That stretches our theology, but it makes an essential point. The works we do are not the essence of the relationship. The relationship is a matter of sharing His Spirit, knowing His heart, and stepping into His purposes. It isn't a supernatural sideshow, though it's certainly supernatural. It isn't a record of performance, though it certainly involves works and fruitfulness. The heart of the matter is . . . well, the heart. If He doesn't have ours, we don't have Him. And that's a tragedy with devastating consequences.

Jesus, know me—in every sense of the word. I open
myself up for You to fill me with Yourself. I want to do
miracles, but only with You truly as my Lord. I want
to bear fruit, but always and only Yours.

September 7

I saw a door standing open in heaven. . . .
The voice said, "Come up here, and I will
show you what must happen after this."

REVELATION 4:1

In spite of human limitations, a mortal man is given an invitation to "come up here"—into the throne room of God. Even "in the Spirit," how can a human respond? Though the logistics are baffling, God gets him there. It's a vision, after all. Strange things can happen in the Spirit. The even more remarkable truth in this vision is that we serve a God who wants to open up and show His secrets.

Hear the heart of the Lord in this invitation: "I invite all My people into My throne room. In fact, you've been there without knowing it. This particular occasion was just for John, and this particular vision was unique. But I invite everyone to 'come up here.'

"You want to know how? That's the wrong question. Logistics are never your concern. I didn't explain how the walls of Jericho would fall or how the mechanics of a virgin birth can work. I'm not asking you to 'come up here' by figuring out the steps and then taking them. No, I'm looking for a desire and a hunger in you. If you call to Me with a heart that wants to come up here, I'll get you here. Just don't turn away and say, 'Well, I asked and nothing happened.' Give it time. Let Me work. You'll be surprised at the ways I can get you into My Presence.

"Understand that I'm a revealer by nature. I have mysteries, but I show them to those who seek. Do you really want to encounter Me? When I say 'Come up here,' don't say, 'How?' Say, 'Yes.' When I hear that answer in you, I begin to heighten your spiritual senses and prepare you to encounter Me in new ways."

Lord, I say yes. I know John's vision was unique, but
Your desire to reveal was not. Share Your heart with me.
Let me experience Your mysteries. Let me come.

September 8

It is the glory of God to conceal a matter, but the
glory of kings is to search out a matter.

PROVERBS 25:2, NKJV

For a God who loves us, pursues us, and calls us to draw near, He seems awfully obscure sometimes. In fact, we experience this seeming contradiction almost constantly. The God who made us for Himself keeps Himself hidden—not completely, of course, having revealed Himself in Scripture and in Jesus, but still invisible to natural eyes. Why? What possible reason could reconcile divine love with divine obscurity?

"I want those who are interested in Me, who respond to the ways I draw them. Do you think I came to you to remain hidden? To keep My ways a mystery? Paul wrote of mysteries that have been revealed in My Son. What makes you think I wouldn't continue to reveal them to those who seek Me? Have you asked Me? Have you sought the secret counsel of My heart? Or have you just assumed I won't share the treasures I've concealed? Don't accept the human limitations you think you have, as though My work through you is bound by them. I created you for eternity. I've given you a book full of encounters with Me that went well beyond human limits. Whenever you read or hear of them, I'm inviting you to step into what others have experienced.

"I've often whispered invitations you haven't answered. Yes, most of them would have been quite a stretch for you to pursue. But why don't you stretch? That's how I measure your hunger. Will you make sacrifices to seek Me? No one finds Me conveniently. Whenever someone seeks Me out, the process is inconvenient. Even when I come to someone who wasn't seeking Me, the encounter is inconvenient. Either way, it isn't easy. I'm always testing people in how desperately they want Me. I sort out the semi-serious from the truly serious and reward the latter with My Presence."

Lord, I'm serious about knowing You better—
about seeking until I find. It's the glory of Your
royal children to seek out the things You have
concealed. Please reward my search.

September 9

*And after the fire there was the sound
of a gentle whisper.*

1 KINGS 19:12

Elijah had gone to Mount Sinai, back to the place where Moses had received the law against which all of Israel had recently been rebelling. After a fierce windstorm, a violent earthquake, and a raging fire, God spoke to the prophet in the stillness, as quietly as a whisper. Why?

"I speak in the quiet. People want Me to write My words to them in the sky or thunder them from heaven or send an angel with a message, but that doesn't measure hunger or desire. It dictates My will. I'm not a dictator; I'm a wooer. I draw you, and only those who respond can come. That's how it works.

"Sometimes in history I've been more aggressive with My voice. Moses needed to be startled, for example, and so did Gideon. But normally I speak faintly enough that only the hungry and thirsty will risk failure and follow. They are desperate enough. Those who shrug off My voice as a whisper will often miss Me. Those who assume that every voice they think they hear is a whisper from Me will be wrong sometimes, but they won't miss Me. Sometimes they will be right, and over time I will fine-tune their hearing so they will know the difference between My real whispers and their own inner voices. But their desire to hear Me, even knowing they could be wrong, pleases Me. Moses and Paul expressed My heart when they wished everyone could prophesy. I want My voice to be heard by all who have ears to hear."

*Father, I want to hear You at all costs. I'm willing
to risk failure to step out on a limb and believe
that I've heard. Help me discern which whispers
are Yours and which are not. But let me never be
so "discerning" that I deny Your voice along with
others. Please, Lord, give me ears to hear.*

Blessed is he who is not offended because of Me.

LUKE 7:23, NKJV

Naaman the Syrian was offended. A slave girl from Israel had suggested he go see the prophet Elisha to be healed of his leprosy, so he went. A servant of the prophet came out to meet him and told him to wash seven times in the Jordan River. Naaman was furious. No personal greeting from the prophet himself? Washing in Israel's Jordan River, though Syria had plenty of its own? But Naaman had nothing to lose, so he complied—and was stunned to find himself healed (2 Kings 5).

This isn't rare in Scripture. God's calling at first offended Moses, then many around him. Jesus offended a Gentile woman—He called her a dog—before delivering her daughter and commending her faith. Prophetic words often offended the vast majority of those who heard them. God is in the habit of offending those who have sought or cried out to Him.

Why would God use such a strange strategy? "I don't often reveal Myself in inoffensive ways. I always allow hurdles—in your mind, in your heart, in your traditions—that challenge you and force you to face a choice. Haven't you noticed? Whenever you choose Me, you have to choose against something else. You have to leave behind a tradition or a preconception or a pet doctrine or an expected answer. I'm not convenient, and I'm not easy to find. I'm *certain* to be found, but that's different from being easy. I guarantee you'll find Me if you seek Me, but the search isn't simple. I promise understanding, but the questions may make you uncomfortable in the process. I promise answers to your prayers, but the processes toward those answers may press you. I give assurances, not red carpets. But blessed are those who are not offended by Me and press through to the end."

Lord, I know You reward persistence. Help my heart be strong and not fail. I choose not to be offended because I know Your blessing is on the other side of the offenses.

September 11

Be filled with the Holy Spirit.
EPHESIANS 5:18

Perhaps you need a little more patience. Or a lot more love. Or a deeper prayer life, or some more specific direction, or . . . well, a whole range of pieces in this vast puzzle we call "the Christian life." The problem is that a lifestyle can't be parceled out into bite-size sections, even though much of our discipleship approaches seem to imply that it can. The truth is that being a Christian means being filled with Christ. We don't need more of this virtue or that characteristic. We need Jesus.

We have Him, of course—as completely as we ever will. But we still need more experience with or more realization of the Presence we already have. If the fruits of the Spirit are in any way deficient in us, it isn't because we only have part of the Spirit. We have all of Him, but maybe He doesn't yet have all of us. Our life in Christ is a continual stepping into more of what we've already been given.

What would happen if we unceasingly prayed, "Lord, fill me with You"—not "give me patience" or "strengthen my faith" or "help with this problem" or "heal this disease"? What if we stopped viewing the gifts and fruit of Jesus as separate entities and began seeing Jesus in us as an integrated whole? What if we simply prayed—boldly and persistently—"Be present, manifestly so, in me and around me"? We might be surprised at how comprehensively His Presence meets our needs. All of His attributes come with Him as parts of the package. When He is allowed to express Himself freely within us, we experience all the growth we seek.

Jesus, I know that if I have You, I have Your character,
Your gifts, and Your attitudes. I don't need more faith
or patience or love, I need more of You. Be all You
want to be in me. I welcome Your personality fully.

September 12

If you are walking in darkness, without a ray of light, trust in the LORD and rely on your God.

ISAIAH 50:10

In the New Testament, Paul tells us we see in a mirror dimly, but there are times when it seems that we hardly see at all. John of the Cross once referred to a "dark night of the soul," and many believers can relate. We long for a personal touch from God, but it isn't there. We listen for His voice but hear nothing. We pray without confidence and can detect no concrete answers. We feel alone.

Why God allows such seasons isn't clear, but they have a way of establishing truth in us if we let them. Nothing tests our beliefs more severely than the complete absence of evidence or lack of spiritual support. Will we rely on what we know is true or jettison it somewhere in the darkness? Choosing faith in spite of feelings will strengthen faith in surprising ways.

It will also make a statement to every observer—human, angelic, and divine—about what God means to you. God enjoys our faith in any season in life, but the trust we display in the dark is far more precious than gold. Nothing overcomes the enemy's tactics or thwarts his desires more clearly than that. When everything seems stacked against us and we trust God, praise Him, and lean on Him anyway, we have won invisible victories that are visibly celebrated in heaven. Our faith in the dark is treasured by God.

Whenever you find yourself in darkness, let your trust in God pierce it. Choose to rely on Him. Those seasons don't last forever, but you have an opportunity in them to create an eternal testimony to His goodness. You become a trophy of grace on display in heavenly places. And when the season passes, your faith will bear unusually sweet fruit.

Father, I feel lost, but I know I'm not. I know You're with me—guiding, providing, and protecting. I trust You, even when I can't see. Please lead me into places of peace and abundance.

September 13

He canceled the record of the charges against us.

COLOSSIANS 2:14

When it really sinks in just how present God is—that He knows every crevice in creation and even every movement of every atom—our first reaction is often fear, guilt, and shame. After all, if God knows every corner of our hearts, He knows the secrets hidden there. He knows every thought we've had, every mistake we've made, every flaw we've tried to cover up. He sees through the image we put out there for everyone else to see. All the junk in our lives is an open book to Him.

That's why it's crucial to know that God removed everything between us and Him. Jesus' sacrifice actually canceled our sins. He still welcomes us with open arms. He is passionately, relentlessly committed to forgiving us. In spite of all the garbage, He still says, "I want to be with you. I want you to feel my breath and hear my whispers. I want to walk with you and talk with you. Yes, I know everything about you, much more than you know about yourself. And I love you deeply." There's nothing—absolutely nothing—standing between us and Him.

Guilt and shame have a unique ability to suffocate our sense of God's Presence. Refuse to let them. God has done everything to get them out of the way; we undermine His purposes when we hang on to them. Though it goes against our instincts to forget our offenses and assume intimacy—though it feels presumptuous on divine grace—assume intimacy anyway. Deal with issues, but don't hang on to them. God has already let them go.

Father, it's hard for me to grasp that there are absolutely no barriers between us. Let that truth sink into my heart, and help me live by it. You have paid an enormous price for our intimacy. I don't want to waste a moment of opportunity to experience You.

September 14

*The Spirit of the Sovereign LORD is upon me,
for the LORD has anointed me to bring good
news to the poor. He has sent me to comfort the
brokenhearted and to proclaim that captives will
be released and prisoners will be freed. He has
sent me to tell those who mourn that the time of
the LORD's favor has come.*

ISAIAH 61:1-2

The words of the prophet certainly applied to his time, but they were more directly relevant to the Messiah, who quoted them centuries later. Jesus read this part of Isaiah's scroll at the synagogue in Nazareth, ending the quote before it took a turn toward God's wrath. That's because when Jesus came, it was indeed an era of favor. Judgment would be deferred for a much later time and an altogether different appearance of the Son. But on this Sabbath in Nazareth, Jesus declared a mission reflecting the compassionate heart of God.

Think about the implications in terms of God's Presence. If the Spirit was upon Jesus to accomplish these things—delivering good news to the poor, comforting the brokenhearted, announcing the release of captives—and if the Spirit of Jesus is now in us, surely His mission and ours are one and the same. The Presence hasn't changed agendas or personalities. The Spirit of the Sovereign Lord is still of the same character as when He spoke to the prophet and when Jesus quoted the prophecy. Like the Spirit of prophecy and the Messiah who quoted Him, we are to declare the time of the Lord's favor. He lives in us specifically for that purpose.

Many Christians don't know that or have forgotten the mission. They declare more of God's judgment than His favor. But the Presence within us has come to shine and bless and draw others to Himself. And He leads us to do the same.

*Holy Spirit, this is my mission because it's Your mission.
The judgment will come, but this is a time of favor. Help
me declare it well and demonstrate it clearly.*

September 15

To all who mourn in Israel, he will give a crown of beauty for ashes, a joyous blessing instead of mourning, festive praise instead of despair. In their righteousness, they will be like great oaks that the LORD has planted for his own glory.

ISAIAH 61:3

Despair is a common human feeling. It isn't, however, part of our original design. Neither is it part of our redemption. We are clothed in joy instead of mourning, beauty instead of ashes, praise instead of despair. Though we may dread many of the problems or people we face, we aren't meant to. Though we lose hope in many of the trials of our lives, we aren't intended to. Though we forget that God sees the end of a situation even when no end is in sight, we aren't supposed to. Despair is supposed to be foreign to a relationship with Him.

That's because we serve a God of hope and read Scriptures filled with hopeful promises from beginning to end. While the church wallows in low expectations and defers hope into the far-too-distant future, God's Spirit fills us with hope and expectation in His goodness now. He reminds us of His benefits, His promises, and His Presence. Despair cannot thrive or even survive when we are in close fellowship with Him and are seeing Him well. God, who is not discouraged about anything, won't allow it.

Learn to see despair and its related emotions—discouragement and dread—as symptoms of distance from God. His Presence is a powerful immune system against poisonous thoughts of hopelessness. And hopeless thoughts are a weapon of the adversary to blind us to His Presence. Cultivate fellowship with God and choose hope. God's purposes are good enough to fill us with joy and leave no room for despair.

Lord, I lose hope far too easily, which means I lose sight of You far too easily. If I saw You clearly, I would be encouraged. Please come close and fill me with truth. Give me the joy of Your Presence and the hope of all Your promises.

September 16

You will be called priests of the LORD,
ministers of our God.

ISAIAH 61:6

A biblical priest stands in a unique position between God and humanity. He represents the words and purposes of God to human beings and the needs and petitions of human beings to God. It's a role of interceding, of functioning as a mediator between the human and divine. Like an agent between two parties in a negotiation, the priest seeks to represent the interests of both in a way that brings them together.

God designated priests within Israel to represent the nation to God and to speak God's words to the nation. He also designated Israel as a priestly nation for the other nations of the world—a global go-between to make Him known and through whom salvation would be revealed and offered. Then He sent Jesus as the High Priest who forever lives to make intercession for His people. But in Him, every believer becomes a priest in his or her sphere of influence. We are priests to one another within the church and a nation of priests to the world (1 Peter 2:5, 9). The Presence of God resides within us for a vital cosmic purpose.

Learn to see yourself as a go-between standing in the space that separates God and a needy world. Your role is to intercede for the nations and to represent God to their people. As a priest, you are called to be holy—not detached from the world or impossibly righteous, as many interpret holiness, but to be set aside by God for a specific purpose. For many people, you are a link to the divine. You may not have realized you were chosen for that role, but the Presence within you mandates it. You are a minister of God.

Lord, I know I'm called to "the ministry"—we all
are. How do I do that in my work? In my family?
In my community? Show me. Empower me to
represent You to others and lift up others to You.

September 17

I am overwhelmed with joy in the LORD my God! For he has dressed me with the clothing of salvation and draped me in a robe of righteousness. I am like a bridegroom in his wedding suit or a bride with her jewels.

ISAIAH 61:10

Throughout the Old Testament, uncleanness had a corrupting influence. Leprosy was contagious, infecting the ritually clean with its impurities. Death and disease were kept outside the camp because of their contaminating nature. Sinners and scoffers were a bad influence, impacting the behavior of the righteous. Evil was a leaven affecting the whole lump of dough.

Jesus defied this dynamic. He touched lepers, and instead of Jesus becoming unclean, the lepers became clean. He touched dead and diseased bodies, and instead of being defiled, He gave them life and health. He hung out with sinners and unsavory characters, and instead of being corrupted, He changed them. Righteousness became the leaven affecting the whole lump of dough.

Isaiah foresaw this dynamic at work, and God's Presence overwhelmed the prophet with joy. God turned Israel's mourning into dancing. He covers His people with the clothing of salvation and dresses them in a robe of righteousness. He has completely switched the direction of influence. Having needed light, we become lights. Having needed forgiveness, we become forgivers. Having dressed as mourners, we are clothed for a wedding.

Choose to live in the reversal. Don't be defeated; overcome. Don't be victimized; be victorious. Don't just receive; give. Don't be easily influenced; be an influencer. Yes, the reversal can be a process, but it's largely a matter of perspective, and perspectives can be chosen. The laws of the Spirit now work in your favor. Choose to take full advantage of them.

Father, show me the power of my perspective. Help me live in the reversal, where my attitude and internal state are impacted only by You. Clothe me in the joy and celebration of what You have done in me.

*If only I knew where to find God,
I would go to his court.*

JOB 23:3

Job had questions. Painful ones. He was going through an excruciating season of disease, calamity, and conflict. He felt abandoned, although he had no idea why. He had always been faithful to God, and God seemed distant. He would have gladly pleaded his case before the divine throne, if only he could have found it. But God was nowhere to be found.

This God who has promised us His Presence—and, since Pentecost, has promised that His Spirit dwells within us—allows us to go through dark and painful seasons. Our pleas for His intervention seem to go unnoticed; our questions remain unanswered; our problems linger. Where is He in our pain? He doesn't say. We have theological answers to such questions, and we trust that He is near. But we long for His touch—and His solutions. We want Him to fix things for us.

Job 23 ends with a lament that "thick, impenetrable darkness is everywhere." How do we respond to God at such times? We may not have the same friends Job had, but we hear their voices: "You must have sinned." "He has abandoned you." "You made the wrong decision." "God doesn't work that way." "His promises don't apply the way you thought they did." And on and on. The accusations and doubts are relentless. They seem to speak much louder than God does.

Don't listen to them. The voices lie. Yes, there are dark times in a believer's life, but God is still there. He honors faith that survives the darkest nights. He strengthens souls with the most painful instruments. And in the end, His gifts and glory compensate for any hardship we had to face.

*Father, thank You that seasons of darkness are rare,
and thank You for the knowledge that they are only
temporary. Do what You need to do in me, but please let
me feel the encouragement of Your touch often.*

September 19

*He knows where I am going. And when he
tests me, I will come out as pure as gold.*

JOB 23:10

Life didn't make sense. This God had promised to reward the obedient with
blessings and to curse the disobedient with disaster. And yet an obedient man
was experiencing disaster. Perhaps Job knew the divine orders of blessing and
curse, or perhaps he didn't. Either way, he knew the character of God, and
God's actions didn't seem right.

Even in the midst of his darkest season, Job knew that the apparent
absence of God was not a sign of His disfavor—or even worse, that He was
somehow unjust. Job knew his own heart, he trusted God's, and he believed
everything would work out in the end. He couldn't explain why bad things
were happening or how a good God would allow them. But in the dark, he
trusted what he had learned in the light.

There are times when we have to either make that choice or walk away
from what we believe. Perhaps that's one reason God allows dark, disorienting
moments—to see whether we trust His heart regardless of what we see or
decide He isn't who He said He is after all. In the face of contradictions, true
faith will decide that the human perspective is flawed and God's purposes are
still good—even if the "evidence" says otherwise. This decision, this declaration that God is good anyway, is His ultimate victory over the enemy. The
tempter has lost when he has made his best case that God is not good and
we insist that He is anyway. A soul that makes that choice is built for eternity.

In your times of darkness, cling to what you've learned in the light. Refuse to accept the adversary's spin on your circumstances. Know that when
you are tested in the fire and your faith in God's goodness stands, you will
come through to a place of honor and blessing.

*Lord, I believe. Even when I can't see, I know who
You are, and I cling to You always.*

September 20

He will do to me whatever he has planned.
He controls my destiny.

JOB 23:14

This statement of faith can be either extremely comforting or extremely terrifying. To Job, it was the latter. He was in a difficult season, and his pleas had not moved God. From all appearances, God's plans would continue on this dreadful course for the foreseeable future. Job's destiny appeared unalterably headed in a frightening direction.

When we're in a season of abundance and promise, Job's declaration is exactly what we want to hear. A hope-filled soul is delighted that God will follow through on His plans and unswervingly control a destiny. We want to know that nothing can thwart His good purposes, that He is keeping us from evil influences and calamitous events. If "whatever he has planned" is positive and in line with our desires, nothing could be more encouraging than His sovereignty.

It's important for our attitude toward God's sovereignty to be influenced by hope regardless of the season we're in. That's easy when we've been seeing the encouraging side of God, but it's profoundly difficult when His goodness has been obscured by a dark season like Job's. Our sense of destiny is only inspiring to us when we fully trust God's goodness. Otherwise, it can be a source of dread.

Expect good things from God—even when you haven't seen many of them lately. Know that He has given you a future and a hope. Let that hope, no matter how hard it is to envision, fill your heart with anticipation. However things look today, the future—your God-ordained future designed by His sovereign purposes—is bright.

Lord, fill my vision with hope—the expectation of
goodness from Your hand. You've given promises and
offered hope even when I can't see what's ahead. Help
me walk in the good purposes You've planned for me.

September 21

Against all hope, Abraham in hope believed and
so became the father of many nations.

ROMANS 4:18, NIV

God gave Abraham a promise and then let him sort it out over the next twenty-five years. That seems cruel. Abraham tried to do his part, but God kept refining his part out of the equation. Would he have his many descendants through a nonbiological heir like his servant? No, they would come from his own offspring. Would those offspring come through his wife's maid? No, they would come from his wife's own body. God hadn't spelled everything out; Abraham sought clarification through trial and error and time. Eventually, all he could do was wait.

That's a position God often puts us in, and it's extremely frustrating. What do you do when you have a promise for a yes but you're living in a no? When day after day the opportunity for fulfillment passes and God seems to do nothing to take advantage of the opportunity? What do you do when God fills you with hope and then moves you into more hopeless circumstances? Like Abraham, you hope against hope. When everything seems impossible, you remember that God doesn't bow to impossibilities. That kind of faith produces great people and great nations.

Choose hope. Against all hope, hope anyway. Believe whatever God has promised. Long delays and circumstances moving in the opposite direction of your vision are normal, even confirming. This is how God works. He did so with Abraham and with others in Scripture. If you want to have biblical faith in the God who is working in your life, this is what it must look like.

Lord, faith is hard. The ways You dealt with
people in the Bible are difficult to endure. But
You rewarded the faith of those who endured, and
I know You'll do the same with me. Against all
hope, I'm choosing to hope and believe.

September 22

*Learn to know the God of your ancestors
intimately. Worship and serve him with
your whole heart and a willing mind.
For the LORD sees every heart and knows
every plan and thought.*

1 CHRONICLES 28:9

David was nearing the end of his life with an unfulfilled dream still in his heart. He knew the promise about the dream, of course—that God would enable David's son Solomon to build the temple David had envisioned. So the dream would be fulfilled, just not through David. Nevertheless, the man after God's heart knew that such dreams are accomplished when the heart is right. God's promises come to pass for those who prioritize Him.

That's the strange dynamic with dreams and destinies. Our hearts can be filled with some great hope or vision, yet God must remain greater within us if that hope or vision is to thrive. That's why David told Solomon to worship and serve the Lord with a whole heart and a willing mind. Not only is this the core of a relationship with Him, it's a necessary condition for receiving all the benefits of that relationship. When the relationship is broken or supplanted by greater desires, we miss the Presence and all the blessings that come with it. Even if the object of our dream or vision is fulfilled, it's less than it could have been. It's only fulfilling when God comes with it. And God only comes with it when He is our greater desire.

Whatever is in your heart to do, even when you're confident it's from the Lord, don't let it grow larger than Him. Get to know Him above all else. He already knows every thought in you and invites you to search out the thoughts in Him. That's how He imparts His dreams, and that's how dreams get fulfilled.

*Lord, I have so many desires, so many dreams of
things I want to do and want You to do in my life.
Help me keep my desire for You above them all.*

September 23

*"Every part of this plan," David told
Solomon, "was given to me in writing
from the hand of the Lord."*

1 CHRONICLES 28:19

David dreamed of building a temple for God (2 Samuel 7 and 1 Chronicles 17). Nathan the prophet assured him that it was a good idea, that God was with him. Then God told Nathan otherwise. In fact, God said it wasn't His idea to build a temple at all and that He didn't need one. But He would allow one of David's sons to build it, and the result was integrated into God's plan.

We aren't sure how this works. Who initiated the Temple? Did it come strictly from David's desires or from desires God had put into David? Why did the prophet assume it was God's plan and then hear otherwise from God Himself? How did the word of the Lord come? And fast-forwarding to the verse quoted above, how did God give David the plans in writing from His own hand?

We wish the Bible were more specific about the mechanics of revelation—how God speaks, how much uncertainty is involved, and how we can tell if our desires are God-given or not. But these things aren't spelled out. All we know, at least in this episode, is that David's desire somehow became God's plan, that hearing God was an uncertain process at first, and that David and Nathan were convinced they got it right over time, down to the details of the plans. The rest is for us to speculate about. Or experience—if we pursue such interactions with God ourselves.

Don't assume that every word from God was crystal clear at first. Jeremiah heard a word from God but wasn't certain until circumstances confirmed it (Jeremiah 32:6-8). But believe along with the prophets that God's voice can be crystal clear with faith and confirmations over time. Details of His plans can be revealed to you from His own hand.

*Lord, grant that I might hear You as clearly
and confidently as David did when You gave
Him plans for the Temple.*

September 24

Be strong and courageous, and do the work.
Don't be afraid or discouraged, for the
LORD God, my God, is with you.

1 CHRONICLES 28:20

Life is full of bullies. Intimidators. Tasks, trials, temptations, and even people with a disproportionate ability to keep us feeling beaten down and victimized. They remind us of our limitations and weigh heavy on our hearts. They seem to drain "abundant life" from us. They can even paralyze us in fear.

God's people often face monumental tasks or overwhelming opposition. Those in Scripture who found themselves in such situations—Joshua, David, Solomon, and others—were told not to fear but to be strong and courageous. Why? Because the God who is bigger than any and all giants was with them.

The Presence of God is always an immediate game changer. When David was surrounded by thousands, he slept in peace because he plus God outnumbered an intimidating army. When Jehoshaphat was threatened by a coalition of three armies, he turned from worry to worship and enjoyed victory without even having to fight. When Elisha's servant was panicking because of a hostile Syrian army, a vast array of God's horses and chariots and fire was behind the scenes preparing a defense. In every case, God's Presence and His solutions turned apparent victims into victors. And they still do.

This isn't automatic. It requires not being afraid or discouraged by the size of the task—that is, faith and courage. In other words, we find God's Presence has more impact in our lives when we're actually aware of it. A shift in perspective makes Him more tangible and accessible. When we make that shift, we can "do the work" with confidence and trust in Him.

Lord, I trust You with the mountains I face. They are
often overwhelming, but You are infinitely larger. Help
me put more confidence in You than in my obstacles.
If You are with me, nothing is impossible.

September 25

I am the LORD who heals you.

EXODUS 15:26

My young son lay in bed asleep—seemingly at peace. But I knew the traumas he had experienced that day and the words that had pierced his heart. They were the kinds of wounds that all of us receive every day. We become battered, bruised souls that learn to survive. But simply surviving doesn't seem ideal, especially for your own children. So I prayed for healing. More than that, I declared Jesus' Presence in the place of every trauma and wound.

Jesus demonstrated on earth that all sickness and infirmity must bow before His Presence. He clearly didn't heal everyone in the land—there were plenty of people left over for the disciples to heal after His ascension, even in places where Jesus had passed before—but according to the report of the Gospels, He did heal everyone who came to Him and asked. In His Presence, wounds and diseases are healed.

When we become carriers of God's Presence, we can speak words of healing too. We can impart His Presence into all kinds of wounds, including the deep emotional traumas that stick with us for a lifetime. The God who comforts (2 Corinthians 1:4) wants to be present in our pain, not just to walk us through it but to heal us from it. His desire is to touch, to soothe, to heal. His processes can be slow, but His work is thorough. He heals completely.

Receive the healing that comes with the Lord's Presence. Let Him touch every raw wound and lingering scar. But also speak His Presence into the wounded places of others—words that comfort and heal with kindness and mercy. Pray for His touch and, wherever possible, be the one who gives it. The Lord who heals is still reaching out—to us and through us.

Lord, I have needed Your healing so often, and I still do. Please speak Your restoration into all my wounds, and give me wisdom and words to speak Your Presence into the wounds of others.

September 26

You have tested us, O God; you have
purified us like silver.

PSALM 66:10

The psalm begins with God's great miracles that He has done for His people. It ends with praise for the God who answers prayer. But in the middle is testing and hardship and long, painful endurance. The psalmist observes of the God of great power and deliverance and mercy, "You captured us in your net and laid the burden of slavery on our backs. . . . We went through fire and flood" (vv. 11-12). *Then* He brings us to a place of abundance.

God pressed Jacob down in a wrestling match, allowed David to be driven into the wilderness, confined Joseph in an Egyptian prison for years, and let Paul suffer from some situation that kept him weak and broken. But in these seasons of stressful dangers and crushing weights, they learned of God's faithfulness and power on their behalf. They grew to depend on Him even when circumstances were harsh, threatening, and constantly shifting. Like newly poured concrete, their faith settled and hardened over time and became impenetrable to corruption and hostile forces. They leaned into His Presence and found Him always near and always working.

Let Psalm 66 be a marker on your journey. This testimony of a season of hard endurance sandwiched between two testimonies of God's great power and blessing is an accurate summary statement of life in Him. His Presence is a blessing, but one that comes with trials and tests. It isn't easy. Experiencing Him is certain but not simple. He gives promises for the destination but not smooth highways for getting there. Endure patiently, press ahead, and don't ever for a moment assume that the Christian life or a relationship with God was meant to be a bed of roses. It's a long journey and an epic battle, and there are ample rewards for those who persevere.

Yes, Lord, the seasons of testing are hard. And painful.
But purify me well. Let my faith endure. And remind
me often that You are with me every step of the way.

Peter and John laid their hands upon these believers, and they received the Holy Spirit.

ACTS 8:17

Several times in Acts, people received the Holy Spirit when someone already inhabited by Him laid hands on them. Timothy received a spiritual gift when the elders of a church laid hands on him (1 Timothy 4:14). Paul longed to visit the Roman church in order to impart a spiritual gift to its members and make them stronger (Romans 1:11). Apparently, a very spiritual experience can be transferred to others through a very physical Presence.

We might like to think of God's Presence as a completely private experience, and sometimes it is. But it's never exclusively so. God has made us to be interdependent in our relationship with Him so that much of our experience comes through others. He is not only to be known, He is to be shared.

This is hard to fathom in a culture of independence, but it's solidly biblical. God inhabits His people and then spreads through them to others through prayer and physical Presence. In spite of all the flaws we notice in others, in spite of all the friction we experience in our relationships, those who are born of His Spirit are also bearers of His Presence. We receive and then impart what we have been given.

Receive the Spirit and His gifts from others, and impart them to others too. You are a conduit of power, a minister of the resurrection life. Freely you have received, freely give—not only by distant prayers but by physical impartation. Cultivate God's Presence within you and take Him everywhere you go.

Lord, You are a Spirit who inhabits flesh—in Jesus and now in Your people. Help me open myself to receiving the gifts You have given others. Fill me with all Your fullness and let me share Your Presence with others, too. Inhabit my touch, my words, my prayers.

September 28

The Lord said to her, "My dear Martha, you are worried and upset over all these details! There is only one thing worth being concerned about."

LUKE 10:41-42

It's a familiar story with a familiar message. Jesus is visiting the home of some friends, and Martha is busy preparing a big dinner for the honored guest and others who have gathered. Mary, as a cohost, is expected to help with all the preparations; that's normal in this culture. But Mary departs from normalcy and sits at the feet of Jesus, listening to Him teach. Martha is offended by the unfairness, but Jesus commends Mary for forsaking busyness and investing her time in what's most important.

God wants us to fulfill our responsibilities, of course, but only with the right perspective. What would He say of our fast-paced times? "I see people striving for so many things—to fulfill their responsibilities to their families, to earn an income—but often doing these good things in a way that shows a motivation for status, comfort, pride, protecting themselves in the future, impressing people, or even simply greed. They envision a dream and then spend themselves on reaching it, but they never really do. They pursue 'needs' that aren't needs. All the while, they neglect Me, the one who could give them status, security, promises for fulfillment, comfort, and so much more in a moment's time. They have real, deep-down desires but are trying to fulfill them in misguided and inefficient ways. If they invested more time in Me and less time in their strategies, I would give them better results, both internally and externally."

We know this is true. We tell ourselves often that we need to slow down and prioritize the Lord's Presence. Still, we keep running the rat race, spinning our wheels, chasing the wind, or whatever other metaphor describes our condition so well. We have to stop. Literally. Sitting and listening is more important than anything else we can do.

Lord, forgive my busyness. Whatever it costs, help me not to skip my time with You.

September 29

I will not abandon you as orphans—
I will come to you.

JOHN 14:18

Jesus' heart behind this verse is clear: "From the foundation of the world, I was near while you remained distant. Eyes had not seen the Presence right next to them. Do you know how I longed to be clothed in flesh and live among you? Finally I could be seen—not by a handful of prophets tuned in to My Spirit, but by anyone with natural eyes. They could listen to My voice and see My works. Why would I limit that awareness of My Presence to three years of ministry? That enormous expense for one small moment in one small country? No, My desire is to dwell with you—all of My people— closely and unmistakably forever.

"I understand when you say you wish you had been alive when I walked among you. But it grieves Me when you don't realize how I walk among you now. Your awareness of Me sometimes reverts to pre-Pentecost levels, but it is meant to be so much more. You make decisions without hearing My voice, pray without sensing Me in the room, and talk about Me as though I'm not listening. Why? I said I would come to you. I said My Spirit would be in you. I promised My Presence at all times. If you aren't aware of Me, it isn't because I'm not there. It's because you aren't paying close enough attention. I show Myself clearly to all who seek Me without giving up."

When the Lord seems distant, remind Him—and yourself—that He not only promised closeness but implied that we would experience Him in practical ways. Refuse to live like an orphan. Ask Him to make His Presence known in some way today, and keep the eyes of your heart open to see what He will do.

Jesus, I know You are with me. Please show me how.
Help me live in constant communion with You and with
an awareness of Your Presence. May my words and
actions always acknowledge that You are in the room.

September 30

When I am raised to life again, you will
know that I am in my Father, and you
are in me, and I am in you.

JOHN 14:20

In John 14:8, one of the disciples asked Jesus to show them the Father. In the only kind of language one can use to express infinite thoughts to finite minds, Jesus explained that the Father was in Jesus doing His work and that Jesus was in the Father—and that anyone who believes these things can do the same works Jesus did. It's a mystery—hence the lofty verbiage—but it's true. Jesus and the Father are united as one, and those who believe are united with them.

The Resurrection is confirmation of these things. It was a testimony confirming all that Jesus did and said, but it was also a spiritual explosion of power that continues to ripple through the centuries. It's evidence that the God who rules over creation has entered human history and reoriented it. Through the power of the Resurrection, we are now united with Jesus and with God—as one. We are in Him and He is in us. Life is new.

Are you living a new life? Few Christians feel Resurrection power coursing through them, but according to the Word, we are one with the risen Lord. That doesn't mean ease or comfort, but it does mean we walk through trials and tribulations with an ability to overcome them. Today's troubles are tomorrow's trophies for those who are filled with God's Presence. Recognize the power at work in you and choose to live in it.

Jesus, show me what it means for You to be in me
and for me to be in You. Enable me to live my life in
Resurrection power—in Your strength and wisdom
and love. Help me do the works that You did and
share in the unity You have with the Father.

October 1

*Those who accept my commandments and obey
them are the ones who love me. And because
they love me, my Father will love them. And I
will love them and reveal myself to each of them.*

JOHN 14:21

We know it's possible to obey God without loving Him. The Pharisees and
plenty of religious people since have proven that. But the reverse isn't true.
It isn't possible to love God without obeying Him—or to put it in more
relational terms, without sharing His heart and carrying out His desires. And
that's what obedience is, in its truest biblical sense. It's a heart connection
with God that heeds His will and produces His fruit.

Jesus gives a profound, twofold promise to those who have that kind of
relationship with Him. He and the Father will love them, and He will reveal
Himself to them. Both sides of that promise are remarkable: one implies that
the God who loves unconditionally has a unique, conditional love for those
who love Him, and the other implies that love is a condition for greater
revelation. If we are lacking either—a sense of His love or a clear view of
Him—then this may be the reason. Perhaps our love for Him is the problem.

If that's the case, the solution isn't to try to muster up more love. That's
futile. We can stoke it and stir it up, but we can't manufacture it. No, the solution is to ask His Spirit to fill us with His love so that we understand how
deeply He loves us. "We love Him because He first loved us" (1 John 4:19,
NKJV)—meaning that a glimpse of His love will prompt a similar response in
us. When we are filled with that love, obedience becomes natural and revelation increases. We begin to see Him as He is.

*Jesus, I do love You; help me love You more. I want to
step into the relationship You have with the Father, to
live out Your will, and to see a greater revelation of You.*

October 2

God is our refuge and strength, a very present help in trouble.

PSALM 46:1, NKJV

In C. S. Lewis's *The Horse and His Boy*, Bree (the horse) and Shasta (the boy) were chased through the night by a terrifying lion. They found out much later in the story that the lion was the good Aslan, who was actually guiding them, protecting them, and spurring them on in their journey. His terrifying presence was really their salvation.

That's often how we experience God. When we're in trouble, He seems distant. That's because we hold an underlying assumption that hardship is a sign of His having abandoned us. Our minds know that isn't true, but our hearts say otherwise. God seems far away when we're struggling.

This psalm promises the opposite—that He is very present when we need Him most. He was present in delivering Israel out of Egypt, through the wilderness, and into the Promised Land. He was present in delivering Peter from Herod's grasp and Paul and Silas out of a Philippian prison. But He was also present *in* the troubles of Jacob as he and God wrestled, *in* the painful words of the prophets, and *in* the trauma of the Cross. His Presence is often for our rescue but also often for difficult correction, teaching, or transitions. Either way, He is there for our good.

God is your refuge and strength—a refuge to protect you and a strength to help you overcome. Both defense and offense. Even when you are wrestling with Him, He is there to preserve and empower. The times you think He has departed from you are often the times He is most powerfully present. Whatever hardship you are struggling with, He is in it—guiding you, protecting you, and spurring you on in your journey.

Lord, I depend on You—even when You seem far away. I know You are with me in every circumstance, no matter how difficult or traumatic. Please let me experience You as a very present help in trouble.

October 3

Do not banish me from your presence, and don't take your Holy Spirit from me.

PSALM 51:11

David wrote the famous words of Psalm 139: "I can never escape from your Spirit! I can never get away from your presence!" (v. 7); "You saw me before I was born. Every day of my life was recorded in your book" (v. 16); "When I wake up, you are still with me!" (v. 18). In other words, God is always with us, always aware of our every thought, always by our side.

This is the same David who, having sinned and been disciplined, pleaded with God not to banish him from the Presence. He begs for the Holy Spirit not to be taken from him. That's because David knows the difference between God's omnipresence and His relational Presence. He knows his sin has cost him some degree of intimacy with God, and he wants that intimacy back. The comfort and peace he once felt with God's Spirit are gone.

We live in a different age and know that being born of the Spirit makes for a different relationship—a relationship in which we are united with Him. He doesn't leave us. Still, the experience is similar. It's possible for us to lose intimacy with Him and to feel distant through our own neglect, indifference, and sin. We may not be banished from His Presence, as David feared, but we can certainly feel alienated. We sense a breach when things aren't right.

Our own sin adds an unwanted dynamic to our relationship with God. We know He always accepts us when we turn to Him, but we remain unsettled about the possibility of discipline and correction. It's easy then to slip into performance mode, trying to make things right by our behavior. And it never works. When necessary, repent and trust that His Presence is still with you. Rest in His mercy and enjoy His peace.

Holy Spirit, remind me of Your Presence, even when I sin. Restore me to deeper intimacy with You than ever before.

October 4

From there you will search again for the LORD
your God. And if you search for him with all
your heart and soul, you will find him.

DEUTERONOMY 4:29

Israel's falling away and exile were foretold long before it happened. God knew when He made His covenant with the Israelites that they would not be able to keep it. Moses presents the consequences as an if/then proposition—as though their apostasy is a hypothetical possibility at any given point in history—but the wording implies that it's going to happen. Unaided, human nature tends to rebel.

Even so, God gives a sweeping promise in the midst of Moses' warning. In the place of exile—in our times of deepest, darkest alienation from Him—a desperation-induced search for Him will be rewarded. Though He hides Himself from casual or proud observers, His purpose is always to be found by those whose hearts are ready for Him. A chastened, humble soul is perfectly primed for the Presence. And God obliges as though all offenses have been forgotten.

If this is God's reward for the rebellious who have rejected Him and then turned back, imagine how He responds to those who already belong to Him, already follow, and want to seek Him at a deeper level. If He is willing to bring close those who have strayed, He certainly brings close those who are already there. But those who are far away are aware of their need to seek Him; those who are in a good relationship with Him often don't realize how much better the relationship can be if they press in even further.

Awaken to the opportunity of coming even closer—of seeking the One you might think you've already found. However familiar you are with Him, He invites an even greater familiarity. Always seek it.

Lord, how do I seek You? My heart is turned toward
You. I'm grateful for Your Presence, but I want more. Let
me find You in new and deeper ways today.

October 5

Let us go right into the presence of God with
sincere hearts fully trusting him.

HEBREWS 10:22

In the days of the Tabernacle and the Temple, the place of God's Presence was designated as a small "Holy of Holies" in which the Ark of the Covenant was placed. Only the high priest could enter, and then only once a year, and even then only after a series of purifying rituals that would protect the priest from death. No one just waltzed into the place where God dwelled.

But a greater High Priest came, and at His death, the thick curtain of the Holy of Holies was torn from top to bottom. God removed the barrier between the hearts of His people and His dangerous but awesome Presence. An encounter that once would have consumed us now enlivens us. We can enter the throne room of God confidently.

What does that mean for us practically? Long before Jesus came, God's people prayed, and He heard. Anyone could speak with the invisible God at any time. And we still pray to an invisible God and know that He hears us. So what's different now? How does access to the Presence change the way we relate to Him? What does it mean to "go right into the presence of God"?

For one thing, it means that we pray not to a distant God but to a God who lives within us. For another, it means that we pray with complete assurance that there is no obstacle between us and Him. And finally, it means we can expect to experience His Presence if we ask. Instead of relating to Him as someone sitting across the table trying to negotiate an agreement, we connect with Him as a partner working on the same project. Or instead of knowing Him as someone else's father, we can crawl into His lap with full confidence that we are welcome.

Father, let me never take my access into Your
Presence for granted. And let me never relate to You
as though You stand at a distance.

October 6

There has never been another prophet in Israel
like Moses, whom the LORD knew face to face.

DEUTERONOMY 34:10

Moses was the first and greatest prophet to meet with God face-to-face, though other prophets, like Isaiah, Daniel, and Ezekiel, would later see visions of the Holy One. Moses foretold another Prophet who would come from within Israel one day, and he instructed the people to listen to Him—the same instruction that a voice from heaven spoke when Jesus was transfigured on the mountain (Matthew 17:5). Jesus knew the Father face-to-face, and many have known Jesus, the Lord of glory, face-to-face. Since the era of Moses, God has issued repeated invitations to know Him deeply and personally.

How do you respond when you hear of someone having this kind of relationship with God? Do you assume it's an exception or see it as an invitation? Does "face-to-face" seem like a once-in-a-Testament phenomenon or a prototype for a new creation? When we see this possibility fulfilled in Moses and others, and then long to pursue it for ourselves, God seems to set the potential for our relationship with Him at a much higher level. He gladly opens doors into His Presence for those who boldly believe they can enter.

Ask God what "face-to-face" means with Him, and don't rule out any possibilities. Never look to the experiences of those around you as a standard; let others' experiences motivate you, if they will, but never let them lower your expectations. There is no "normal" with God. Seek the exceptional, and boldly enter where He leads.

Father, I don't want an average experience with
You. I want "face-to-face." Show me how I can
have it and let me not miss any open doors.

The LORD your God is living among you. . . .
He will rejoice over you with joyful songs.

ZEPHANIAH 3:17

What would a God who sings over His people say to them? "I want My people to see Me through the right lenses. Most of them don't know that I rejoice over them with singing. They don't recognize My heart in everyday life. They think obedience is My ultimate goal for them, but it's really the means to an end. Do they really think all of history led up to a point of My coming to demand greater obedience simply for the sake of having more servants and accomplishing My plans? Is My glory really just about getting My way?

"No, I'm after your hearts. My glory is revealed in your delight in Me. The way I'm demonstrating My glory and treading on My enemy is by winning your affections. My blood wasn't spilled just to get you saved so you can go to heaven when you die. You have to understand that there's a greater *reason* I save you—that I want to know you intimately, to commune with you, to gaze into your spirit and have you gaze back into Mine. I made human beings to feel the joy of romance because *I* feel the joy of romance. My heart beats faster with love.

"My sacrifice was never just to prove My power or My wisdom. People eventually realize that relationships matter more than their achievements or status. Yet they suggest that My glory is a matter of establishing My Kingdom or demonstrating that I'm sovereign. What would be the point? I could establish My Kingdom and prove My power without a sacrifice on a cross. There's a deeper heartbeat behind this creation than that. I want to know and be known. That's why worlds were created."

Lord, let me hear You singing over me. Fill my heart with Your song. Draw me into the depths of Your heart and let me love You completely.

October 8

*When the Spirit of truth comes, he will
guide you into all truth.*

JOHN 16:13

We hear voices. They aren't audible voices—at least not for most of us. But despite their subtleties, we have the ability within us to hear three distinct messengers: our own thoughts, God's voice, and the adversary's lies. The problem is that all three voices clothe themselves in our own vocabulary and speech patterns. They sound like us. If we aren't discerning, we can hardly tell the difference.

That's where the Spirit of truth comes in. He is the arbiter among these voices, distinguishing His own from ours and the enemy's. If we listen to Him, the flaws in our own thinking are revealed and the lies of the evil one are exposed. The more we focus on His truth, the more we recognize the variations from it. Intimacy with Him makes voices clearer.

As always, our question in matters like this is "how." We want a step-by-step pathway to cultivate intimacy with Him and to hear His voice. Entire books have been written on the ways God speaks, though His ways can't be limited to a finite number of pages. But as usual, God's answer to our "how" is "keep asking, keep seeking, keep knocking." Don't look for steps; look to a Person. Pursue Him in faith. Ask the Spirit to be an alarm signal in your heart to alert you to false perceptions and to clothe His words in such vitality that they come alive as you hear them. Expect Him to do verbal surgery within you, separating corrupted and cancerous ideas from the life-giving inspiration He gives. You may never notice His process, but you'll see the results: a greater discernment and sensitivity to His leading. It's a promise. The Spirit will guide you into all truth.

*Holy Spirit, only You can sort out the voices in
my mind, and I'm trusting You to do that. You
promised to keep me from deception and to lead
me in truth. Please fill me with the ideas and
inspiration of Your heart and Your Kingdom.*

October 9

He will tell you about the future.

JOHN 16:13

We hunger for a glimpse of our destiny. That's why psychics, clairvoyants, and fortune-tellers remain in business. Most of them are frauds, and those who aren't receive their information from ungodly spirits. But they give hints of the future and stir up expectations, and desperate hearts long for such hope.

The desire to dream is a good and true desire. It was put into us by a Creator who wants us to dream with Him—according to truth. He wants us to see our potential in Him, envision the growth of His Kingdom, and to partner with Him in faith to accomplish it. He is a forward-looking God with great plans and a desire to share them. He longs to give us glimpses of our future.

The psychics and fortune-tellers offer a counterfeit of what the Spirit truly gives. And He gives it to all who believe in Him. Most believers apply this verse to a few select prophets and apostles, but we all have the ability to envision with God. No, He doesn't tell us everything about the future and satisfy all our curiosity; we still have to walk by faith. But He does guide us into tomorrow, give us cues about what we need to prepare for and what we will need to face, and fill us with pictures of His plans for us.

Don't quench the dreams and visions the Spirit puts inside of you. Human nature is to subdue our hopes in order to protect ourselves from disappointment, but God gives longings and hopes in order to fulfill them. Jesus' promise applied not only to a few apostles but to all who would read His Word. The God who knows the future will lead you into yours by giving you glimpses of it. Notice them and follow His lead.

Spirit of God, You know my future and how it fits with Your Kingdom plans. Please show me enough to draw me into Your purposes. Give me God-sized visions that we can fulfill together.

October 10

He will bring me glory by telling you
whatever he receives from me.

JOHN 16:14

Many in our age wish we could have seen Jesus when He walked among us. We want to see His miracles firsthand and hear His words directly. If we could hear His tone of voice when He preached or observe His interaction with His disciples, we would know a lot more about Him than we do. We long for the personal experience of being there.

The eyes of our spirit can still see and hear Him. He communicates with us regularly. The Spirit receives things—words? gifts? assignments?—from Jesus and reveals them to us. He interacts with us at a level that caused Jesus to tell His disciples it was better for them if He went away (John 16:7). His ascension was by no means the end of the relationship. It was only the beginning.

We now have access to greater truth than the disciples had when Jesus was physically present. But notice that Jesus didn't define the Spirit's role simply as a guide to our intellectual study of Scripture. Just as Jesus did and said many things that were never recorded in the Gospels (John 21:25), God has many thoughts that haven't been written in the Word. The Bible is the lens through which we see the realms of heaven and earth, and all that the Spirit says will be consistent with it. But He leads us into deep mysteries and shares His heart in personal ways. He directs our steps individually and opens our eyes to the ways God works in our lives.

Jesus' glory is made more visible in us when we receive His revelation through His Spirit. If our current relationship with Him causes us to long for the "better" days of His physical Presence, we have much more room to grow. His Presence is as real now as it was then.

Jesus, let the Spirit bring You glory in me by revealing
Yourself—Your truth, gifts, and mission—to me. Help
me experience You as personally as the disciples did.

October 11

It is no longer I who live, but Christ lives in me.

GALATIANS 2:20

Hudson Taylor, the pioneer missionary to China's interior, wrote of the sweetness of the rest he felt in being fully identified with Jesus. He said he was no longer anxious about anything—that no matter where God put him, no matter how hard the constraints or pressures, God's Presence within him would be equal to the task. Somehow he had learned how to rest and let the Spirit flow through him.

That's one of the benefits of the Presence, if we can learn to rest and let the Spirit live in us fully. In order to do that, we have to be able to trust in the goodness of His purposes, even when our path takes unexpected turns. We have to be able to believe that He is living and working within us. And we have to be able to let go of all competing props that would hold us up or tempt us to rely on our own resources. In some respects, it can be hard work to rest in Him.

The "hard work" ends when we get the right perspective and establish new habits and thought patterns. Resting in Him gets easier with practice. At first it goes against our normal tendencies, but over time it becomes less of a conscious choice and more of a default posture. We're so used to striving and straining that the idea of resting in Him seems irresponsible and unnatural. But when we see the fruit of it, we realize it was irresponsible and unnatural to do anything else.

Choose rest. Let Jesus live in you. Insist that the vine bear fruit through the branch. Not only is that your true desire, it's His, too.

Jesus, do You really live Your life in me? Can I really depend completely on Your strength? have Your desires? display Your purity and character? walk in Your power? Show me how. Become all You want to be in me.

*This left Jacob all alone in the camp, and
a man came and wrestled with him until
the dawn began to break.*

GENESIS 32:24

Jacob had issues, particularly that nasty episode with his brother that had never been resolved. Years earlier, he had tricked his father into proclaiming Esau's blessing over him instead. Then Jacob fled in fear that Esau would kill him. Now, after marriage, children, and years in a far country, Jacob was returning home. He would soon see his brother face-to-face. And he feared the prospect of his past catching up with him.

Jacob was left alone in the camp, and God (as a man) came and wrestled with him all night. It's one of Scripture's strangest stories—until we reflect on the picture and realize we've been there. There are times when we are left alone to wrestle with God, when past issues loom over our psyche and threaten to burden us with consequences and conflicts we don't want to confront. At such times, God's Presence is painful but purposeful, provoking a catharsis or cleansing from old wounds. It can be an intense, exhausting struggle, but eventually dawn comes and we receive a blessing for having contended with God—and ourselves—face-to-face.

For your relationship with God to arrive at any depth, it has to include some of these wrestling matches. Old wounds must be healed, and it's sometimes a messy process. When your past and your God come face-to-face, it can be an intense encounter. But it's a necessary one, and it leads to blessing—sometimes even a new name. The struggle lasts until dawn, but *only* until dawn. And with it comes a new day.

*Lord, the dark night can be overwhelming. Sometimes
You seem to oppose me and strengthen me at the same
time. But I know there's blessing—and the dawn of a
new day—at the end. Let it come quickly.*

Then the man said, "Let me go, for the dawn is breaking!" But Jacob said, "I will not let you go unless you bless me."

GENESIS 32:26

Some people see surrender as the purpose of Jacob's wrestling match with God—that Jacob had to come to the end of himself and submit to God's lordship. But there seems to be no surrender in this episode, or even a need for it. Jacob had already arrived at the end of himself, unable to face his brother in his own strength and willfulness. No, the "man" who wrestled with Jacob "saw that he would not win the match" (Genesis 32:25), and Jacob refused to let go until he was blessed. And God gave him a new name because he had "fought with God and with men and [had] won" (Genesis 32:28)—even on his back. No, this wasn't about surrender; this was about contending with God and knowing His heart even in the intensity of a battle.

God honors spiritual tenacity. His Presence can provoke turmoil within you for a time, but those who press through the struggles and hang on to faith in Him will be blessed. God has many sides to His face, and sometimes He seems to show a harsh one. But what do you really see—a harsh face or a tender heart? Whichever you see more clearly determines whether you can endure being on your back for a while, as well as what blessing you see at the dawning of the next day. Only the tenacious hold on to God in the midst of a wrestling match with Him and the relentless issues of life.

Hold on. Go ahead and wrestle; God doesn't mind. But if you've been put flat on your back, keep holding on anyway. Stay in close contact with God, no matter how intense, and see into His heart. He wants to bless. He's waiting for the dawn. And He wants you to wait for it too.

Lord, may I be as bold as Jacob. I won't let you go until You bless me. And even then, I'll cling to You forever.

...no longer be Jacob," the
...om now on you will be
...e you have fought with
...h men and have won."

GENESIS 32:28

We get down on the
..., grunt and gasp, and
...o know who is stron-
...le competitive streak.
...bond.

...because He wants to
...rating His mastery—
...e first came to Him.
...le to all the twists and
...times lets us "win." In

...tling match. Sure, He
...lory would rightfully
...ated in His image to
...age to relate to Him.
..., to enjoy Him—and

...ormal or a sign that
...er to Him, knowing
...will end, and even if
...r for it and feel closer

...u—even in the difficult
...uggles of life. When I'm
...ge me with Your words.

LINE NO.	PRODUCT AND DESCRIPTION	QUANTITY ORDERED	QUANTITY B.O.	QTY. SHIPPED	UNIT PRICE	PRICE U/M	AMOUNT (NET)
1	CUTBR2020B100 1PH 100A LDCTR	1.00	0.00	1.00	76.25000	each	76.25
2	CUTBR230 2P-120/240V-30A CB	3.00	0.00	3.00	10.00000	each	30.00
3	CUTBR220 2P-120/240V-20A CB	1.00	0.00	1.00	10.00000	each	10.00
4	CUTBR240 2P-120/240V-40A CB	1.00	0.00	1.00	10.00000	each	10.00
5	CUTBR115 SP-120/240V-15A CB	3.00	0.00	3.00	4.25000	each	12.75
6	CUTBR120 SP-120/240V-20A CB	2.00	0.00	2.00	4.25000	each	8.50
6 Lines Total			Qty Shipped Total	11.00	Total		147.50
					Taxes		8.85
					Invoice Total		156.35

October 15

Jacob named the place Peniel (which means "face of God"), for he said, "I have seen God face to face, yet my life has been spared."

GENESIS 32:30

The Israelites at Sinai didn't want God to speak to them directly. They were afraid they would die, so they begged Moses to go into the Presence and then tell them what God had said (Exodus 20:19). When Daniel heard Him speak, he trembled, fainted, and lay facedown (Daniel 10:3-11). When John saw a vision of Jesus, he fell at His feet as though dead (Revelation 1:17). None of them were harmed, but all were severely traumatized. The Presence of God can be frightening.

Some people confuse God's Presence with a warm heart and a positive attitude. Others confuse it with emotional swells, tears of joy, or deep burdens. Though God certainly can prompt all of these, there's another side to the experience: awe. When He comes close, we are overwhelmed. The things we were preoccupied with seem suddenly irrelevant, the insurmountable problems we faced suddenly seem like minor speed bumps, our self-will bows to His majesty, our imperfections come to the surface of our minds, and all we can think about is how to relate to Him properly. God's Presence is always good, but never quite safe.

Jacob's encounter wasn't a majestic view of God's glory, as the visions of many others were, but he still understood the gravity of it and marveled that he survived. We need to have the same perspective: joy that we have access to Him, but an understanding of the radical nature of meeting Him face-to-face. In other words, a sense of wonder and awe. We need to recapture the ability to marvel at the amazing position we're in. And we should be grateful that our lives have been spared.

Lord, help me recapture the awe of Your Presence. Show me Your glory and then fill me with wonder at seeing it. May my encounters with You always be frequent but never taken for granted.

*God has made a home in the heavens
for the sun. It bursts forth like a radiant
bridegroom after his wedding. It rejoices
like a great athlete eager to run the race.
The sun rises at one end of the heavens and
follows its course to the other end.*

PSALM 19:4-6

Psalm 19 gives us a picture of the glory of God being revealed in His creation—particularly through heavenly bodies. The skies are continually speaking of His greatness. And in the middle of the psalm, the rising sun becomes an illustration for His own movements.

The Presence of God is like the dawn. When we wake up to the reality of the Presence, it's like a sunrise in the heart. Every area of life—circumstances, relationships, responsibilities, plans, and goals—is seen in a new light. We get new eyes. We see the limitless possibilities offered by the beginning of the new day. The hidden features of the landscape are unveiled. The cold night air begins to warm. Dawn is full of hope.

The "dawn" theme shows up often in Scripture because we crave newness and God offers it. We're told that God's mercies are new every morning, and so are His blessings and promises and life. He spoke entire worlds into being and began a re-genesis with the Cross. "New" is what He does best.

Whenever you feel stagnant or stuck, ask for the rising of the Presence to come like the dawn. Petition Him for a new season of refreshing. Receive new eyes from Him and see the world in a new light. Then go explore His Kingdom in that light. Try things you haven't tried before. Pray bigger than you've prayed before. Worship more zealously than you have before. Expect all things to become new.

*Lord, You make all things new. I need refreshing from
You. I need to wake up to a new day in life and see
things in a new way. Give me new eyes, show me new
mercies, and take me on new adventures.*

October 17

*We also have the prophetic message as
something completely reliable, and you will
do well to pay attention to it, as to a light
shining in a dark place, until the day dawns
and the morning star rises in your hearts.*

2 PETER 1:19, NIV

The excitement of a new day comes with the rising of the Presence within us. Many of us interpret verses like 2 Peter 1:19 in the context of Jesus' second coming, and it's true that Scripture often points us toward that event. But the light of prophetic and apostolic testimonies is meant to shine in the night of our soul until the Morning Star—Jesus, according to Revelation 22:16— rises *in our hearts*. In other words, we hang on to the Lord's promises until we experience the fulfillment of them within us. The words are the signposts; His Presence is the goal.

This is what we long for. That feeling of excitement about life, of adventure and exploits—these are the possibilities of a new day dawning within us. The things that excite us—about the world, God's creation, a new relationship, a new interest, a new goal or ambition or dream—do so because of some characteristic or attribute of God reflected in them. We scarcely realize it, but we are drawn to the creativity and beauty of God in the people and things He has made and the ways they function and interact. He has placed His personality in creation. All things in the world that are truly interesting for their beauty or creativity or intrigue are interesting because they reflect something about Him. Our enthusiasm for life, when we have it, is really about Him.

The more He dawns in our hearts, the more we wake up to a new day with enthusiasm. The Kingdom adventure to which we are called can only be enjoyed when He is directing it from within us. And He promises that He will.

*Jesus, rise up within me and live the joy
of Your life through me.*

October 18

Arise, shine, for your light has come, and
the glory of the LORD rises upon you.
See, darkness covers the earth and thick
darkness is over the peoples, but the LORD
rises upon you and his glory appears over
you. Nations will come to your light, and
kings to the brightness of your dawn.

ISAIAH 60:1-3, NIV

First Jesus arises and shines *on* us. Then He arises and shines *within* us. Finally, He arises and shines *through* us. These words of God through Isaiah speak glory over Jerusalem and, by extension, over all whom the Lord calls His own. We needed a great light, and Jesus came to us. Now people dwelling in "thick darkness" need a great light, and Jesus comes to them—through us. And nations and kings will come to that light in the same way the world wakes up to each new day.

The Lord speaks to us about the world: "I've called you to arise and shine because My glory is coming upon you. You have received Me as a rising sun in your life; now become a rising sun to others. You can introduce and impart My Presence to others. When people really see Me in you—when you have immersed and saturated yourself in Me—they are drawn to Me. Even those who are hostile to My Presence in you are drawn to Me, but they resist and run because they are afraid to change. But those who are honest and hungry are drawn openly, without resistance, just like they were drawn to Me when I was with you in the flesh. Now they are attracted to the Me who is in you.

"Know that I rise up within you for your sake and for the sake of others. Believe that I have glory to reveal through you. And live in a way that lets Me shine on others."

Jesus, I want You to shine in me. I don't know how
that happens, but I'm trusting You to cover me in Your
glory and draw others to You through me.

October 19

He raised us from the dead along with Christ and seated us with him in the heavenly realms.

EPHESIANS 2:6

James and John had a lot of nerve. They wanted to sit on each side of Jesus' throne in His Kingdom. Jesus didn't tell them no, but He did explain how authority is granted in His Kingdom. It would be given to those who suffer and serve (Mark 10:35-45). Ruling with Him wasn't a privilege to be granted lightly.

The other disciples were indignant that James and John had even asked. Was it because of their audacity, or because they got the idea before the rest of them did? Either way, the other disciples were appalled at the idea of two disciples being chosen above others to rule in the Kingdom. The request seemed so arrogant.

Surprisingly, the New Testament makes some remarkable statements about our role in the Kingdom. It tells us that we have been raised up with Jesus and seated with Him in heaven—already (Ephesians 2:6). It says we will judge the world (1 Corinthians 6:2). It encourages us to endure because we will reign with Him (2 Timothy 2:12). It calls us royal priests (1 Peter 2:9) and a Kingdom of priests (Revelation 1:6). And it says those who overcome will sit with Him on His throne (Revelation 3:21) and will reign on earth (Revelation 5:10). For some unfathomable reason, we are destined to reign.

We need to remember that not only is Jesus present with us, we are present with Him. That means we are with Him on His throne—and that, in some sense, He shares His authority with us. It's an authority based in the humility of servanthood, but it's high above all earthly authority. Even though we are by nature weak and can do nothing without Him, His Presence results in power. Whenever we find ourselves in a low place, we can appeal to a higher realm. Our prayers and faith are based on a heavenly position.

Jesus, thank You for raising me up with You.
Teach me what it means to live in two realms
and to exercise the authority of heaven.

October 20

[He] has made us kings and priests to
His God and Father.

REVELATION 1:6, NKJV

Most of us are happy just with getting to heaven by the mercy of God and haven't given much thought to a throne. And unless we're filled with pride, we aren't preoccupied with exercising dominion over any earthly realm, much less a heavenly one. It's hard to know what that would even look like. We've envisioned a death or rapture that takes us away from earth, never to endure this planet again. But reigning? With the only true Lord? On earth? That stretches a lot of people's theology.

At the very least, we know this: by adopting us into His family, God has given us (1) a royal status and (2) a priestly function. We are priests/kings, or as Scripture describes it, a nation of priests or a royal priesthood.

A priest has the privilege of representing God to humanity (expressing His will, declaring His forgiveness, displaying His heart, for example) and of representing humanity to God (confessing sins, praying for His help, for example). It's a vertical relationship, a position at the intersection between divine and human interaction. A king, on the other hand, has the privilege of implementing God's government and policies on earth. It's a horizontal relationship, a position over human affairs on behalf of a higher authority. Combined, the two roles carry both heaven's and earth's authority. And according to God's Word, we have been given both.

How do you exercise those roles? Begin to see yourself as one of God's representatives on earth, knowing the authority in which you stand. Wherever you see something that does not reflect the Kingdom of God, pray and act to bring the Kingdom into that place. Persist in the Spirit until the earthly situation bows to heaven's rule. Live and speak as a child of the King.

Father, show me how to live as a priest and
as a king. Help me speak Your will and live
it out in every situation I see.

October 21

And we shall reign on the earth.

REVELATION 5:10, NKJV

Many of the verses about our ruling with Jesus are future-oriented, but some of them aren't, insisting that we are already a royal priesthood or a nation of priests. Even those that are future-oriented imply that we are preparing for that position now. They give us some sense of present authority to pray and implement God's mission in this age. Yet most of us pray tentative prayers without any sense of authority and carry out God's mission as though we are already defeated by the overwhelming tide against us. We may *be* royal priests, but we don't act as if we know it.

We need to understand that we are inhabited by the God of the universe and carry His Presence with us wherever we go. We bear the seal of His name. We host His Presence. Instead of letting our external environment shape whatever we feel inside, we need to let our internal environment shape whatever we encounter outside. That may just be a shift in perspective, but a changed perspective can result in changed actions and increased faith. It can have a powerful effect on how we live our lives—and what God does in them.

Look in the mirror each day and remind yourself that you are royalty. Tell yourself that you have priestly access to heaven's answers for earth's needs. Remember that this kind of authority is granted to those who drink the cup of Christ and who serve in humility—just to make sure your royal identity doesn't turn you into a head case on a power trip. Your authority is unlike any the natural world has yet witnessed through its human leaders. But don't underestimate the privilege given to those who are truly in Him and whose attitude is right. You, your royal highness, are destined for a throne.

Lord, how can I reign with You? That's hard for me to fathom, but I want to walk in every bit of authority You offer in this age. Please show me how.

October 22

*I am confident I will see the LORD's goodness
while I am here in the land of the living.*

PSALM 27:13

We have a pesky habit of expecting that anything truly good and lasting from the Lord will be given to us only in heaven, when the Kingdom has come in its fullness. In other words, we get the good stuff only after we die. Meanwhile, everything on earth is a heavy burden and a cross to bear.

Scripture is clear that this world is broken and won't be completely renewed until Jesus comes again. But it is also clear that God's promises are good in this age as well as the next. We can experience Him now, we can receive answers to prayer, we can enjoy the redemption of past mistakes and difficult situations, and we can taste of His gifts and goodness. He is a present God in present circumstances. He means for us to experience abundance in the land of the living.

God tells us about heaven so we'll look forward to it, and there's nothing wrong with envisioning its perfections when life gets difficult. But never let the promise of heaven distract you from the promises of today. No matter how complicated or heavy life becomes, God is able to deal with it. His Presence is available. He can turn any situation around in a moment. He may do that today, or He may take some time to accomplish His thorough work. Either way, He wants us to hold on to hope—to keep our focus on who He is in spite of what we see right now. He wants us to know that we can and will enjoy His goodness in the land of the living.

*Father, I know everything will be perfect one
day—that I'll see You face-to-face and experience
all the abundance and completeness I can handle.
But I also believe Your goodness and Your promises
apply to this age, on this earth, in this lifetime.
Please help me keep my hopes focused on You.*

As for me and my family, we will serve the LORD.

JOSHUA 24:15

You've experienced God's Presence. It's a beautiful thing between you and Him. And that's the way it should be—at times. But God's Presence, as personal as it is, isn't entirely private. He fills you with Himself not only to fellowship with you. You can actually *be* the Presence in the world.

Where do you do that? You house His Presence in every area of society, first and foremost in your family. As a member of a Kingdom of priests, you represent your family to God and minister His gifts and graces to each of its members. You help shape the environment of your home through your attitude, your actions, and your spiritual connection with Him. (You've likely noticed how contagious your moods and outlook can be.) Your worship affects the atmosphere anywhere, especially where you live and among those closest to you.

Many people find family members to be the most difficult people to live the gospel around. That's because they know all of our issues, and that can cause us to feel that we've lost all credibility with them. But being both transparent and humble has a powerful effect on others, especially those close to us. And when our transparency allows them to see the Presence of God, even through all our flaws, lives can change. Even without words, we can impact the environment of a home.

Whatever your family situation—whether you live alone, with parents or siblings, or with a spouse and children—God has put relatives in your life that can benefit from your relationship with Him. Be His Presence among them. Let your attitude shape the atmosphere. Treat Him as an honored family member. Let the Kingdom come in your home.

Lord, Your Presence brings peace to a home. Of all the places You want Your Kingdom to grow, families are a priority. Help me carry Your Presence around those closest to me.

October 24

Let us not neglect our meeting together.

HEBREWS 10:25

One might think the Presence would be most easily felt in the body of Christ, the church, but that isn't always the case. In fact, there are times and places when it's actually hard to see Him in His body. Yet He insists on being found there, working and moving through the gifts, callings, and desires of His people. When we look at a fellow believer's face, Jesus is behind it somewhere.

Though it may be hard to see His face in others at times, make sure it isn't hard for them to see His face in you. One of the key environments we're called to shape is the church—both inside and outside the walls of the building. We are to be the Presence of Christ among other believers, not only when we worship in one place, but also when we serve together in the world. Whether at church buildings, in homes, or in other venues, we are to give and receive the Presence to and from each other.

How can you *be* the Presence of God in your church? The same ways you can be His presence anywhere: by expressing His attitudes, speaking His words, seeking His wisdom and revelation, offering His solutions, and exercising His gifts. Anytime you operate in His Spirit, you are offering His Presence to others. And others need that from you as much as you need it from them. That's why meeting together is vital: the Spirit in many is stronger than the Spirit in one.

Bring the Presence into your fellowship with other believers. Learn to see yourself as a bearer of the Spirit—not a perfect one, of course, but an essential one. Learn to see others that way too. The church must be shaped and directed by those who are filled with Him and understand why.

Holy Spirit, please overflow from me and let me see You overflowing from others in my relationships with other believers. Let my church be known as people who display You and Your amazing works.

October 25

From the day Joseph was put in charge of his master's household and property, the LORD began to bless Potiphar's household for Joseph's sake.

GENESIS 39:5

Joseph was put to work in a difficult situation. This heir of God-given dreams and destiny had been sold into slavery and forced to manage the household of an Egyptian official. But God's favor—His blessing, support, and even Presence—seemed to be on Joseph, and he became a blessing, a supporter, and a carrier of God's Presence to others. In Potiphar's household, in prison, and then in all of Egypt, he kept rising to the top of his situation.

That happens when we bring God's Presence into our work situation. Our job and economic relationships are one of the vital sectors of society we're called to impact. We enter the workforce as employers, employees, or even just as participants and consumers, and God gives us favor there when we function in His Spirit. That doesn't mean we all rise to the top positions—that is, the "top" as the world perceives status—but we do all have spiritual authority and influence in the workplace. In fact, if we work among unbelievers, we're spiritually the highest-ranking people there. In the Kingdom, that's a significant influence.

Know who you are in the Spirit. Just as you have influence in your family and church, you carry the Presence of God into every area of life, including your occupation. You can ask God for solutions to difficult problems, serve a priestly function to those who don't know Him, sense God's heart for them and express it, and affect the environment with your words and attitudes. There's more to taking God's Presence into the world than overtly witnessing, on one hand, and quietly being salt and light, on the other. Demonstrate His character, feelings, and ways. Be the visible Presence of the invisible God.

Lord, help me be a Joseph—a person anointed by You to serve others well, to bless them, and to demonstrate Your ways. Give me Your favor and put me in a position of great spiritual influence.

October 26

Pharaoh said to Joseph, "I hereby put you in charge of the entire land of Egypt."

GENESIS 41:41

Not only did Joseph represent the Presence of God in his workplace, he eventually represented God at the highest levels of government. Like Daniel, Esther, and others strategically placed in kings' courts, Joseph was able to access God's revelation for Egypt's needs. Pharaoh had a dream and no means of interpreting it. Joseph asked God, received an interpretation, saved a Gentile nation from famine, and prepared the way for God's people to settle there. And he did it from a prison cell. He became an apt picture for what any of us can do in our world.

God can use any available, faithful person to impact the highest levels of society. Most Christians don't expect Him to do that—we don't normally ask for His solutions to national or global problems—but perhaps that's the problem. We assume that unless we sit in an executive boardroom or a political office, or aren't an absurdly talented trendsetter, we aren't influencers of our culture. We forget that Joseph, Daniel, Esther, and Nehemiah were put in strategic positions by extremely unlikely means. Strategy is God's business; a response of faith and expectation is ours.

If you've never asked God for divine solutions to the problems of your community, city, nation, or world, try it. Open your ears to revelation from Him. One of the most effective ways to represent His Presence is to receive and implement His wisdom. The world is hungry for solutions, and being able to apply wisdom from above gives you favor and glorifies Him. Learning to hear may be a process, but the benefits to you, to society, and to the Kingdom are ultimately rewarding. When God's people access God's answers, it impacts the world.

Lord, give me divine solutions to human problems.
Put me in a position through divine appointments to
share them with whoever needs to hear them. Help
me bring glory to You by being a blessing to others.

October 27

The lips of the righteous nourish many.

PROVERBS 10:21, NIV

The world is full of negative news. Words of criticism, discouragement, bitterness, and condemnation spew out of people's mouths regularly—even through broadcast, electronic, and print media. Highly influential spokespeople can put a distorted spin on whatever is going on in the world, and we drink it in like irresistible poison.

Negative words are one of the enemy's most effective strategies. Human nature accepts a cynical or critical spin much more easily than news that sounds "too good to be true." And not only is that the case in mass-market media, it also applies to our personal relationships. God calls us to be a kingdom of blessers, yet our own nature and the adversary's influence conspire to create a culture of cursing. Instead of our words nourishing life, they quench it.

You can shape the world around you with your words, probably more radically than you think. Spoken words are one of the vehicles for God's Presence. His Spirit actually backs those words that are in line with His heart and purposes. Our speech isn't neutral or meaningless. It's substantial and powerful to impact our environment. Jesus warned strongly against "idle words" (Matthew 12:36), and Proverbs assures us that they can kill or nourish life (18:21). Words matter. A lot.

Become a vehicle of the Presence through your own broadcast medium—your mouth. Wherever the enemy spreads news of despair, meaninglessness, condemnation, and bitterness, choose to counter with a Kingdom perspective and spin it with hope, purpose, redemption, and possibilities. As Paul wrote, bless and do not curse (Romans 12:14). As your personality is filled with God's Presence, let your tongue express it. Fill the Kingdom with words of a hopeful King.

Father, fill my mouth with Your words—with meaning
and hope and peace. Inspire me to pronounce blessings
on those around me, even when they are unaware.
Change the atmosphere according to my speech and let it
set people up for an encounter with You.

October 28

*I have specifically chosen Bezalel. . . . I
have filled him with the Spirit of God,
giving him great wisdom, ability, and
expertise in all kinds of crafts.*

EXODUS 31:2-3

One of the most powerful shapers of culture is the arts and entertainment industry. Music, movies, sports, literature, and other forms of creative expression form the opinions of the age far more effectively than speeches, sermons, and instructional books do. It's tragic, then, that Christians have often isolated themselves from influence in these important areas of society. Many have decided that secular entertainment is too corrupt for a Christian to be involved with. So we've left it to voices that don't reflect anything approaching a biblical worldview. And those voices are usually more dominant than ours.

We've missed enormous opportunities to take the Presence into the secular marketplace through entertainment media. Many are trying, some effectively, but we have a lot of ground to regain. Reentering a sector of society we long ago abandoned is a battle. So we struggle to produce "Christian" works for a "Christian" market while the world continues to produce powerful messages with little influence from us. Times are changing, but it's slow.

God is creative. You've probably noticed that in the things He has created. The first people mentioned in the Bible as being filled with His Spirit are two artisans, Bezalel and Oholiab, whose job was to craft the Ark of the Covenant and the articles of worship for the Tabernacle. As children of a creative God, we can be filled with His Spirit for creative purposes too. Inspired works of art can be vehicles of His Presence, messengers of the Kingdom and the King.

Create with whatever creativity God has put within you. Your expression makes you like Him—an Artist whose heart overflows into the works of His hands. The world needs inspired creativity. And His Presence inspires greater works than the world can conceive.

*Spirit, fill me with Your expressiveness. Inspire me and
equip me—and all of Your people—with the skills to
influence culture with the creativity of Your Kingdom.*

October 29

He is the one we proclaim, admonishing and teaching everyone with all wisdom, so that we may present everyone fully mature in Christ.

COLOSSIANS 1:28, NIV

God revealed His truth to Israel and told them to keep His words in their hearts. "Repeat them again and again to your children," He urged. "Talk about them when you are at home and when you are on the road, when you are going to bed and when you are getting up" (Deuteronomy 6:7). In other words, His voice was meant to resonate deep in the souls of His people throughout the generations. They were to teach in a way that kept His Presence in view.

We can do that easily in our churches, instructing people toward spiritual maturity. But a crying need of our generation is for a widespread impartation of God's wisdom. How can we get the Presence into the intellectual discussions of our day? Into schools and universities? When we remember that our presence is a vehicle for His Presence, the answer is simple. We go there. God's desire is to display Himself through His people. We carry Him into learning institutions and into discussions through our attitudes, prayers, and communion with Him. We season our words with the salt of His truth, even when overt references to our faith aren't accepted. We aren't limited by biases and restrictions. We have the limitless God within us; wherever we are, there He is.

Do you want to impact a generation for the Kingdom? Be the Presence of God in whatever schools you attend, influence, or even drive by. Engage in public discourse with the attitude of Jesus and a heart of compassion. Offer up prayers in the Spirit for the wisdom of God to fill the culture. There's no limit to the ways you can infiltrate society with the Presence that dwells within you.

Spirit, fill me with wisdom from above. Fill our schools, educators, and students with insights and revelation. Let Your Kingdom come—on earth as it is in heaven—even through people who don't know the source.

October 30

Enoch walked with God.

GENESIS 5:22, NKJV

We don't know much about Enoch other than that he walked with God—or "lived in close fellowship with God," as one translation puts it—but we know that God was present in his life in substantially different ways than He was in others. A chapter later, we're told that Noah walked with God too, and God also did exceptional things in his life. Apparently walking with God sets a person up for unusual treatment.

The Gospel of Luke tells us of two travelers on the road to Emmaus who walked with the resurrected Jesus and had a long discussion with Him before recognizing who He was. He unveiled scriptural truths to them and finally revealed His identity just before disappearing. This same Jesus, who apparently stepped in and out of the visible realm at will after His resurrection, is just as present with us as He was with the disciples on the Emmaus road. Is it possible that we walk with Him without recognizing Him, just as they did? And if so, can we become aware so that we aren't walking in ignorance?

God makes Himself more tangibly real to those who choose to walk with Him—to be conscious of Him, to converse with Him constantly, to enjoy a close relationship with Him—than He does to those who simply have knowledge about Him. Fellowship with God is a cultivated condition, and it's deepest among those who are alertly watching for Him to step into their visible realm at any moment in whatever manner He chooses. He is neither silent nor detached, but normally only vigilant eyes detect His voice and His Presence. He walks with those who choose to consciously, deliberately, watchfully walk with Him.

Lord, I want to walk with You as Enoch, Noah, and the disciples of Jesus did. But I want to be fully aware at all times. Sharpen my senses to recognize You in every moment today.

October 31

You hide them in the shelter of your presence.

PSALM 31:20

The promise is given to those who honor God, who come to Him for protection from the dangers of the world. We find ourselves in spiritual battles and physical hardships, and the enemy doesn't fight fair. Though we aren't spared from our definition of harm, those who trust God and lean on Him are spared from His definition of harm. He is a God who protects His people.

That's what this psalm is about, from beginning to end. David felt besieged; his city was under attack, and he fled into God's Presence for protection. He acknowledged that God alone was his defender, that God had not handed him over to the enemy but had set him in a safe place, that God cared about all his anguish and turmoil, and that God had treated him faithfully. Yet he also acknowledged that he was in distress, miserable, full of grief, and held in contempt by many. It's a clear statement of two sides of our experience: we're desperate, but God is trustworthy. Outside of His Presence, we're vulnerable to the worst kind of harm; but in His Presence, nothing can touch us. He is our place of safety.

That's why we can go wherever God calls us—into dangerous mission fields, war zones, or even the jungle of our workplace—without anxiety. His Presence makes all of those places safer than our own living room. God doesn't call us to be reckless, but He does call us to be fearless. No refuge is more secure than He is.

In whatever decisions you face, take fear out of the equation. If you trust God and honor Him, He hides you in the shelter of His Presence. He allows the war, but guards you from defeat. He protects those who are loyal to Him.

Lord, hide me in Your Presence. Protect me in the battles I'm facing. As I honor You with my trust and cast myself on You, please deliver me—not just with survival but with complete victory.

November 1

Fix your thoughts on what is true, and honorable, and right, and pure, and lovely, and admirable. Think about things that are excellent and worthy of praise.

PHILIPPIANS 4:8

What fills your mind in your mental downtime—when your head hits the pillow at night, when you wake up in the morning, when your thoughts wander while you're driving? Often those mental wanderings will reflect your highest priorities or your deepest worries. Unless things are going perfectly smoothly in your life, your thoughts will swirl with concerns.

What if you chose to dwell on the Presence of God within you during those times? What if you fixed your mind on Him, His blessings, His Kingdom agenda, and the multitude of ways you can enjoy Him at any moment? What if you turned those mental adventures into relational experiences with Him—not necessarily deep, heavy conversations, though those are appropriate at times—but casual conversations about His goodness and love? Relationships are enjoyed most when both parties share their dreams, talk about common interests, and express appreciation for each other's qualities. And though we talk often about having a relationship with God, most of us rarely have these kinds of conversations with Him. It's often a relationship that doesn't meet the criteria for most familiar, loving relationships.

Mental wanderings like these may revolutionize our lives and, in fact, deal with those concerns more effectively than our worrying does. The swirling thoughts and what-ifs that often churn within us don't accomplish very much, but a vibrant relationship with God certainly does. His Presence in us, when cultivated, probably accomplishes much more through indirect influence than we can accomplish directly by planning, plotting, and worrying. Our thoughts can weigh us down, but communion with Him gives life.

Lord, I fix my thoughts on You—on Your goodness, Your love, Your Kingdom, Your ways. I choose today to focus not on what seems like the highest priority but on what really is my highest priority—You. And I trust You to deal with all the things that concern me.

November 2

*My nourishment comes from doing the will of
God, who sent me, and from finishing his work.*

JOHN 4:34

Jesus and the disciples had been traveling, and He was tired. So He sat down
by a well to rest while the disciples went into town to buy food. When the
disciples came back, Jesus was apparently reenergized. They kept offering
Him food, but He wasn't hungry anymore. "I have food you don't know
about," He told them. Then He began two days' worth of ministry in the
town where they had stopped to rest.

Jesus wasn't refreshed simply by doing more work. That's an exhausting way to try to live. He wasn't refreshed by getting back in touch with the
Spirit, as though He had been out of touch before. No, the Spirit was fully
present in Jesus at all times. But when the Spirit manifested the work of God
through Jesus in an encounter with a woman at the well, He was energized.
That's what happens when the Presence gets stirred up. We get filled with His
enthusiasm and strength.

We've all experienced the boost of energy that comes when something
captures our interest. But we aren't used to thinking of God—or Jesus or the
Spirit—as having various levels of enthusiasm. He seems to be above such
swells of emotion. It's hard to understand His fire rising and falling with certain ideas and events.

Scripture is clear that God has zeal for specific purposes and plans (Isaiah
9:7; 37:32). And when we line up with God's purposes for us, we're reenergized
too. That's why it's essential to notice the passions God has put within you.
That's where He has designed you to work and build His Kingdom. Your food
is to do His will, and whatever His will is for you, it will refresh you.

*Father, I know my food is to do Your will. Please
fill me with the right passions and then refresh me
as I live from my heart for Your purposes.*

November 3

Looking at the man, Jesus felt genuine love for him. "There is still one thing you haven't done," he told him. "Go and sell all your possessions and give the money to the poor, and you will have treasure in heaven. Then come, follow me."

MARK 10:21

The rich young ruler can at least be glad he wasn't named in Scripture. He goes down in history as someone who turned down the opportunity of a lifetime—or an eternity—by not following Jesus. He came with a question about how to inherit life, and Jesus felt compassion for him. But the man was more attached to his possessions than he was to truth. He went away sad. He had an opportunity to live in Jesus' Presence and instead he chose his personal status quo.

An invitation into God's Presence—or into any new level of relationship with Him—almost always involves such a choice. Perhaps it isn't as dramatic as a whole new lifestyle, as the rich young ruler faced, though it may be. But it at least involves a choice between Jesus and our current schedule, or Jesus and our current employment, or Jesus and the way we currently spend our free time, or . . . well, you get the picture. Whether a heart-idol is involved or not, the logistics of priorities dictate a choice. When we want more of Him, we almost always have to have less of something else.

How much do you want more of Jesus? Your heart probably gives one answer and the current constraints of your lifestyle another. And something has to give. But the rewards of knowing Him more deeply always outweigh the costs. And He always responds to those who say yes to His Presence.

Jesus, I never want to make the same choice that the young man made—at any level of my life. I do say yes to Your Presence and always want to go deeper, whatever it costs.

November 4

*By his divine power, God has given us
everything we need for living a godly life. We
have received all of this by coming to know
him, the one who called us to himself by
means of his marvelous glory and excellence.*

2 PETER 1:3

No matter how much contempt the world has for those born into a silver-spoon existence, there's almost always a hint of jealousy behind it. We're envious of those who are sheltered from all harm, whose problems are always solved for them, who never need to give a second thought about whether they will have enough. While we stress and strain to make a living and navigate the treacherous waters of our lives, some people seem to breeze through their days with ease. We long for that level of provision.

We have it. In the spiritual realm, everything is provided for us. We have been given "all things that pertain to life and godliness" by His divine power, as one translation puts this verse (NKJV). That doesn't mean we're spoiled children spiritually, but we do have the wealthiest Father in the universe. There is no shortage of any provision for those who are born of Him. His Presence within us gives us an abundance of spiritual power and authority, faith for both spiritual and material needs, all the fruits and many gifts of the Spirit, and much more. We may go through plenty of hard times, but we won't go through them without what we need. As we grow in Him, we tap into more and more of our Father's accounts.

With that in mind, why worry? Why be jealous of those who seem to live a life of ease? Seriously, what situation could you find yourself in without having His abundant help? He is always there, always working within you, and always working through you. His supply is limitless, and what He provides is always more than enough.

*Jesus, exercise Your divine power within me. Teach
me how to tap in to Your limitless supply so that I'll
never find myself lacking in anything You offer.*

November 5

*Since you have been raised to new life with
Christ, set your sights on the realities of
heaven, where Christ sits in the place of
honor at God's right hand.*

COLOSSIANS 3:1

Scripture says Jesus lives in those who have been born of His Spirit. We also know He is seated at God's right hand in heaven—and that we are seated there with Him (Ephesians 2:6). Unless one of these statements is false—and being inspired Scripture, they aren't— then both Jesus and we are in two places simultaneously. He is in heaven and in us, and we are on earth and in Him. The result is not only a dual citizenship but also a dual Presence. In His incarnation, He became an on-earth God; in our resurrection with Him, we became in-heaven people.

What does that mean for us? We're used to the mysteries of the God-head, so it's not hard for us to imagine Jesus being in two places at once. He is, after all, a Spirit as well as a man. But then so are we. Our natural eyes see only the limits of location, but our spirits are capable of existing in different realms simultaneously Our physical senses dictate thoughts and feelings related to the material world, and most of us heed those senses without much resistance. But Scripture calls us to lift up the eyes of our spirit and see differently. We are to think the thoughts of heaven and function in that realm.

You'll have to choose which senses to heed: your physical senses or the spiritual perceptions given through God's Spirit in you. Most Christians don't know how to exercise those senses, but you can learn by asking and trying persistently. Paul's instruction is to think the thoughts of the Kingdom and set your sights on the realities of heaven. Immerse yourself in another way of thinking, feeling, seeing, and doing. Wherever Jesus lives, you live too.

*Spirit, open my spiritual senses to know the realities
of Your Kingdom. Help me see myself here, in
heaven, and everywhere else Jesus dwells.*

November 6

*Think about the things of heaven, not the
things of earth.*

COLOSSIANS 3:2

The things of earth get right in our face and speak to us relentlessly. We have
things to pay for, plans to arrange, people to please, and responsibilities to deal
with—all of which make our to-do lists long and our bodies and souls tired.
There's no way to avoid the things of earth—we do actually live here, after
all—but we can't be totally preoccupied with them. They drain us of energy
and resources if we are.

What does it mean to think about the things of heaven? It means knowing heaven's agenda: God's purposes and His ways. It means seeking visions of
Him and His plans. It means living with heaven's values: a Kingdom culture
of integrity, honor, purity, peace, generosity, and blessing. We understand that
heaven is filled with radical worship right this moment, and we join in the
praises. We learn to treat other people as eternal beings, even if we aren't sure
of their eternal destiny—to see the treasure God has put in them rather than
the junk that comes to the surface now. And we need to know that we are
surrounded by spiritual beings: angels that minister to us and deceptive spirits
that try to seduce us. Heaven's realities are described in Scripture, and we are
fully encouraged to let them become the realities in which we live and move
and breathe.

Whatever is happening visibly in your world today is only a fraction
of your true life. The rest of the story—the most important parts of it—are
invisible to your physical eyes. But they aren't invisible to your spirit or your
thought life. Choose where to dwell, and fill your mind with the reality of
heaven. Live out its culture, its values, its relationships, and its activities.

*Spirit of God, fill my mind with heavenly thoughts. Let
me see what's truly real and really true. Help me live out
my citizenship as an influencer in Your Kingdom.*

November 7

*You died to this life, and your real life is
hidden with Christ in God.*

COLOSSIANS 3:3

When people enter a witness protection program, they are given a new identity. Their old name, accounts, places, daily routines, and even relationships have to be put in the past. They become someone new.

When we are born in Christ, we become someone new too. We may look the same as we did before, but a fundamental change has occurred. The Christian life is an exchanged life. Jesus took our identity to the cross and then filled us with His identity. Instead of living our own self-oriented lives, He lives His life through us. He took all that we have upon Himself and gave us in exchange all that He has—His name, His authority, His inheritance, and more. As Paul said, we no longer live; He lives in us.

That means we don't have to depend on our own wisdom, love, faith, or any other quality. We don't even pray in our own name anymore. We use His. His Presence within us provides all we need. We can claim *His* faith, *His* ideas, and *His* solutions for everything we need. We can have His humility, patience, boldness, compassion, and any other of His attributes we need. Instead of focusing on the *how*, we focus on the *who* and let Him be Himself within us. Over time, we begin to love or forgive or have bold faith not because we should but because that's who we are. The life of God within us will be expressed if we will let Him express Himself.

If you think you're in need of a new identity, remember how radically Jesus can shape you from within. Ask Him for a complete makeover, and then live according to the Jesus inside you. The more He fills you, the more you become your true self.

*Jesus, make me new. Live Your life through me. Only
You can empower the life I was meant to live.*

November 8

You are the salt of the earth. . . . You are the light of the world.

MATTHEW 5:13-14

God created human beings in His own image, watched us fracture and distort that image through sin, worked throughout ages to prepare to restore the image, sent the perfect image of Himself to live among us, and then put the Spirit of that perfect image into the beings that had fallen. The result is a renewed race not only made in His image long ago but remade in His image and enabled to house His own Presence.

If you had gone to such lengths to create people who reflect your likeness—that is, to put your glory within them—how would you want them to use their identity? Your ultimate goal would be fellowship, of course; that's what love desires. But you wouldn't want it to be a purely private relationship. If you make such extraordinary sacrifices to display your own characteristics in others, you want the display to count. If your motive is to be known, you want to be known widely.

God's motives for creating and recreating people in His image were (1) to share His thoughts, emotions, and goals with creatures who could understand them and relate to Him in love; and (2) to make Himself known using creatures who could reflect His character and ways. We know this from the major themes of Scripture and from His instructions that point to these purposes. His command to know and love Him, as well as His calling to go into the world with His Spirit and His truth, show us His heart. His desire is for us to be influencers in a fallen world—to be salt and light, affecting others with the image He has put within us. Amazingly, He has left the display of His glory largely to repaired and restored vessels like us.

Lord, it's an awesome responsibility to reflect Your image and Your glory to the world, but it's an awesome privilege, too. Give me opportunities to do so and help me reflect You well.

November 9

The glory of the LORD will be revealed, and all
people will see it together. The LORD has spoken!

ISAIAH 40:5

God calls His people to be salt and light, to be influencers for the sake of His Kingdom. He puts His glory and His Presence within us so we can reflect His image to the world. And He inspired prophecies about His glory filling the earth as the waters fill the sea (Habakkuk 2:14). There's an obvious connection between the calling and the prophecy. The earth will be filled with God's glory because God's glory-reflectors—His people—will cover the earth.

We live in a day of widespread depravity and agendas hostile to God's Kingdom. But we also live in a day of unprecedented revival and growth in the Kingdom itself. Once-resistant mission fields are being penetrated by an increasing awareness of Jesus, His people, and the power of His Spirit. Secular institutions are being influenced by people filled with God's Presence. In many respects, the knowledge of God's glory is spreading throughout the earth. And according to prophecy, it will continue to do so.

God's favor rests on those willing to carry His Presence into their world each day. If we gaze at Him, are transformed to be like Him, are filled with Him, and become one with Him, His glory will be on us and in us. He will put us in strategic positions as influencers; He will make Himself visible in us. Some won't recognize His glory for what it is—or will choose to be blind to it—but others will see and be drawn to Him. And His Kingdom will continue to grow until He comes with even more visible glory.

Lord, I want to experience Your favor, and I know You
give it for purposes as worthy as displaying Your glory.
Give me assignments and put me in position to reflect
You. Display Yourself visibly in me.

November 10

The devil took him to the peak of a very high mountain and showed him all the kingdoms of the world and their glory. "I will give it all to you," he said, "if you will kneel down and worship me."

MATTHEW 4:8-9

Satan tempted Jesus by trying to get Him to fulfill godly desires by ungodly means. His offer of the nations of the world was legitimate; they were currently under his influence, and the nations had been promised as an inheritance for Jesus by Old Testament prophecy. But Satan's offer was a shortcut to fulfillment and would come at an unreasonable cost: the Son worshiping the enemy. That was a high price that would have subverted the order of the universe.

But hidden in Satan's statement is a curious fact: the nations have glory. Already. Even in their brokenness, even under the enemy's influence, glory is already in them. If God's glory is going to cover the earth as His people take His Presence into nations, and if nations already contain some measure of glory, the mission will involve an unveiling of things already on earth. Before Jesus comes down in a visible demonstration of ultimate glory, His glory can rise up in His people and in the kingdoms of the world. He will be revealed from above and from below—a victory as resounding as He deserves.

What does that mean for us practically? It means there's a glory to be unveiled in society, and we can be instrumental in the unveiling. We carry God's Presence not only into our churches but into governments, businesses, arts and entertainment, schools—every social structure known to humanity. Scripture never tells us to sit in our living rooms waiting for glory to be revealed in the sky. We are called to influence our world with the glory we have been given.

Lord, I know every sphere of society is already filled with the seeds of Your Kingdom. Give me eyes to notice what others don't see and help me reveal Your glory wherever I see it.

November 11

I ask you again, does God give you the Holy Spirit and work miracles among you because you obey the law? Of course not! It is because you believe the message you heard about Christ.

GALATIANS 3:5

Paul preached the gospel of grace throughout the region of Galatia, and many believed. Jewish Christian teachers came through the region later and insisted that righteousness, even for believers, was a matter of keeping Israel's law. Paul debated this idea vigorously in Galatians, making the valid point that if we're saved by grace through faith, we should continue to live by grace through faith, not by keeping the law. The work of God was accomplished in their lives not because of obedience to the law but because they believed.

This verse in Galatians 3 comes in the context of that debate about the role of the law versus the role of faith. That theme takes center stage. But do you see what gets lost in the discussion? One of Paul's best pieces of evidence is that the Holy Spirit is present in them and working miracles among them because of their faith. It's clear that this isn't strictly a theological argument, an exchange of unprovable hypotheses. No, God has given visible confirmation of their faith. When people believe, the Holy Spirit's work can be seen and miracles happen.

Why don't we see more miracles? Perhaps because we don't believe we will. We have two millennia worth of rationalizations to explain all the times we haven't seen one when we expected to, and the explanations may undermine our faith. Or perhaps it's because we don't cultivate the Spirit's Presence as the Galatians did. Regardless of the reason, we can believe and expect to see evidence of the Spirit's work. He responds to faith in the message of Jesus. There is power in His Presence.

Holy Spirit, I believe in Your power to do miracles, and I want to see the evidence of Your work. Help me believe fully and expect great things from You.

November 12

*Then I went into your sanctuary, O God, and I
finally understood the destiny of the wicked.*

PSALM 73:17

The psalmist Asaph has been observing the wicked and noticing that they
often seem to have easy, prosperous lives. Meanwhile, God's people struggle
and suffer. Why? Is a godly life for nothing? Asaph asks all the questions we
tend to ask when life doesn't seem fair. But when he enters God's sanctuary and meditates in the Presence, the truth sinks in. In the grand scheme of
things, the prosperity of the wicked and the suffering of the righteous are
both very, very short. The eternal picture makes the life of the righteous look
so much better than the life of the wicked.

God's Presence is the place to ask hard questions. Our minds can go
to a lot of dark places on their own, and we never really arrive at the truth
by our own reasoning. But sitting in God's Presence, asking for His wisdom,
and meditating on the truth of His Word seems to make cloudy issues much
clearer. He may not give immediate or even thorough answers, but He does
give us perspective. He fills us with faith and turns our hearts in the right
direction.

Do heavy questions hang over your head today? Do God's ways seem
obscure and confusing? Does life seem unfair? Whatever issues you need clar-
ity about, take them into the Presence of God and ask Him about them. Sit
with God with a request for understanding, a patient heart, and an openness
to whatever words and images He brings to mind—especially those from
His revealed Word. He loves to impart His perspective to His people and to
enlarge their hearts with His wisdom and vision. And He turns your heart
toward Him.

*Father, there's so much I don't comprehend. Your
ways don't seem to make sense. I'm choosing to
trust You, but I also want to understand. Please
teach me truth and give me Your perspectives.*

November 13

Nevertheless I am continually with You;
You hold me by my right hand.

PSALM 73:23, NKJV

That the psalm turns on a "nevertheless" implies that the psalmist has felt some distance or separation from God. In fact, his musings were off base until he entered the sanctuary and spent time in God's Presence. But the "nevertheless" is not only a hinge moment for the psalmist, it's a repeated hinge moment in our lives too. We have to be able to shift from that sense of separation to a deep-down knowledge that we are still with Him. We have to know, even when we don't feel it, that He holds us by the hand.

It's true; God holds us in His heart. His gaze is continually on us. He takes pleasure in the vision He has for us, in the knowledge of who we are becoming and the plans He will fulfill for us. He watches our steps and brings us back into the right path when we stray from it. He isn't constantly scanning the past and defining us by what we've done; His eye is on the present and future to draw us into His purposes and define us by who we are becoming. He sees His Son in us and is exceedingly pleased.

Knowing this simple truth is essential if we're going to fulfill His purposes for us. It's so basic that perhaps we feel we should move on to deeper truths, but what can be deeper than His Presence and constant care? In a world in which multitudes feel isolated and alienated, we have the permanent companionship of the most loving and powerful Being in the universe. Nothing could be more important and life shaping than that. Whatever difficulty we go through, He nevertheless holds us by the hand.

Father, I know You are with me and are holding
my hand. I don't always feel it—thank You when
I do—but I depend on Your Presence anyway.
Remind me often that Your eyes are on me and
that You are working on my behalf.

November 14

*You guide me with your counsel, leading
me to a glorious destiny.*

PSALM 73:24

Soldiers on the battlefield have to be able to receive communication from headquarters in order to follow the right directions and tactics. A pilot has to receive clear communication from air traffic control in order to position the plane for safe takeoff and landing. A good marriage has to have good lines of communication in order to stay healthy and strong. In virtually every area of life, clear expression is important.

That's true of our relationship with God, too, but an alarming number of Christians believe we can't hear God with any certainty. In fact, those who claim to hear from God are viewed suspiciously by those outside the church as well as by many within it. But Scripture is clear that God communicates with His people—both through His Word and in many other ways consistent with it—and that we can receive His counsel. He has a long history of speaking to His people in a way we can understand.

Not only that, God's counsel leads us to "a glorious destiny." Those who fear His voice haven't understood His purposes. Whether He speaks to correct or to encourage, His plan for us is good. Those who trust Him and listen for His voice need not fear condemnation; He has already assured us that there is no condemnation for those who are in Christ (Romans 8:1). His voice comes to us for growth, encouragement, and comfort (1 Corinthians 14:3). He is an effective communicator who is very positive about our future. We have everything to gain by listening to Him.

Lord, let me hear You clearly. You promised that I can, and Your voice is vital if I'm to carry out Your will and fulfill the destiny You've planned for me. Please speak in a way I can understand, and give me faith to believe what I have heard.

November 15

Whom have I in heaven but you? I desire
you more than anything on earth.

PSALM 73:25

Religious teachers from all religions throughout the centuries, including Christianity, have looked down on desire as an unspiritual attitude. In Buddhism, it's the root of all suffering; in some Islamic and Christian teaching, it has often been considered the root of sin. Perhaps desire is held in such contempt because human nature points it in so many wrong directions. But good desire—the deep and true longing of the heart—is a God-given attribute designed to lead to fulfillment. When we turn our longings in the right direction, God satisfies them with Himself.

Jesus told His disciples to seek first the Kingdom of Heaven, and all their other concerns would be taken care of (Matthew 6:33). That's because we were designed to love Him above all else, and life doesn't work well if we don't get that right. His purpose is relationship. That's the driving force behind creation. God loves to be longed for and delights in those who delight in Him. The attitude of the psalmist is music to His ears.

Let this verse be a personal statement of desire. You can have meticulously correct doctrinal beliefs and strong faith, but if a longing for God doesn't drive you, you've missed His heart. That would be tragic—for Him and for you. The God who is love and who says His name is Jealous wants your passion above all else. He has the works of many servants and the thoughts of many theologians, but He doesn't have the hearts of many lovers. Not fully. Be one of those whose desire connects with His.

Lord, I know You want my passion more than You want
my doctrine, my understanding, my obedience, or even
my faith. I realize these things are related, and You really
want them all. But above all else, You want my love. I
really do desire You more than anything on earth.

November 16

My health may fail, and my spirit may grow weak, but God remains the strength of my heart; he is mine forever.

PSALM 73:26

"If you don't have your health, you don't have anything." Perhaps you've heard such nonsense before; it's a common enough statement from people who can't see past our current physical existence. Perhaps those who say it haven't thought through the implications, but plenty of terminally ill patients can testify that there's a hope greater than our health. Even when we're wasting away, an eternal flame burns within those who are born of the Spirit.

Paul said as much in describing the afflictions he bore in his own body (2 Corinthians 4:7-12). There's a glorious power within us, an imperishable treasure contained in these perishable vessels. If we walk through life with a limp, we still walk with the strength of God showing up in our weakness. If we are attacked by a disease, it cannot touch our spirits. Though we taste death, we overcome it. Yes, God gives us wonderful promises for healing and often does miracles in our bodies. But even when we don't experience that blessing, we have greater promises for more lasting blessings. If God is the strength of our heart, no weakness really matters.

Embrace the psalmist's statement: "he is mine forever." There really is no other passion that lasts forever, but this one not only lasts, it grows. When the world shakes—and it often does—only one relationship, one security, one truth can't be shaken. He is the stability and permanence we long for. No matter what is happening in your world today, hang on to the imperishable, unending Spirit within you. He is your life, and nothing can take Him away.

Lord, You are the strength of my heart, and I know I can rely on You in any situation. I face threats to my health, safety, and security in this world, but that isn't my life. You are. Help me stay anchored in You.

November 17

But as for me, how good it is to be near God! I have made the Sovereign LORD my shelter, and I will tell everyone about the wonderful things you do.

PSALM 73:28

Everything in the Christian life comes by faith. That doesn't mean it's all in our heads; we can actually experience the fruits of this life in tangible ways. But not before we exercise faith. That's the currency of this Kingdom. So when the psalmist speaks of being near God and making the Lord his shelter, he isn't stating universal facts that apply to everyone. He's stating particular facts that apply to himself and anyone else who makes a similar choice to believe. He *made* the Lord his shelter. It didn't happen automatically.

That's the difference between knowing the truth that God is everywhere and experiencing Him practically at certain times. Faith fills our hearts and minds with an awareness, a focus, and expectations, and God responds to that posture. Yes, there's a psychological dynamic at work in that approach, but experiencing Him is so much more than a psychological effect. Faith primes us spiritually to receive Him in deeper ways, and it prompts His response to come to us in deeper ways. The psalmist experienced God's nearness and benefited from His sheltering because he believed he would.

Don't assume that God will do what He wants to do regardless of whether you believe. Sure, He often protects us and provides for us in spite of our awareness of Him—He's a good and merciful Father—but faith makes a difference in how much of His protection and provision we receive. That's why Jesus attached significance to faith as it relates to prayer, seeing God's glory, receiving salvation, and much more. You can choose how much of God you will experience by what you believe.

Father, by faith I make You my shelter. I also accept Your Presence and receive all other blessings You offer. Grow my faith to be as big as the gifts You want to give.

November 18

I asked the LORD to give me this boy, and
he has granted my request. Now I am giving
him to the LORD, and he will belong to the
LORD his whole life.

1 SAMUEL 1:27-28

Not only did Hannah desperately want a child. She also desperately wanted her husband's other wife to stop taunting her for being barren. She was depressed, frustrated, and bitter. So she prayed, crying out to God with many tears and a desperate vow. If God would give her a child, she would give the child to God.

God answered her prayer, and a nation was changed. The child grew up to be a prophet who restored integrity to Israel's priesthood. Samuel became a key figure between the period of judges and the kingdom era, anointing both Saul and David as Israel's first two kings. God entered Hannah's desperation, fulfilled her longing, and glorified His name.

Our desperation often becomes the platform for God's Presence and glory. He's always with us, of course, but He seems to enter into our deepest needs in a unique way. The cry of a desperate heart appeals to Him, not because He likes our desperation but because He likes our dependence. As the heart of a parent goes out to a hurting child, the heart of God goes out to those who cling to Him in their pain. When we grab hold of Him and refuse to let go because of our desperation, He hangs on to us, offering His comfort, strength, and solutions. He responds to the spirit of desperate arms around His neck.

Invite God into your desperate moments. Cry out to Him and ask Him to use your desperation for His glory. Expect Him to respond in His mercy. He may use your plea not only to change your life, but also to change a nation.

Lord, hear my pleas. Enter into my needs and
fulfill them. Use my desperation as a platform
for Your glory. And like Hannah, may I see Your
provision and praise You for it.

November 19

*Jesus said, "Come to me, all of you who
are weary and carry heavy burdens,
and I will give you rest."*

MATTHEW 11:28

A lot of Christians feel a certain ambivalence toward this verse. That's because in following Jesus, we take on certain responsibilities toward family, church, work, and friends that, when added together, weigh heavily on us. Being a good, dutiful Christian isn't easy.

Perhaps in following Jesus we take on more responsibilities than He has actually laid on us. We may assume the Christian life to be something other than it was meant to be. But even if we are laden with heavy loads, Jesus offers a lightness in the way we carry them. As the strength within us, He assumes responsibility for how circumstances turn out when we trust Him with them. When we roll our burdens onto Him, listen for His instructions on our role in addressing them, and do only what He tells us to do, we can be fully confident that He will work them out for His purposes. As our burden-bearer, He is responsible for outcomes.

Jesus spoke specifically to those who were under the heavy burden of performing for God. Right standing before Him isn't earned. But if we thought this performance mentality was unique to the Pharisee culture of Jesus' time, it's simply because we don't notice how it has seeped into Christian teaching today. We easily slip into approaching the Christian life as principle-based standards of behavior rather than as Presence-based fruitfulness. The result, whether we're adhering to religious standards or cultural expectations, is a heavy burden.

Refuse to be crushed by the weight of life and even of Christian responsibility. Be responsible without being burdened. Jesus frees you from heavy burdens—if not from the responsibilities themselves, then at least the weight of carrying them in your own strength. When you come to Him—intentionally into His Presence—He lightens your load.

*Jesus, life is heavy, but Your burden is light. As I rest in
Your Presence, please carry my loads. I'm trusting You
with every detail of everything that concerns me.*

November 20

*I keep asking that the God of our Lord Jesus
Christ, the glorious Father, may give you
the Spirit of wisdom and revelation, so that
you may know him better.*

EPHESIANS 1:17, NIV

Wisdom, from a biblical perspective, is the ability to apply God's truth to life's situations. Revelation, on the other hand, is the knowledge that comes directly from Him that may or may not make sense to the natural mind. And we desperately need both.

God makes it clear that human wisdom is foolishness to Him, and His wisdom is foolishness to the natural human mind (1 Corinthians 1:18-25). We need the thought processes that tune us in to the truths of heaven. But He also makes it clear that we have the mind of Christ, a state of revelation that imparts God's truth to us apart from common sense and natural reasoning (1 Corinthians 2:16). We need to see the reality of things above, the heavenly perspective that gives us a picture of supernatural power, of angels and demons, of the big-picture plan that hurtles toward a final unveiling of the Son of God and those He calls His own. Without a picture of the throne room of God and the purposes He has ordained, we won't know the direction of history or the power of His promises. But without the wisdom that comes from above, we won't be able to apply His purpose in real-life situations. We'll default to human reasoning and limit His works. We need a mind (wisdom) and a heart (revelation) that comprehend the purposes of God.

Seek wisdom *and* revelation—the thoughts of God and the visions of God. Ask for the eyes of your heart to be enlightened with truth from above. Make this prayer the cornerstone of your thought life, the centerpiece of your internal conversations with God. And let your life be guided from above.

*Lord, I need to have Your mind. I also need to see Your
Kingdom. Give me wisdom and revelation to discern
what Your Spirit is doing in every situation around me.*

*I keep asking that the God of our Lord Jesus
Christ, the glorious Father, may give you
the Spirit of wisdom and revelation, so that
you may know him better.*

EPHESIANS 1:17, NIV

Many have spent years in faithful service with a focus on the service—the sowing and reaping. Many have spent years in study of the doctrines and precepts of Scripture—the nuances of theology that explain who God is in an intellectually satisfying way. Many have spent years jumping from church to church with a deep desire to taste inspiration and see the supernatural—the manifestation of the gospel in power. All spring from good intentions. None are enough.

To know Him is the goal. God's desire is for us to say, "I want to know You and be with You." If we miss that in life, church, family, or any other area of life, the rest doesn't matter. We can zealously pursue the things of God without knowing God. We can study His Word and even teach it without knowing Him. We can major on the truths and actions of the gospel without knowing the heart behind it. It happens all the time, and it's tragic.

Sure, those who believe in Jesus and His saving work are welcomed into His Kingdom. Many have focused on the works, the study, and the miracles without knowing Him deeply and still have a saving relationship with Him. But why stop there? The true purpose of Jesus' coming and dying for us was bigger. It was to know Him—to deeply relate to Him. This is why He makes His Presence known.

When we focus on God rather than the things of God, we can live in power. We can say to the world, "God wants to know you and be with you." The message is simple. So is the lifestyle. But many miss it. By all means, don't. This is why He came.

*Lord, forgive me for missing the mark. I want to
know You—not Your Kingdom, not Your gifts, but
You. Please help me see Your face.*

November 22

Give thanks to the LORD, for he is good!
His faithful love endures forever.

PSALM 136:1

This last phrase shows up often in the Psalms, but it's especially prominent in Psalm 136. The first half of each verse shows a reason to be grateful to God, then the second half declares, "His faithful love endures forever." The repeated refrain pairs God's works with God's motivation—mighty acts and the love behind them. The overall message is that we have an awesome God who works on our behalf.

If we look closely enough, we see another common theme in God's mighty works. Not only are they motivated by His love, they are prompted by our need. He delivered His people out of slavery, led them through the wilderness, gave them a path through deep waters, defeated their enemies, gave them a land where they could live, and remembered their weakness. Each incident refers to the Exodus, a time when Israel was helpless to save herself and needed intervention every step of the way. God stepped into their gaping needs and saved.

That's what He does with us, too. We each have canyons of need that beg to be filled, and instead of being our downfall, those needs become opportunities to know who He is, see how He acts, and grow closer to Him in the process. His Presence doesn't fill those who are already filled; it fills those who are empty. Wherever we experience lack or obstacles, we can experience Him. And whenever we experience Him, we thank Him—not only for what He did but for the motive of love behind it.

Father, thank You for filling my needs with
Your provision and Your Presence—and for
the love behind all of Your mercies.

November 23

*Enter his gates with thanksgiving; go into
his courts with praise.*

PSALM 100:4

We want closer encounters with the Lord. We ask for them and wait for them. We position our hearts to receive them. Still, we hunger for a "how." We want to know the secret to experiencing more of His Presence.

Perhaps a key is found in this familiar psalm of praise. We often read it with the assumption that it describes the attitudes we should have when we approach God—that as we go into His Presence, this is how we should respond. But what if it's an instruction for how to get into the awareness of His Presence in the first place? Reading it through the first lens says, "When you come to God, you should be thankful and worship Him." Reading it through the second lens says, "If you really want to come into God's Presence, gratitude and praise are the keys that open the door." The whole purpose shifts.

Clearly, the first reading contains truth. We *should* be grateful and worshipful as we come to God. But the second reading seems to be true as well, as experienced by many who have not sensed His Presence until they chose to express gratitude and praise to Him. Many testify that God felt distant when they were discouraged or confused or apathetic and that waiting to be filled with gratitude and praise got them nowhere. But when they chose to find *something* to give thanks for and decided to praise Him in spite of their mood, the spiritual atmosphere shifted and God showed up. Thanks and praise led them into a deeper experience with Him.

Be intentional about your thanksgiving and see yourself entering His courts as you express it. Let that response to God open the door into His Presence. He comes to us when we come to Him with thanks and praise.

*Lord, thank You for the things I normally
take for granted. I can find much to be
grateful for. You have poured many blessings
out on me, and I rejoice at Your goodness.*

November 24

Jesus was filled with the joy of the Holy Spirit, and he said, "O Father, Lord of heaven and earth, thank you . . ."

LUKE 10:21

Jesus gave thanks. A lot. He thanked God for hiding truth from those who are proud of their "wisdom" and revealing it to those who are humble and childlike (Luke 10:21). He thanked God for food—the loaves and fish He fed multitudes with (Matthew 15:36) and the bread and wine representing His own body and blood (Matthew 26:26-28). He thanked God for hearing His prayer to raise Lazarus from the dead (John 11:41). And He received thanks from those He healed and marveled that nine cleansed lepers neglected to express their appreciation (Luke 17:17-18). In His relationship with the Father and with others, Jesus established a culture of gratitude.

As always, we need to remember that Jesus is more than an example to follow; He's the living Presence inside of us. When we're in fellowship with Him and synchronized with His heart, a culture of gratitude will be formed within us. It's helpful to develop and practice habits—vital, in fact—but it's even more important to cultivate our union with His Spirit. The more we sense Him, commune with Him, and enjoy His Presence, the more our hearts will fill with a spirit of thanksgiving.

The flip side of this truth is that when we aren't feeling very grateful, it's a sign that we're out of sync with Him. Let that drive you further into His Presence. Fellowship with Him reshapes our perspectives and restores all the right attitudes. And it reminds us that all He has done and continues to do for us is worthy of our gratitude.

Jesus, stir up gratitude within me. Fill my heart with Your praise. May my life always reflect the culture of gratitude You established.

November 25

*Let your lives be built on him . . . and you
will overflow with thankfulness.*

COLOSSIANS 2:7

Rivers and streams overflow when the rains are either intense or persistent. The amount of water running into them is greater than the capacity of their banks. We overflow with thanksgiving when God's mercies and blessings fill us up. The amount of favor being poured into us is greater than the capacity of our hearts. When we realize the size of God's generosity, we can't help but be grateful.

But how do we let our lives overflow with thanksgiving when we feel dry and dusty? What if we're going through a season of lack? That's when gratitude is the last thing on our minds. We know we *should* be grateful to God; He has saved us and blessed us with many spiritual blessings. But the burdens we bear and the needs we have tend to outweigh the memory of His favor. In the absence of a tangible or recent touch from Him, we lament our difficult situations. We may even grumble about them.

Gratitude is a matter of perspective. The road back to it can begin with a conscious choice to notice what God has given. Even the basics—breath, a roof over our heads, the last meal we ate—are worth appreciating. We can thank Him for the things He has provided that He didn't have to or for things that haven't happened to us but could have. In every situation, there is something to be grateful for. When we find it and express it, our faith and gratitude increase. The attitude seems to have a positive snowball effect in our hearts.

Choose gratitude. Find something to give thanks for, and then say so. Out loud. The more you do, the more your life begins to overflow.

*Father, You are worthy of a heart that overflows
with thanksgiving toward You. When I think of all
You have done and put it in perspective, I'm filled
with gratitude. You have filled me up. Help me
always remember to express my thanks.*

November 26

*The tongue can bring death or life; those who
love to talk will reap the consequences.*

PROVERBS 18:21

You constantly have a script running through your mind. We all do. That script is filled with thoughts about the past, present, and future. The backward-looking thoughts may be either regretful or satisfying, the present-oriented ones may be full of doubts or decisiveness, and the forward-looking ones may be full of anxiety or hope. Usually, all of the possibilities, both positive and negative, weave in and out of our thought life. And with most of us, they come out in our words.

According to Scripture, words are powerful. They can kill or nourish life, wound or heal, and even shape our future. The script that plays in our minds and on our tongues has major consequences. If we're full of doubts, fears, regrets, discontentment, bitterness, criticism, or despair, our outward circumstances and relationships will tend to line up with what we say and expect. But if we're full of gratitude, words of encouragement and blessing, worship, contentment, and faith, the same is true—our outward lives will tend to match our inner lives. We shape our surroundings far more than we think we do.

This is opposite of what many of us believe. We tend to assume that our outward lives dictate our inward emotions and that we are victims of our circumstances. But when we invite the Presence into our inner lives, and when we choose to think and speak according to His truth, the inward life shapes our outward experience. The truths we hold on to in faith are the truths that play out in our lives. The words we speak become a pretty accurate script for our story.

Guard your story well. Be intentional in your thoughts and careful in your words. Fill them with gratitude and blessing and faith. And enjoy the change in your experience.

*Father, let my words and my thoughts reflect who You
are and the truth You have spoken. And let them shape
my life and the lives of others for Your glory.*

November 27

I will praise the name of God with a song, and will magnify Him with thanksgiving.

PSALM 69:30, NKJV

The mountain near my house used to be huge. It was the biggest hunk of rock I'd ever seen. Today it's pretty small. It hasn't changed in size over the years, but my perspective of it has. How? I've seen bigger ones. Much bigger ones. By comparison, the mountain that used to seem enormous is now unimpressive in its size.

The same dynamic applies to our problems and our God. When we are focused on the enormity of our circumstances, they fill our vision and overwhelm us. They seem huge. When we get a glimpse of a bigger God, the problems that once intimidated us are no longer impressive. He has a way of turning mountains into molehills.

How do we get our perspective to shift? We can't actually magnify God. Being infinite means He's already immeasurably large. But we can magnify Him in our perspective, and one of the best ways to do that is through worship and giving thanks. The more we focus on His power, wisdom, love, compassion, mercy, strength, glory, abundance, favor, and any other of His many attributes, the larger He becomes in our eyes. Gratitude and praise change the way we see.

That's one of the most powerful keys to living a life of faith: changing the way you see. Most discouragement and doubt come from a false perspective. If you're a child of God but aren't hopeful, you've listened to a lie somewhere along the way. Thanksgiving has a way of recalibrating your perspective so that you see correctly. Focus on His goodness and see what it does to your heart—and then how your heart affects your outer world. You'll be amazed by the ways your mountains change.

Father, I want You always to be the biggest object in my line of sight. I want to see Your glory and be unimpressed with the size of everything else. Give me visions of You and fill my heart with thanksgiving.

Father, thank you for hearing me.

JOHN 11:41

We ask God for something. We wait for Him to answer. If and when we receive what we asked for, we thank Him. That's our normal pattern.

But what if we take literally His promises about prayer—that whatever we ask in His name, it will be done for us (John 15:7)? Or His instructions about praying in faith—that whatever we ask for, we should believe we have received it (Mark 11:24)? Assuming we've met the conditions for abiding in Him—not an impossible standard by any means—the promises are pretty straightforward and assure us of answers. Why wait to give thanks?

When we pray in faith, we can give thanks for the answer at the same time we offer the request. If we're unsure about whether the request is God's will, we can ask Him for confirmation that it is, or we can thank Him for whatever answer He will give, even if He has to redirect our desire. But in light of all the assurances He gives us about asking and receiving, the wait-and-see approach seems far too hesitant. We can thank God in advance for His goodness and the ways we will see it.

Jesus took that approach. Before breaking the few loaves of bread that would feed thousands, He gave thanks—presumably not just for the food but for the miracle of multiplying it (John 6:11). And before He called Lazarus out of the tomb, He thanked God for hearing Him, knowing what was about to happen (John 11:41). Jesus thanked God in advance.

Gratitude at the front end of prayer presumes faith and, in fact, stirs it up within us. When we pray in that kind of faith, God responds accordingly. In Scripture, He doesn't answer doubtful prayers nearly as often as He answers bold and faith-filled ones. Thanksgiving is based on faith, builds our faith, and leads to faith's results.

Father, thank You for hearing me and for the
answer You are going to give.

November 29

Jesus was sleeping at the back of the boat with his head on a cushion. The disciples woke him up, shouting, "Teacher, don't you care that we're going to drown?"

MARK 4:38

The sea was stormy, waves were splashing into the boat, the disciples were in a panic, and Jesus was sleeping through it all. He must have been tired—Galilean fishing boats were small enough to get tossed around harshly in a storm, and no one could sleep under those conditions without being exhausted. But the disciples had enough energy to be frantic about the situation, so they woke Him up with an accusation: "Don't you even care?"

The disciples seem to have already assumed a disastrous fate, but they at least wanted the Savior to act like He might be able to save—or even to care. So Jesus got up, rebuked the wind, and commanded the water to be still. The elements obeyed, and Jesus questioned His friends about their fear compared to their faith. Apparently, the storm had only appeared to be a threat. In reality, it wasn't. Especially when someone with faith and divine authority commanded it to stop.

Are there moments in your life when you wonder if Jesus is asleep? When a storm is raging and you can't understand why He doesn't seem concerned? It isn't an uncommon situation in our relationship with Him. Even when He is assuredly present with us, it often seems like He isn't. But you can rest assured that He isn't worried about your situation like you are. He knows how it will turn out, and He wants your faith to win out over your fear. Doesn't He care that you're going to drown? Yes, He cares; and no, you aren't going to drown. Trust Him to speak to your storm at the right time.

Jesus, I know You care, and I know You aren't really sleeping on the job in my life. Please speak to my storms and tell them to be still. Until You do, please fill me with faith instead of fear.

November 30

Nothing is impossible with God.

LUKE 1:37

You may have difficulties in your life. Perhaps they have lingered far too long and disguised themselves as permanent. Maybe they have masqueraded as impossibilities rather than the difficulties that they are. Even so, you can remind yourself often that when God is involved, nothing is impossible.

Scripture affirms this again and again—the same truth expressed in various ways. It tells us that nothing is too difficult for Him, that His arm is not too short to save, that all things are possible with Him. No matter how it's phrased, the point is the same: no problem is beyond His ability to solve, and no task is too great for His power. In fact, He actually prefers to work in "impossible" situations rather than very far-fetched or somewhat unlikely situations. He specializes in solutions that have no explanation other than Him.

It's easy to understand why, from His perspective. These are the situations in which His attributes are most visibly displayed. When Joseph and Daniel interpreted dreams that were impossible for others to interpret, God's ability to reveal truth was clearly seen. When the sea parted and the walls of Jericho fell down, His power was obvious. When older women like Sarah and Elizabeth or a virgin like Mary conceived, His creative ability was revealed. The most impossible circumstances set up the clearest displays of His glory. In the words of Jean de La Bruyère, "Out of difficulties grow miracles." Miracles don't happen if impossibilities don't happen first.

Don't get discouraged by the long, unyielding situations in your life. God has solutions for them. He may not have revealed those solutions yet— He let many people in Scripture endure long periods that required faith and patience—but He is never late with His answers. Wait, believe, and hope. Nothing is impossible with Him.

Lord, I need You to overcome the impossibilities in my life. Fill me with faith and hope and help me to be patient. Show Your glory in my circumstances.

December 1

The word of God is alive and powerful. It is sharper than the sharpest two-edged sword, cutting between soul and spirit, between joint and marrow. It exposes our innermost thoughts and desires.

HEBREWS 4:12

I woke up in one of those dreadful moods, already prejudiced against the day ahead. I spoke to the Lord about it—asked Him to jump-start my spirit and help my attitude shift. Nothing. I still felt like the day was out to get me.

Sometime later, I decided to pull out some index cards with Scripture verses on them, words that God had used to speak encouragement to me at critical moments in various situations. I read through each one, remembering the power I felt when they impacted me at those moments. Little by little, my attitude shifted. The day wasn't out to get me; I was sent into the day by a powerful God who had already ordained my steps. Whatever happened on this day, I would overcome.

The Spirit of God is always with us and in us, but sometimes we can sense His practical Presence only in the Word He inspired. God is present when we read His Word and affirm its truth, when we let the living power of the Word sink into us and shape us. It's entirely possible to read and study the Bible without experiencing this living power—plenty of Pharisees, philosophers, and skeptics have done so throughout history, and so have we at times. But when the Word lands in the fertile ground of faith in our hearts, things change. God goes to work. He inhabits the words He has spoken, and they take on a vitality that transforms.

If you're in need of God's Presence, you can always find it one way or another in His revelation. Don't just read His words; let them speak. Let them change your day—and your life.

Lord, I need to experience the living power of Your Word. Whenever I thirst for You, lead me to the verses that reveal Your voice for that moment. Use them to shape me from within.

December 2

I pray that God, the source of hope, will fill you completely with joy and peace because you trust in him. Then you will overflow with confident hope through the power of the Holy Spirit.

ROMANS 15:13

Some days, it's hard to keep it together. You try to maintain the right attitudes, to stoke your faith and expect God's goodness, but circumstances seem to be winning the war of the heart. It feels like an enormous effort to keep the internal peace. And that effort sometimes takes energy we don't have.

That's okay. God understands those "I can't keep it together" days. There's always mercy and the strength available in His Presence, when we can find it. But what we really long for, and what He longs for on our behalf, is that we have the deep-down peace that isn't an effort to "keep together" because it's who we are. Sure, trying to maintain the right attitudes is important, but we want to get to the point where we don't have to try. We want them to come naturally because our hearts have been transformed. We don't want just to tell ourselves to be at peace; we want to actually have it.

God is getting us to that place. It's a process; the attitudes of the Spirit don't come to us instantly. But the more we soak in His Presence and fellowship with His Spirit, the more He fills us with hope and peace. At some point these attitudes are no longer self-imposed. They overflow from within.

Seek that ideal. You won't be perfect at it, but you can certainly grow in that direction. His Presence calms the storms within you without your having to keep a lid on them. He stirs up hope without your having to manufacture it. He cultivates joy without your having to talk yourself into it. By faith, let Him overflow.

Lord, I want to overflow—naturally, through what You have done in me. I accept Paul's prayer as my own. Give me hope, and keep me happy and full of peace as I believe.

December 3

When he heard that Lazarus was sick, he
stayed where he was two more days.

JOHN 11:6, NIV

Scripture is full of seeming dead ends. Joseph, with dreams and destiny in his heart, was cast into slavery and then prison. The Israelites, pursued by a hostile army, were led by God to the edge of an impassable sea. Paul and Silas, in their efforts to spread the gospel throughout Asia Minor, were twice forbidden by the Spirit to go in their intended direction. Lazarus's sisters wanted Jesus to come and heal their dying brother, and Jesus lingered far away. At times, God seems to specialize in boxing His people in.

We serve a God of the tight spot. There are times when we feel stuck, long for alternate scenarios, plead with Him either to move us or move the mountains in our way, and still find every path to be shut off. He gives us no options, so we sit still, pressed on every side, stuck in a vise grip of brutal circumstances and unyielding limitations. And when we look to God to deliver us, as we're told to do, all we see is a divine poker face. No expression. No hint at what He's going to do. Just a powerful God who apparently refuses to move.

Why does the ever-present God feign absence? We don't know, but what we choose to believe in those moments is crucial. Those who reject the adversary's lies about God's goodness and choose to trust His favor will eventually see a breakthrough—a new freedom, some parted waters, an open door of opportunity, even a resurrection. Our subtle beliefs in our tight spots have powerful implications for what God does next. Hang on to faith, even at seeming dead ends. The God of power is still standing by.

Jesus, I choose to believe in Your goodness, even in my
tightest spots. I know I'm never stuck when You're
at work. I trust You completely and know You have a
solution. And I'll wait as long as necessary to see it.

December 4

As surely as the LORD lives and you yourself
live, I will never leave you.

2 KINGS 2:2, 4, 6

Elisha was a spiritual pest. At least three times on the day of Elijah's depar-
ture, the younger prophet rebuffed requests to let the older prophet depart in
solitude. Elijah was about to be "taken" by the Lord—though no one seemed
sure exactly what that would look like—and he told his protégé to stay behind. But Elisha insisted on following his master through Bethel, through
Jericho, and through the Jordan River. He would not be absent while God
was doing something amazing.

God honors that kind of persistence, as pesky as it seems at the time.
In fact, He strongly urges it. "Give the LORD no rest," He urged the praying
watchmen of Jerusalem (Isaiah 62:7). "Keep on asking. . . . Keep on seeking.
. . . Keep on knocking," Jesus commanded His disciples (Matthew 7:7). Jesus
told parables of a noisy neighbor asking for bread at midnight (Luke 11:5-8)
and a widow relentlessly pestering a judge for justice (Luke 18:1-8), describing them as pictures of prayer. He responded to a blind man who wouldn't
quit yelling at him (Luke 18:35-43) and to a woman who kept asking for a
favor, even after He had spoken discouraging words to her (Matthew 15:22-
28). Both were rewarded with miracles. Apparently, God welcomes pests.

If you aren't content with a casual relationship with God and pester
Him for something more, you are honored in His Kingdom. Never arrive at a
place of saying, "Okay, that's enough. That's all of Him I need." Pursue higher
levels, deeper depths, more of the Presence. You are promised that those who
seek will find. And those who seek persistently will find more.

Lord, Elisha's words to Elijah are my words to
You. I will never leave You. I will always want
more and will always keep asking.

December 5

Let me inherit a double portion of your spirit.

2 KINGS 2:9, NIV

Elisha was a spiritual glutton. He had observed the power of God in his prophetic mentor—the miracles of healing, fire from heaven, the divine authority to command and rebuke kings—and he wanted it. He had also seen the costs—rejection and persecution, moments of exile, discouragement, and even depression—and he still sought the same spirit. The costs didn't seem to outweigh the benefits. He knew God was at work in Elijah, and he wanted God to be at least as powerfully at work in him.

The choice between the benefits and costs of experiencing God is a choice we all face. Jesus spoke of the costs of discipleship on several occasions, pointing out that His suffering is an integral part of following Him. Being in God's fellowship in view of the world is indeed "a difficult thing," as Elijah called it in 2 Kings 2:10. But what about the costs of not following Him? They are greater. The Spirit may add a whole new dimension to our lives, layers of uncomfortable trials, temptations, and intense assignments. But missing out on life with Him? That's much worse. The easy way is ultimately the harder way.

God honors those who know that. He rewards sincere spiritual gluttons—those who pursue a double portion not for their own glory but because it's right and good to do so. He enjoys the fellowship of those who choose greater costs for greater fruitfulness, and He honors their wishes. He gives them more of the weight of His glory.

Ask God for the double portion—for more of His Presence, His gifts, His assignments. Ask boldly and often. Then *expect* boldly and often. God's favor comes to those who weigh the costs and willingly accept them.

Father, it is truly a costly thing to follow You—especially to follow You fully. But I want Your Presence and power more than I want freedom from the burden of having it. Please, Lord, more. Always give me more of You.

If you see me when I am taken from you,
then you will get your request. But if not,
then you won't.

2 KINGS 2:10

Elisha was given a sign. Elijah told him he would know if the spiritual double portion was granted if he saw Elijah as he ascended. As they were walking, a chariot of fire came between them, and a whirlwind took Elijah up. And not only was Elijah visible, Elisha was able to keep his eyes on him as he ascended.

That must have been no small task. In the commotion of such a startling supernatural event, staying focused on one person involved couldn't have been easy. Perhaps there was design in that divine test: if a prophetic apprentice could follow his mentor's instructions in the midst of such chaos, he was fully prepared to follow his Lord's instructions in the chaos of a prophetic ministry, with all its rejection and persecution. Whether that was the purpose of the test or not, Elisha passed. He remained focused. He kept his eyes on his master.

If we want the greater portion—more power and Presence in God's Spirit—we must be people of focus. We need to be able to look past the distractions of the day, the opposition against the Kingdom, and the obstacles we inevitably encounter and see only the Master. Our gaze must be continuous. If we look to the side, we'll get discouraged or distracted easily. If we don't, we'll have what we're looking for. We receive what we behold.

Watch your gaze. We have been told to keep our eyes on Jesus and run with endurance (Hebrews 12:1-2)—no easy trick in an age of many distractions. Don't let your mind be filled with less worthy visions. Those who refine their focus are rewarded with what they see.

Jesus, let me see only You. Help me look past
distractions, deceptions, and difficulties. With my eyes
on You, I can fulfill any purpose You set before me,
and I'll know Your Presence is with me always.

*Be careful how you live. Don't live like
fools, but like those who are wise.*

EPHESIANS 5:15

Socrates said that the unexamined life is not worth living. That's the heart behind the "prayer of examen," a spiritual practice of looking back each evening at the events of the day. What gifts and joys were worthy of my gratitude on that day? What careless words and actions might require confession and repentance? How did the Spirit lead, and did I follow Him well? The reflection can result in a treasure hunt of God-moments, retrospectively. It's a way of examining life in order to live it wisely and worshipfully.

One of the most encouraging aspects of a prayer of examen is seeing where God was in each moment of the day. The ever-present Father was somehow in every moment of each circumstance, but what was He doing? What signs of His Presence did we miss? What patterns of His Presence show up only in retrospect? What does His work in our lives seem to be pointing toward? What was He wanting to do through us in each situation to represent Him to others? When we ask these questions and hear the Spirit speak to us about them, God's purposes for our circumstances are often unveiled for us. In that sense, looking back can be one of the best ways to look forward.

Look back over your last twenty-four hours. What has God been doing in your life? Where was He in that disappointment you faced or that bright idea that popped into your head? What divine appointments did He arrange? How might He have wanted to reveal Himself and His goodness in each situation? The answers to those questions may convert discouragements into encouragements, closed doors into open ones, distractions into directions. And they will probably reveal His Presence in a new way.

*Lord, where were You in my last few hours? I want
to see. Show me what You have been doing so I'll
know where You are leading. And thank You for
every moment of Your Presence.*

December 8

*I saw the Lord. He was sitting on a lofty throne,
and the train of his robe filled the Temple.*

ISAIAH 6:1

Use your holy imagination for a moment and picture this: awesome, terrifying, winged creatures shouting in voices loud enough to shake the foundations of a massive stone temple. A loud chorus booming across the heavens, compelled to cry out in amazement that this infinite Being is completely different from any other being, indescribable in radical perfection and power. Hollywood's best special effects pale in comparison. This scene plays out on the largest of screens: the sky.

This is what Isaiah saw for a moment in time. As he worshiped in the Temple, the curtains were pulled back on this heavenly vista, and the prophet was overwhelmed with the majesty of it all. In Presence so intense, it's impossible to get deep enough into the floor; Isaiah the prophet cried, "Woe is me" (v. 5, NKJV), desperately craved cleansing, and volunteered to do anything this God wanted. In such a moment, he surely understood why Scripture suggests that no one can see God and live. Yet Isaiah lived, as Moses had and other prophets like Daniel and Ezekiel soon would. Still, the vision was enough to overload human senses.

Though Isaiah saw this scene for a brief moment in time, it's occurring at this very moment. The seraphs are even now shouting about God's otherness, He's still on His throne, and the universe is still charged with His glory. It's important to hold such scenes in our minds as we worship; we don't want to be out of sync with the heartbeat of creation. And we can know that Isaiah's deep humility and desperate desire to serve this God are always an appropriate response. The Presence provokes radical, self-sacrificing allegiance. Envision what is truly happening around God's throne, and worship the One you see.

*Lord God, You are holy—far beyond what I'm able
to imagine. But I can still sense the awesome majesty
of Your Presence and the thunderous shouts of amazing
creatures. May such scenes draw me into true worship.*

December 9

"Stand up, son of man," said the voice. "I want to
speak with you." The Spirit came into me as he
spoke, and he set me on my feet.

EZEKIEL 2:1-2

The first verse calls Ezekiel to his feet in order to hear God. The next verse implies that the Spirit compelled Ezekiel to stand as a reaction to God's voice. And both are true; Scripture is full of people who had to change their posture to hear God's voice but also of people who heard His voice and then had to change their posture (see Daniel 10:11 and Revelation 1:17, for example). The physical response is symbolic. An encounter with God always provokes movement from one point to another.

Clearly God can speak to us in order to calm us and give us peace and rest, but He generally does so only when we're restless and anxious. Even then, His voice provokes movement from one state of being to another. God speaks to shift our direction, get our attention, correct our attitude or behavior, settle our heart, call us into a new mission, open our eyes to His purposes, and prompt us to reach out to others. In every case, we are somehow different than before. The heart of His voice is change.

Position yourself for an encounter with God by standing to hear Him. But when He speaks, reposition yourself because of the encounter in order to do what He has said. The necessary change may be subtle—perhaps nothing more than an encouraging word that causes you to embrace a deeper level of faith or dispense with an unnecessary fear—but it is change nonetheless. Both before and after, your posture has a lot to do with your experience of hearing God. And when you respond appropriately, you position yourself to hear Him the next time as well. Move toward God, and also move with Him. Then you will find Him moving on your behalf too.

Lord, I'm standing at attention to hear You, and
I'm standing ready to move at the sound of Your
voice. I want our encounters to change me, no
matter how subtly or radically You want them to.
Help me live in sync with You.

December 10

The LORD is my shepherd; I have all that I need.

PSALM 23:1

"Yes, I am your Shepherd—your *good* Shepherd. But don't assume you will never feel need in this world. You've seen many who love Me and submit to My shepherding go through seasons of lack. That isn't a contradiction to My promise. I allow you to have needs and expect them to drive you to Me as your Provider.

"Understand that there's a difference between having provision and knowing a Provider. You've heard the saying that it's good to give someone a fish but better to teach him how to fish. It's good when I give you something you need, but it's better when I teach you to walk with Me. My material gifts are used and then gone, but My heart as your Provider never fades. When the Provider is your constant companion, you never worry about whether you will have what you need.

"That's what David meant when he said he would not want for anything—not that he would never experience lack, but that he would never experience lack without confidence that I would be available to him. You can have that same confidence. Yes, you will have needs, but you will never be in a place of unaddressed need, wondering if I am going to come through for you. My Presence with you means that you can be at peace about your future. I see all the days in front of you, and you won't be forsaken in any of them. Your worst-case scenarios aren't in My plans. I take care of My sheep, and you are one of them."

Lord, although I do have everything I need to survive right now, I don't have everything I need to thrive or to fulfill Your calling. But I know all of those things are in You, and I have You. Please show me how to discover and experience Your provision at each step in the journey.

December 11

*He lets me rest in green meadows; he leads
me beside peaceful streams.*

PSALM 23:2

"You need balance. Yes, there's a time for pressing in to Me and My purposes for you. I love the hunger of your heart and how it drives you deeper into Me, and I don't want your pursuit to wane. But you need to understand that pursuing is not striving. You can seek without being stressed, expect without being impatient, need without being unhealthily needy. The key lies in your focus. Are you intent on fulfillment or on self-fulfillment? Receiving or seizing? These are subtle but substantial differences.

"One of the ways I keep you in balance is to insist on rest and peace. You can find Me only when you cease striving and know that I am God—when, in your desperate search, you relax and receive. I've decreed that your salvation is in repentance and rest, not in climbing and achieving. That's the only way you can get what you need. You have to learn how to wait and receive.

"That doesn't mean being passive and inactive. Actively believe. Anticipate. Continue to focus your gaze on Me. But when your search for fulfillment becomes dependent on your own seeking and striving, you will miss it. I hold you and speak peace to you. I calm your heart and prepare you to receive. Not every path in My Kingdom is treacherous. I guide you into meadows and lead you beside streams. Learn to discipline yourself to actively rest, to intentionally accept, to zealously be at peace. Seek the balance I offer, and I will lead you gently and calmly where you need to go."

*Lord, help me know how to ask without being
demanding, how to receive without grabbing, how
to seek without being obstinate. Help me find You
in Your strength, not mine. And teach me to live
and work, even diligently and persistently, with a
sense of peace and rest.*

December 12

*He renews my strength. He guides me along
right paths, bringing honor to his name.*

PSALM 23:3

"You depend on Me for strength. Some days you feel strong, but you also go through many seasons of feeling weak. I actually accomplish more through you during those times of weakness, although you usually don't see the results until much later. When you're weak, you have to lean on Me. That's a position of fruitfulness. And as you lean on Me, you grow stronger—not in your own strength but in Mine. You learn to let My energy flow through you. That's the kind of renewal you seek.

"You depend on Me for guidance. You think this is entirely for your sake, but I have a stake in your direction too. I want you moving in the right direction for your good and for My glory. Both are important to Me. That's because I've given you My name; you are known as someone who believes in Me. For reasons I won't fully reveal, I have chosen to let My reputation be intertwined with yours. Yes, there are many who don't seek My leading or listen to My guidance, so they reflect badly on My people and My name. But I vindicate those who truly follow Me. I let you represent Me and watch your ways carefully to accomplish My purposes and bring honor to Me.

"I want you to know these things because I want you to embrace your weakness and your need for direction. Look to Me for the right path and the strength to walk it. Don't stress about glorifying Me; I will glorify Myself in you as long as you are depending on Me. Don't try to establish your reputation; leave that to Me. Don't muster up strength; let Me refresh you. Let Me be Me in you."

*Lord, I long for a season of refreshing. I need
renewal. Lead me in the way I should go and
bring honor to Your name.*

December 13

*Even when I walk through the darkest valley, I
will not be afraid, for you are close beside me.*

PSALM 23:4

"Death is the biggest fear you have as a mortal creature. I designed you for eternity, but your forefathers—and you—chose to live outside of My design. The reason I sent My Son was to overcome your greatest enemy and fear—your own death. Now, because death could not conquer Him, it cannot conquer you.

"Notice what My Son and My servants said about death in My Word. Jesus told His followers that Lazarus had only 'fallen asleep.' Paul assured you that departing to be with Jesus was better than living on in the flesh. Peter wrote of your priceless inheritance that is beyond the reach of corruption and decay. I have given you glimpses of My eternal Kingdom and promised that death has no victory over you. Nothing can separate you from My love—ever. And nothing can separate you from My Presence.

"Yes, I am with you, even in your worst times. In the most painful trials, in the most frightening circumstances, in the most tragic events, and on your own deathbed. Do you realize what that means? When you're in My Kingdom, the very worst that can happen to you leads to the very best state of being. Truly you have nothing to fear.

"When your mind begins to worry, when you face danger and your adrenaline begins to flow, when you watch loved ones suffer, know this: I am always with you, I always give you comfort, and I always have a solution. You may not see, but you can know. I am close beside you."

*Father, I know there's nothing to dread in my life—
that my dread comes from the thought of going through
difficulties without Your help. Please remind me often
of Your Presence—even in the face of trials, tragedies,
and death. Help me live absolutely fearlessly.*

December 14

You prepare a feast for me in the presence of my enemies.

PSALM 23:5

"You may have noticed that I sometimes let enemies ride over your head. This is nothing new; I did it with Jacob, Joseph, Moses, Hannah, David, the prophets, and many others. I allow you to experience anguish and humiliation under those who think they have the upper hand, who may even taunt you and gloat. I do that for many reasons, three that you need to know: to expose the arrogance of those who flaunt My ways; to teach you humility and submission, even in injustice; and to give you a point of fellowship with My Son, who suffered from His enemies. There are times when you will have to see your enemies succeed.

"But you'll notice that these seasons of humility and seeming defeat are always temporary. Jacob, Joseph, Moses, Hannah, David, the prophets, and all of My people end up victorious. I do prepare a feast for you in the presence of your enemies—eventually. They will have to answer to Me, and they will regret how they have treated you. Whether in this age or the age to come, you will be vindicated. I will defend you. I will never let you be put to shame. Though you suffer for a time, it is always only that—for a time. No one who trusts Me and depends on Me will be disappointed in the end.

"Be patient. Don't expect always to be visibly victorious at every moment. All who desire to live a godly life will suffer some sort of persecution. In this world, you will have trials. But I have overcome the world. And because My life is in you, you are an overcomer. You will enjoy a feast in the Presence of your enemies, and they will know you are Mine."

Father, please defend me. Please lift me up over those who oppose me. Give me humility to be patient and patience to endure until the time of the victory feast.

December 15

My cup overflows with blessings. Surely
your goodness and unfailing love will
pursue me all the days of my life.

PSALM 23:5-6

"My goodness and love don't just come to those who deserve them. I don't ration out My blessings as though they are in short supply. If you're observant, you'll notice that I pour out blessings and chase you down with My goodness every day. The reason most people don't know that is they aren't very observant.

"Human beings have a tendency to focus on what is lacking. I tell you to focus on what has been given. I deal very harshly with a complaining attitude and very generously with a grateful one. I want you to be able to say, as David did, that your cup overflows with blessings and that My goodness and love will surely pursue you. And in order to do that, you have to be watching. Your fallen nature will magnify all apparent contradictions to My goodness and minimize all evidence for it. My Spirit within you will do the opposite. That's why it's vital to cultivate your relationship with My Spirit and dwell in My Presence. That's where your cup overflows.

"Let your mind dwell on these things. Don't let My blessings go unnoticed. See how your cup overflows. Understand that My goodness and mercy never waver. In fact, they pursue you relentlessly all the days of your life. You couldn't get away from them if you tried. Even when you distance yourself from Me, I pursue. I put gifts in your path and ordain works for you to walk in. I arrange your steps to walk into My grace. Believe that with all your heart and trust Me to do it. And all the days of your life will be much more pleasant."

Father, I don't see Your goodness nearly
enough. I know that's not because it isn't
there; it's because I don't notice. Open my
eyes to see the many ways You relentlessly
pursue me with Your love.

December 16

And I will live in the house of the LORD forever.

PSALM 23:6

"You need to live your life with an eternal perspective. When you are fully convinced that you'll live in My house forever—in My family and in the safety of My hand—you will have a much greater tolerance for discomfort. You'll find yourself much less impatient, much more generous, much less driven by short-term gain, much more willing to sacrifice for the ultimate good. When you finally realize, deep in your soul, that My Presence is an eternal state, your life takes on a whole new meaning.

"David's psalm was a statement of perspective. He understood from his youth as a shepherd that My shepherding changes the way a person sees. He no longer focused on what he lacked, questioned his path, feared death, obsessed about getting the upper hand over his enemies, failed to notice blessings, or planned only for the short term. He knew Me as Provider, Guide, Comfort and Strength, Victor, generous Giver, and eternal Lord. That's why he began his song with a statement of not living in want. He knew that in Me, he had all he needed.

"I want you to live with that perspective. Know that you have all you need—in Me, through Me, or both. Live fearlessly and faithfully. See your losses as temporary and your gains as eternal. Believe—always know, beyond the shadow of a doubt—the depths of My goodness and faithful love. And understand that every benefit of this relationship is forever."

Lord, I want to see with "forever" eyes. I want to live anchored in eternity and have attitudes that reflect ultimate victory and unquenchable life. I want to live as fearlessly and faithfully as You want me to. Help me do that. Shape my perspective. Guide me in Your good and everlasting ways.

December 17

How impossible it is for us to understand
his decisions and his ways!

ROMANS 11:33

Babies learn a language by listening and imitating. They try out words and phrases and come to understand, by trial and error, what works and what doesn't. Over time, the language becomes a part of them—without analyzing verb tenses, without consciously thinking of grammar rules, without noticing the inconsistency of patterns. They don't learn the parts; they learn the whole.

Adults usually try to learn a foreign language by studying the parts—analyzing grammatical patterns, memorizing conjugations, reciting vocabulary. And we try to understand God in exactly the same way. We look for patterns and talk about what God would or wouldn't do based on His methods we discern from Scripture and trying to apply them in predictable ways. The problem is that God isn't predictable. His character never changes, but His methods rarely stay the same. If we try to learn the system, we'll live in the Kingdom like foreigners trying to wrap their brains around the language rather than speaking it from their hearts.

He counsels us repeatedly in His Word, through the stories of people who knew Him well. "I want you to know Me," He seems to tell us, "but I don't expect you to understand Me. In fact, you can't. I'm not predictable, and you wouldn't understand many of My thoughts and reasons even if I explained them to you. They come from a much higher perspective than yours. Your job is to trust Me, not figure Me out. Seek My Presence, not My patterns. Watch My ways, don't define them. As you go through this day, keep your eyes and ears on Me. Watch what I'm doing, listen for My voice, and follow."

Lord, show me what You're doing. I come to you,
recognizing You as a Person, not a system. Give
me glimpses of Your works and let me hear
Your whispers. Tune me to Your Presence
every moment of this day.

December 18

The person who is joined to the Lord is
one spirit with him.

1 CORINTHIANS 6:17

There are difficult people in your life. If they aren't visible right now, they are in the background somewhere. Sooner or later, everyone experiences the frustrations of conflict, even if it's just minor friction. We live in a world where people don't always get along. And that doesn't change when we enter the Kingdom of God.

Even so, anyone who is a believer is one with God's Spirit. That doesn't mean we're always in sync with God's Spirit or expressing His character, but we are always organically united to Him. And that amazing truth applies not only to us; it applies to those in His Kingdom who happen to rub us the wrong way. Even the difficult, abrasive, or insincere personalities who belong to Him are at one with Him. And we need to treat them accordingly.

Find the Presence of God in others—even those who don't remind you of His Presence. The Spirit is there somewhere. If you can begin to see Him in people, you'll begin to see them differently. In place of purely natural opinions about who they are in the flesh, you'll learn to honor them in the Spirit. You'll rise above conflict and be able to call out the treasure that God has placed within them, no matter how hidden that treasure seems to be. And instead of deepening divisions—even those that others have created—you'll help people reach their God-ordained potential and develop a sense of unity. Your perceptions will change. So will theirs. And the Presence of the Lord who is one spirit with all of us will be much more noticeable.

Spirit, unity is important to You. Please help me
recognize You in others. Overcome my biases. Open my
eyes to the treasure You've placed in each of Your people,
and show me how to draw it out of them for Your glory.

December 19

*The wind blows wherever it pleases. You
hear its sound, but you cannot tell where it
comes from or where it is going. So it is with
everyone born of the Spirit.*

JOHN 3:8, NIV

God loves variety. He also loves to keep us on our toes. Our religious instincts always look for patterns and principles to follow, but God won't let
us find them with any sense of lasting satisfaction. That's because we can live
by patterns and principles without Him, even while assuming that we have
"a relationship with God." But a relationship with a system of beliefs is a
poor substitute for a relationship with a person. God won't let us function
on "automatic."

So God rarely does the same thing twice. He spoke through a burning
bush—once. He won a victory by having His people march circles around
a city—once. Jesus healed a blind man with spittle and dirt—once. He has
spoken on numerous occasions, won many victories, and healed many eyes,
but not with any uniform methods. His ways are beyond figuring out.

That's why the Presence is essential. It keeps us in relationship mode
rather than religion mode. When we live exclusively by Christian principles
and patterns—even those we can discern from Scripture—we stop listening
for His voice, hanging on to His every word, watching His every move, and
asking for His specific direction. Instead, we revert to human wisdom, practical
and sensible options, and muted expectations. And we miss the personal touch.

Learn to be blown by the Spirit wherever He pleases. Dwell in the Presence so thoroughly that when the Presence moves, you do too. Take pleasure
in God's variety. Use it as an opportunity to pull away from the practice of
religion and draw close to Him.

*Spirit, blow through me as You will. Redirect me
however You want to. Make me sensitive to Your true
paths, Your varying methods, and Your specific timing.*

December 20

*She will give birth to a son and will call him
Immanuel (which means "God is with us").*

ISAIAH 7:14

All of Scripture, even all of history, points to the Son of God. From God's revealed perspective, all things were created for the Son, the salvation of humanity hinges on the Son, and all things will be summed up and completed in the Son. Scripture ends with a wedding between the Son and a redeemed humanity shaped specifically for His heart. He is the beginning, middle, and end of history.

That the centerpiece of the universe is called Immanuel—"God is with us"—is loaded with meaning. The name points to His deity, it points to our significance as objects of His love, and it points to the Presence uniting us to Him. That means that all of creation was designed to bring us into personal contact with the affection of our Creator. This was evident when the Spirit breathed life into the first Adam, it was clear when Jesus breathed His Spirit into His disciples, and it is apparent in the union of the Son and His bride in the next age. Though many view the gospel through lenses that focus on our depravity and salvation, on our obligation and service to Him, or on the expansion of His Kingdom—all important and valuable truths—His Presence points to a higher truth: affection. He likes us. Our existence is an overflow of His love.

Never reduce the role of the Presence to a matter of simply saving us, equipping us for service, or sending us on a mission. He is with us for all of these purposes, but He is with us for more. He comes close to enjoy us and express His love. That is the driving force behind creation—and needs to be the driving force behind every one of our days.

*Jesus, let me know Your Presence and feel Your
affection, and please receive the affection I have
for You. Help me express it well. May it shape
everything I do all the days of my life.*

December 21

For a child is born to us, a son is given to us. The government will rest on his shoulders.

ISAIAH 9:6

The government will rest on the shoulders of a child. That tells us quite a bit about God: that He is interested in government, now and forever; that a child who is dependent on Him is more powerful than a warrior king who isn't; and that God's greatest gifts come in unexpected, humble packages. The child who is born to us is a powerful Presence.

We know the Christmas story and its universal implications, and we marvel every year at the advent of God's Son. But often lost in the big picture of the Nativity are the personal implications for each of us. Jesus is still an unexpected package in our lives, often disguising His greatest blessings in very humble clothing. Jesus is still a model of childlike dependence on God, the kind of dependence that doesn't appear to be the key to experiencing infinite power, but is. And Jesus is still interested in government, not just of the world and the everlasting Kingdom, but of every inch of our hearts. On both the grand and the deeply personal scales, the child who is born to us is given for comprehensive, life-altering reasons.

The infant in a manger in Bethlehem was a onetime event, but it was also a pattern of things to come. He was God incognito, the One who could be recognized only by eyes of faith, by those who sought out the meaning of a star or who wouldn't have noticed unless they were startled and sent by angels to see Him. Neither He nor His frequent advents into our lives are self-evident. They must be discovered by those who will look for Him. And those who do will be able to cast the government of their lives on His shoulders.

Jesus, give me eyes to see You everywhere. I want to notice every advent, every approach You make into my life. And I depend on You to rule not only my world, but also me.

December 22

He will be called: Wonderful Counselor . . .

ISAIAH 9:6

People write to columnists for advice. They look to horoscopes and psychics for direction. They make lists of pros and cons and consult with friend after friend. They seek professional help for deep, personal issues. Many of the ways we seek counsel are valid and scriptural; many are not. But one thing is clear: we search for the right perspectives and want to know which way to go.

Finite beings with limited knowledge and the scars of a fallen nature need counsel. In God's Presence, we can receive it. Jesus is called Wonderful Counselor, and He calls His own Spirit a Counselor and Comforter. On every page of Scripture, God is reaching out with words of knowledge and wisdom for His people. He has given us much more than an instruction manual; He has given us a guide. He talks us through our dilemmas, gives us perspective on our problems, and leads us in the way we should go.

The Counselor is one of the faces of Immanuel. God is with us not simply to put His arms around us for comfort and encouragement, but also to give us concrete guidance and counsel in the deepest issues of our lives. Discerning that counsel can be a process, but it isn't a shot in the dark. It's guaranteed. While the world relies on human wisdom, we are given the mind of Christ. He gives us revelation, He opens and shuts doors of opportunity, He guides our steps even when we aren't aware of it, and He moves in response to our prayers. In the disorienting events of life, we are never left alone. The Counselor is more than willing to lead.

Lord, as I sit in Your Presence today, make my direction clear. Guide my steps, manage my open and shut doors, impart Your perspective, give me wisdom from above. Give me a heart that understands, then help me live from my heart. Counsel me clearly.

December 23

Mighty God . . .

ISAIAH 9:6

Jesus is the ultimate big brother. He can intimidate the bullies in our lives, if we'll let Him. He's wise, too, so He doesn't go rushing off into every battle we think we have a right to win, but He does stand against our enemies and overcome hindrances that stand in the way of our fulfilling His purposes for our lives. He is the exact representation of the all-powerful God.

But He doesn't seem like it, does He? Whether as a baby in a manger or a criminal on a cross, He doesn't look the part of Mighty God. God declared Himself a mighty Savior in Scripture and proved His power again and again. He delivered His people using plagues, parted waters, a path of provision through the wilderness, and a Promised Land. Then He sent Jesus as His perfect image bearer, and we saw not the thunderous power from heaven but the humility and tenderness of God in Him. But that's by design. The glory is somewhat obscured until His second coming. Only those who believe that this compassionate Jesus portrays God's heart on earth can experience the Jesus of glory who reigns in heaven.

You have to adjust your vision to see the Presence of God in Jesus. He still does miracles and demonstrates power, but often only if you know God's heart well enough to see Jesus where you would least expect to see Him. You're more likely to experience His Presence if you can look past appearances, refuse to dismiss a solution because it looks too humble or unlikely, and get over any assumptions about how He works or who He works with. To know Jesus as your Mighty God, expect the unexpected. Then expect Him to show Himself strong.

Jesus, I need a mighty Savior. I need You to show Yourself as Mighty God—whatever You want that to look like in my life. Open my eyes to see You wherever You are and in whomever You choose to use.

December 24

Everlasting Father . . .
ISAIAH 9:6

It's one of the greatest paradoxes of the Kingdom. A baby born to earthly parents is somehow the Everlasting Father. This is a prophecy of incarnation long before the Incarnation was even understood as such. The eternal housed Himself in a finite body of tiny proportions, experiencing all the trauma of birth, hunger, tears, wet diapers, and the need to be held by human hands. Not until decades later would most people even begin to realize what had happened. The Everlasting Father had showed up as a human son.

What does it mean to us that the Son entered human flesh? Primarily that He became the perfect High Priest to intercede between God and fallen humanity—the familiar Redeemer who spilled His blood for us. But it also means that He can enter *our* human flesh. Granted, the circumstances of Jesus' birth were unique, but the impartation of the Everlasting Spirit into fleshly vessels was not. Because God clothed Himself in flesh, the eternal heartbeat is within us. We are alive forever.

If you as a believer want to sense God's Presence, look within. That's an uncomfortable thought for humble servants of God who don't want to deify themselves, but the truth of Scripture is that the Everlasting Father clothed Himself in the body of a child who grew up, died, was resurrected, and now clothes Himself in the body of . . . you. The promise of the Spirit flows out of the promise of the Incarnation. The latter leads to the former. The baby in a manger offers to endow His servants with the same power He walked in: the life of God dressed in the frailty of humanity.

Jesus, You are the incarnation of the Everlasting Father, and You can fill me with His power. Incarnate Yourself in me, and help me live in all the characteristics of Your life.

December 25

. . . Prince of Peace.

ISAIAH 9:6

In Genesis 14, Abraham pursued a group of invading warrior kings to recapture everything they had stolen. In 1 Samuel 30, David pursued a group of raiders who had destroyed Ziklag and taken his men's possessions, wives, and children. Both men, pictures of Christ in their victories, recovered all that was stolen—everything and more. And both gave credit to God—Abraham even tithing to a mysterious "king of *shalom*" (see Hebrews 7:2). In the end, nothing was lost.

Our Prince of *Shalom* has come to give us peace, wholeness, abundance, fulfillment, and rest. And oh, how we need it. Life can be tumultuous. On this very day, there are people sitting in emergency rooms, living in homeless shelters, wandering back alleys, suffering domestic violence, and receiving lasting scars of emotional abuse. But there are also people overcoming lifelong traumas, repairing marriages, returning to homes and families, finding places to live, and being healed of injuries and diseases. And one way or another, perceived or not, the Prince of Peace is in the middle of those restorations.

That's one of the Messiah's primary missions: restoration. He came to make things right. There's healing in the Presence. Broken places are repaired, wounded places are healed, fragmented hearts are made whole. We don't know how that happens, just that it does. His touch defies explanation, but the effects can be dramatic.

We don't see this on a global scale—yet—although His Presence is discernible in society when His people have shaped it. But we certainly see it in the lives of those who come to Him, in families and communities that invite His restoring Presence into their midst. Whether you have experienced a major trauma or a minor trial—if there is such a thing—the Prince of Peace can restore what was taken and even give you greater plunder from it. Know that He is redeeming all the losses of your life.

*Jesus, I've experienced plenty of losses and have
plenty of regrets. Please restore Your peace and
abundance, Your* shalom, *to every area of my life.*

December 26

Of the increase of His government and peace
there will be no end, upon the throne of
David and over His kingdom, to order it and
establish it with judgment and justice from
that time forward, even forever.

ISAIAH 9:7, NKJV

From the days of Jesus until now, the Kingdom of God has been expanding. And it will continue to expand forever. Though many believe it's shrinking, it isn't. They don't have eyes to see what God is really doing around the world. The truth is that Jesus is growing His Kingdom in numerous hearts, even in many whole communities and societies in behind-the-scenes ways. The small mustard seed is growing; the little bit of yeast is leavening the dough. The government of the Prince of Peace will never come to an end.

Where is the Kingdom of God? Wherever He rules, and it's an inside-out kingdom. That means it begins in the deep recesses of our hearts and works its way outward. There's no limit to its impact other than the limits we impose. If we live freely as children of the King, the Kingdom within us will transform the kingdoms around us. And that's our goal—for the Kingdom to always be expanding within us and around us in our spheres of influence. Our families, workplaces, communities, and churches are to be impacted by what God has done in us.

Let Jesus rule with fairness and justice in your spheres of influence. Carefully cultivate what He is doing in you, knowing that it will work its way outward. As a vessel of the Presence, you are a carrier of the Kingdom. And as a carrier, there is governmental authority to demonstrate fairness, justice, and all the characteristics of God wherever you are. Such demonstrations are never without impact, no matter what little fruit you see at the time. The Kingdom not only expands through Jesus; it expands through you.

Jesus, what can I do to grow Your Kingdom? Help
me do more than tell Your story; help me display
Your character, demonstrate Your ways, and impact
my environment everywhere I set my foot. Expand
Your Kingdom in me and through me.

December 27

The passionate commitment of the LORD of Heaven's Armies will make this happen!

ISAIAH 9:7

God is passionate. Scripture speaks of His zeal and His delight on many occasions, always involving His purposes for His people. When He gives a promise or a prophecy, He watches over His word to perform it. Many of His promises and prophecies are conditional: they require some response on our part in order for them to be fulfilled. But some promises, like the coming of the Messiah and His government having no end, are unilateral purposes that could never be thwarted. The zeal of the Lord *will* accomplish His purposes.

Just as God is zealous about His big-picture plans, He is passionate about His purposes for your life too. He prepares good works for you to step into. He guides your steps even when you aren't aware of it. He redeems your mistakes and actually weaves them into His overall plan to bring glory out of them. Yes, it's possible to rebel or ignore God long enough to miss some of what He has planned, but any heart that is inclined toward Him will be led deeper into His purposes. The more zealously you pursue Him, the more zealously He guarantees that you will fulfill His designs for you. And when the zeal of the Lord guarantees something, it's unstoppable.

Seek the Lord's will, but not with the attitude that finding it and doing it all depends on you. It doesn't. When you focus on Him, He focuses on your issues, your longings, and His plans for you. When you trust, He proves trustworthy. When you have faith in what He has said, what He has said begins to shift from potential to manifested experience. His zeal will accomplish His purposes—for the world and for you.

Lord, teach me to trust in Your zeal for my life—to know that Your purposes cannot be thwarted. In Your presence, let me feel Your passion for me, for the world, and for all of Your purposes.

December 28

*Soon the people began to complain about
their hardship, and the Lord heard
everything they said.*

NUMBERS 11:1

Hardships are . . . well, hard. We don't particularly enjoy them, even when
we know they are producing good fruit in us. We also worry in the midst of
them because we don't know how long they are going to last or how they
will turn out. Sometimes we even question God's wisdom in letting us suffer
from them. They are uncomfortable, disorienting, and a little scary. And when
we feel that kind of pressure, we tend to complain.

God doesn't like complaining. He has a solution for each of the hardships we go through. He knows how they will turn out. He has promised to
be with us in them and to cause all of them to work together for our good if
we love and trust Him. So when we complain about our trials, we are stepping out of sync with God and the environment of heaven. We are declaring
that He might not have a solution, might not know how they will turn out,
or might let them turn out in a way that ultimately harms us. That's a contradiction to His character, purposes, and ways. It's a negative statement about
who we think He is.

Needless to say, this is not an attitude that invites the Lord's Presence. In
Numbers 11, His anger "blazed against" the Israelites who complained about
their hardships. He dealt with them harshly because they had harsh opinions
about Him. He kept His promises to the nation as a whole, but He withdrew
the favor that would have been theirs if they had endured in faith. His Presence itself became a hardship rather than a blessing.

Resolve not to complain. About anything. Ever. Trust God's dealings
in your life, even when they seem torturous or confusing. Know without a
doubt that His plans for you, even when mysterious, are good.

*Oh, Lord—forgive my complaints against You. All
those times I've questioned Your goodness are a grief
to me now. I choose to trust You always.*

December 29

*We all, who with unveiled faces contemplate
the Lord's glory, are being transformed into his
image with ever-increasing glory.*

2 CORINTHIANS 3:18, NIV

Moses' face shone with the glory of God, so he covered it with a veil because the people seemed to have a limited capacity for glory. They knew Moses spoke face-to-face with God, and they saw the glow on him; Paul says the veil kept them from seeing the glory, which was fading away. But in making us alive in Christ and giving us open entry to God's throne, there is no need for veils and glory doesn't fade. The Presence is no longer designated for a holy place in a tabernacle. It's a public-access experience.

Paul says that now that the veil has been removed, we can be mirrors that reflect the Lord's glory. In the process, as His Spirit works in us, we grow to be more and more like Him. As we gaze at Him, His Presence is not just *with* us but *in* us. It becomes more and more real.

We gaze at Jesus, His Spirit works within us, we reflect His glory, and we become more like Him. According to Scripture, that's the process that causes real transformation. But many Christians miss the first step—being face-to-face with Him, being in His Presence—and then are left to attempt transformation by self-effort or a complicated series of spiritual principles. Scripture once presented Moses as a singular exception; the New Testament treats him as a prototype for any Christian's experience. Don't assume God wants less than that. Seek that experience from Him as though there's no limit to the glory He will show you—because, in fact, there isn't.

Jesus, please give me 20/20 vision in gazing at You. Let me have unveiled, face-to-face encounters. I know there are no limits in knowing You and being known by You. I want to reflect as much of Your glory as You will allow.

December 30

This is my command—be strong and courageous!
Do not be afraid or discouraged. For the LORD
your God is with you wherever you go.

JOSHUA 1:9

Joshua was about to lead Israel into the Promised Land, so God gave him some vital instructions. Among those instructions was a command of encouragement: "Be strong and courageous." In fact, God repeated it often enough to indicate that Joshua must have been having some major struggles with fear. He apparently was focusing on the enormity of the task rather than the enormity of his God.

We do that often, and our fear can actually hinder our experience of God's Presence. But when we do encounter God, fear has to flee. When we get a sense of His strength as well as His favor toward us, obstacles seem to become smaller and enemies seem to become less threatening. God becomes our greater preoccupation. As Oswald Chambers once wrote, "The remarkable thing about fearing God is that when you fear God you fear nothing else, whereas if you do not fear God you fear everything else." An encounter with God is the antidote to whatever we dread.

Fear of enemies and obstacles cannot survive in the Presence of God. As your awe of Him grows, mountains shrink and problems unravel. Solutions that once seemed impossible now seem unavoidable. Feeling alone causes you to feel overwhelmed with heavy burdens; but sensing Him causes you to feel overwhelmed only with Him. When that happens, following the command is easy: Be strong and courageous.

Lord, I feel overwhelmed often, but I know
a glimpse of You can radically change my
perspective. Please overshadow my fears and
worries with Your strength. Help me be strong
and courageous in every challenge I face.

December 31

And so we will be with the Lord forever.

1 THESSALONIANS 4:17, NIV

The Presence is not a peripheral issue. It's our destiny. It's what we were made for. Though the Bible ends with a wedding between the Son of God and those made in His image, in a sense that's where the fulfillment of creation actually begins. For all eternity, we will live in perfect union with Him.

There will still be adventures to have, things to learn, maybe even battles to win. We know He wants us to rule with Him on His throne (Revelation 2:26; 3:21), so we certainly won't get bored. Living with Him forever will involve lots of activity and lots of interest. There will be quite a few things to get passionate about. And we will spend plenty of time with the people we knew in this age because we will still know them then. But mostly our eternal state is about a love relationship with the One who made us for Himself. More important than all the things we do is the One we do them with.

That's why spending a year persistently pursuing His Presence has mattered. That's what this collection of devotional readings has been about. And that's a focus that should continue throughout our lives. The more we seek intimacy with Him in this age, the greater our experience with Him will be in the next.

Let this day not be the end of a yearlong exercise in God's Presence but rather just one more day in a lifelong—or actually eternity-long—adventure. He will always pursue you; always pursue Him, too. Cultivate a heart that longs for Him, and it will surely be satisfied. And know that the joy of His Presence will never, ever end.

Yes, Lord—forever. May our intimacy always increase. Let my experience of Your touch never cease to grow. Thank You so much for choosing to love me and letting me know You forever.

SCRIPTURE INDEX

Do-able. _Daily._ Devotions.

START ANY DAY THE ONE YEAR WAY.

Do-able.
Every One Year book is designed for people who live busy, active lives. Just pick one up and start on today's date.

Daily.
Daily routine doesn't have to be drudgery. One Year devotionals help you form positive habits that connect you to what's most important.

Devotions.
Discover a natural rhythm for drawing near to God in an extremely personal way. One Year devotionals provide daily focus essential to your spiritual growth.

It's convenient and easy to grow
with God the One Year way.